1/03

RAVES FOR *A PARENT'S GUIDE TO MONEY*

"I wish I had Alan and Gibora Feigenbaum's book when my kids were growing up! What a difference it would have made. Their book is well-written, to-the-point, and chock full of good advice."

—**Bill Mooney**
Two-time Emmy and Grammy nominee
Author, *The Storytellers Guide*

"Alan helps parents reform their bad money habits and gives them practical ways to help their children avoid making the same mistakes. The book is chock full of useful hints for helping your kids learn how to spend, save, earn and invest wisely."

—**Lita Epstein**
Author, *The Complete Idiot's Guide® to Social Security* and
The Complete Idiot's Guide® to The Federal Reserve

"A wealth of ideas, extensive web sites, specific suggestions for every age and stage of a child's financial life."

—**Judy Miller**
Certified Financial Planner®
Noted Authority on College Funding

"An essential primer for parents seeking help in teaching their children good money habits that will last a lifetime. … With this book, the Feigenbaums may well become the Dr. Spocks of financial child rearing."

—**Cynthia Meyers**
Certified Financial Planner®, MBA
Nationally Recognized Holistic Financial Planner

"This book will inspire parents who are looking for ways to raise financially intelligent children."

—**Robyn C. Morris**
Author, *The Flexible Benefits Answer Book*

"It may be harder to talk to children about money than sex. *A Parent's Guide to Money* demystifies this often taboo subject and provides a learning experience for the whole family."

—**Heather Smith Linton, CPA, MBA, CFP, CVA, CDP**

A Parent's Guide to
MONEY

ISBN: 1-931199-19-1

This book, and all titles in the Parent's Guide series, are available for purposes of fund raising and educational sales to charity drives, fund raisers, parent or teacher organizations, schools, government agencies and corporations at a discount for purchases of more than 10 copies. Persons or organizations wishing to inquire should call Mars Publishing at 1-800-549-6646 or write to us at *sales@marspub.com*.

At the time of publication of this book, all of the information contained within was correct to the best of our knowledge.

Please contact us at *parentsguides@marspub.com*

Edwin E. Steussy, CEO and Publisher
Lars W. Peterson, Project Editor
Michael P. Duggan, Graphic Artist

PO Box 461730
Los Angeles CA 90046

parent's
guide
press

Contents

Contents

Contents

Acknowledgements

To my dear, departed mother, Janet Feigenbaum, for teaching me the value of a dollar and the importance of valuing each and every one. And to my father, Richard Feigenbaum, who for more than 50 years demonstrated daily the value of the unrelenting work ethic needed to earn each and every precious dollar. And to both of them for teaching the values of life that are far more important than the values of dollars, and stressing the value of education in its own right.

—Alan Feigenbaum
August 2002

To my wonderful, hard-working (telecommuting) mother, Janet Levy, for helping me with grammar and empathizing with my constant complaints while trying to maintain major corporate databases from the tiny two-computer office we share. For my father, Alan Feigenbaum, for helping me make the best of this opportunity and helping me develop a more enlightened view about money, while not making me follow all the rules in the book. And to my 11th-grade English teacher, Marjorie Lancaster, for encouraging my writing and giving me a positive attitude about it for the first time. And to the editors at Parent's Guide Press for giving me this opportunity in the first place and giving me and my Dad the freedom to imprint this book with our own style.

—Gibora Feigenbaum
August 2002

Introduction

After you finish this book, you should be well-prepared for every financial aspect of child-rearing: planning for having kids, managing your family with kids, and raising your kids to be financially savvy. But if you want to do even a little better, you might want to follow up this book with some reading about America's 32nd President, Harry S Truman.

After all, Truman was well-known for two things that directly relate to your role as family financial steward. First, consider his famous statement, "The buck stops here," and add the unsaid part, "The buck also starts here." In other words, as parents, you're the family financial stewards who must control the two-way flow of money, rather than having the money control you. Second, Truman made much of being from Missouri, the "show me" state. Because money is the blood supply of your family, and there's only so much transfusing you can do (by adding extra income), you should hold each expenditure up to the light and make it show why you should expend funds for it.

Introduction

If these responsibilities seem overwhelming, consider Truman himself, a relatively modest, plain-spoken man who was the only 20th century President without a college degree. Yet he made the most significant military decision in history, presided over the economic restoration of a war-torn world, and was re-elected to his own 4-year term in 1948, against all odds. If he could do all that, then you can certainly tackle the task of keeping the family's finances afloat without having to be a Wall Street wizard.

Yet, while you can take inspiration from Truman, you can't be blamed for thinking that his presidency made your job a bit harder. When he threw the highly-combustible GI Bill on the fire of returning soldiers' raging hormones, the explosive baby boom erupted. Fifty years later, boomers have proved the most indulgent consumers ever, and their children are following apace. As one of those boomers or boomer children, you're now faced with telling your children to do as you say, not as you did, with regards to spending money.

Your saving grace is that the boomer generation is also unprecedented in fostering redemption – with 12-step programs that span the entire range of human behavior: from chewing your nails or cussing in public to those old standbys – alcoholism, drug abuse, and gambling. So if you're a shopaholic, you can surely find a program to help reform yourself. Our hope is that this book's philosophy, concepts, and practical advice will make it easier for you to become the financial role models that your children need as they move towards adulthood.

How to Use This Book

To accomplish that ambitious goal, the book is arranged to help you understand what you're facing, what tools you already have to meet the challenge, and what you can do to take advantage of these tools.

Chapters One and Two will open your eyes to just what you're in for financially – whether you have young kids already or are planning them. You'll learn how to prepare for the transition from couple to family, and then be given a detailed look at the educational money issues involved in each stage of your child's growth.

Introduction

Once your children are old enough to begin understanding money, you must teach them appropriate skills for each level of maturity. Chapter Three provides an overall perspective on what you should be able to teach your child at different stages. Chapters Four through Seven each provide detailed looks at what your child should learn about spending, saving, earning, and investing, respectively.

Chapter Eight pulls everything together with a look at how to integrate spending, saving, earning, and investing into an overall financial plan, and how to involve your children in family financial planning. It provides guidance on how to improve the "financial literacy" of both you and your children to the benefit of your family and their future families. This chapter also includes a discussion of the financial challenges of divorce, step-families, special-needs children, and other special family situations.

The book concludes with Appendix B, a collection of resources to supplement what you'll learn in this book. Here you'll find web addresses and descriptions of scores of family and kid-only web sites that have a wealth of information on financial issues, as well as specific online tools to help you perform such calculations as how much allowances should be, and how much you need to save for college. You'll find a list of related books that just might include a point or two that this one missed.

So, how much should you give for allowance? Sorry, you'll have to keep reading to find out. While you do, please pardon our leavening the discussion about financial "kidding" with a little good-natured kidding to lighten the mood. And don't worry, unlike "dial-a-joke," we provide the laughs at no extra charge.

Chapter One

Born to Burn Cash:
Kids Are Like High-Tech IPO Startups

The 1990s saw an unprecedented number of small companies grow quickly and rush to go public in order to fund their voracious appetites for cash. As we've seen, these Initial Public Offerings (IPOs) often failed spectacularly because their strategic preparation didn't match their physical growth in facilities, technology, and staff. Consequently, many new endeavors have since retained the option of remaining private much longer – until they're truly ready to "go out in the (Wall Street) world."

As (prospective) parents, you don't have to make that decision about your rapidly growing new enterprise. Even if one of you elects full-time parenting and you later do homeschooling, your children will be out there soon enough; more and more, you must protect them and yourselves from the catastrophe of burning through your cash, and watching your stock as a viable family drop to zero.

So if you'll forgive my IPO (Initial Preaching Offering), it's time to move on to just what challenges you'll face in preparing your child to go public, financially.

1 • Born to Burn Cash

Kids Are a Costly Decision

Regardless of your religious beliefs, in today's world, responsible parenting requires the use of worth control. That doesn't necessarily mean you'll have to settle for a tight-fitting condominium instead of a spacious dream house. But it does mean that before adding to your family, it pays to determine whether your savings, debt, and cash flow add up to enough to cover the immediate extra costs and ongoing higher family expenses.

Average Costs and Your Costs

A recent study by the non-profit organization, Zero Population Growth, showed that a majority of parents didn't even think in advance about reasons for having kids. So it's hardly surprising that two-thirds of parents do no financial planning before becoming a family and are clueless about what kids will cost them. And the one-third of parents that do plan usually underestimate the true cost of raising a child, which (according to the United States Department of Agriculture) typically ranges from $150,000 to $250,000, depending on family socio-economic status; that total also excludes any private and college education, and purchase of a child's own car.

Included in those costs are the obvious: maternity clothes, diapers, formula, baby furniture and toys, and clothing. Then add in the less-obvious breast pumps, baby-room monitors, camcorder, higher life insurance coverage, and short-term home nursing care. Being able to list these helps you start budgeting, but before becoming parents, most couples have no idea just how much of that stuff they'll need, or that a toddler's sweater and shoes can cost almost as much as adults' do. The most serious underestimation, however, comes from not including health items such as higher medical insurance premiums, out-of-pocket deductibles and co-payments, uncovered medical expenses such as well-baby visits, and over-the-counter medicines, creams, lotions, ointments, and powders.

Most couples also fail to consider the need for added family "infrastructure" – starting with the likely trade up to a bigger, safer car. They also don't account for the likelihood of needing a bigger apartment, how soon they might need to buy a condominium or house, or how much remodeling they might end up doing for child-proofing, creating more space, or making the interior more environmentally friendly to tiny air passages.

1 • Born to Burn Cash

Children also cost more than most people think once their lives are no longer centered around the home. The "super-kid" syndrome has parents driving kids all over town to gymnastics, dance, and music lessons – as well as sports and other enrichment activities. They pay hefty fees for these activities, not to mention special clothing, uniforms, instruments, and equipment. Spending time with friends might seem cheaper, but because of contacts made at these activities and less emphasis on neighborhood, parents end up carpooling their kids all over town or to nearby towns, just for play dates.

Of course, what kids cost is different for each family. Although certain basics cost pretty much the same for everyone, a substantial portion of the "baby budget" is discretionary, and usually correlated with a couple's pre-child spending habits. Also, the true cost can be significantly affected by the couple's tax situation, with more child-related tax benefits accruing to those in higher tax brackets.

Top 10 Novel Ways to Reduce Child-Rearing Costs

Don't let the statistics about child-rearing costs get you down. Fight back with these ten terrific ways to reduce those costs:

10. Eliminate the option of your child choosing expensive private schools and elite colleges by refusing to talk to them until the age of six. That's when brain-wave development effectively plateaus, according to new research.

9. Don't treat them for ADD. When they bounce off the walls, it's bound to sometimes be head first, effectively having the same education-cost-reducing result as the silent treatment until age six.

8. Start toilet training at the age of three months. Not only will you save on diapers, ointments, etc. – you'll likely produce militaristic children who will comply readily to your request to "forward march" right out of the store when they've been whining too much about things they want.

7. Buy a computer for their exclusive use by the age of one. It will set you back a thousand dollars or so initially. But your child's early start on the road to hackerdom will pay back big time by age three. By then, she'll have gotten chat pals to reveal parental bank information, enabling you to siphon money from their accounts.

6. Enhance the computer with virtual-reality gear. It's far less expensive spending time in VR ballet and karate lessons, amusement parks and game arcades, etc. than doing the real thing.

1 • Born to Burn Cash

5. Don't spend any money on a new master-bedroom bed or additional bedding. Studies show that most busy parents no longer remember when they last had a chance to sleep.

4. Get your child hooked on phonics; it's far less expensive than booze, crack, or mocha lattes.

3. Start your children on coffee and cigarettes as soon as they're old enough to avoid burning themselves. It will stunt their growth and make it easier to pass them off permanently as 12 or under at restaurants, movies, and other entertainment attractions that give free meals or discounts for children.

2. If your child gets hugged by one of those greeters at the discount superstores, scream "get your hands off him, you sicko," and then threaten to sue for $100,000,000 unless you're given free lifetime shopping rights.

1. Outsource the raising of your children to reduce your parenting costs at least 25%, using this solution offered anonymously on the Internet:

Are you overwhelmed with the cost of raising your children? If so, why not try what I'm now doing – outsourcing my children to a private enterprise specializing in child-rearing as part of my family's comprehensive cost-saving effort. I've sent out requests for proposals and hope to have a contractor in place shortly.

I anticipate saving 25% of our child-rearing expenses by hiring a company specializing in the field. Between things the kids destroy, the wear and tear they put on the family residence and vehicles, and the other expenses such as school and activities, I should be able to pay a private firm about 75% of what I currently spend on the children.

Although my children have expressed concern that being raised by non-parents would be impersonal and would deprive them of some of their current privileges, I've tried to alleviate their fears by holding a family dinner meeting to announce the decision. I told the kids that mere parents don't really know how to raise kids until the kids are grown. This is obvious because every grandparent on the street has advice to give to any parent they meet. A professional child-rearing service would already know how to raise children and not make the mistakes of a rookie parent.

The outsource proposal requires companies to provide the children with benefits at least the same overall level as they receive at home, with some benefits (TV hours for example) expanding, while others (parental attention) decline. The proposal mandates certain "core" benefits, such as food, clothing, and schooling, but leaves the non-core (music, sports, television) at the discretion of the contractor.

1 • Born to Burn Cash

The outsourcing would phase in over a six month period, with the children initially spending daytime hours at their outsource site and sleeping at our home; but, as space becomes available offsite, the children will begin spending all their time away from home except when they are desperately needed at home (for example, when the yard needs "patrolling").

The children originally expressed dismay at residing off-site, but I told them they'd have weekly visitation to the house to retrieve any personal belongings, get new books, 'perform' on their musical instruments, or talk to us. This would also allow the kids to visit their pet (one dog), at least until phase two of my cost-cutting campaign, which includes outsourcing the family pet.

I came up with this idea when my wife and I were having a discussion about family finances that centered on the need to raise the family in a "better, faster, cheaper" mode. Although she was initially reluctant to have the children raised offsite, I convinced her to accept the scheme because she, too, was eligible for "outsourcing."

Don't Forget Opportunity Costs

After you calculate your estimated cost of having a kid, you'll likely shed a few tears for the loss of that dream vacation. You'll be left bug-eyed, though, when you realize that your cost analysis hasn't yet included the opportunity cost of raising a child – the amount you'll potentially lose because parenting will prevent you from taking advantage of certain financial opportunities. Namely, you must consider how kids can derail you from the career fast track, and force you to ride the local mommy and daddy job trains. Similarly, parenting demands so much time that you'll find yourself making slower progress in growing a business or completing advanced education geared to increase your earning power. It also takes first priority when your child is sick or you regard it as essential to be involved in their school and outside activities – taking your attention away from important work meetings and preventing you from staying late the way you used to in order to get ahead. And these opportunity costs will affect the working spouse, even if one spouse becomes a full-time parent.

If you think this won't apply to you, consider the findings about fathers in studies by Cornell University and the non-profit Catalyst organization, and the Radcliffe Public Policy Center. Cornell's study found 20% of men in dual-career marriages had made work or career changes that sacrificed ambition in favor of more time for fatherhood. Catalyst's study showed about 2 of every 3 men desiring the option to gear down temporarily for fatherhood and being able to gear back up later. Finally, Radcliffe's study included two related significant

1 • Born to Burn Cash

findings: the almost 80% of men who claimed a work schedule allowing more family time was a top priority just about matched the women's result; and about 70% of men under 40 indicated a willingness to give up some pay for more family time. (Of course, rumor has it that all three studies refused to publish the result that these men stipulated that an inviolable condition for their involvement was not having to change diapers.)

Staring at Those Financial Baby Blues

"So, kids cost a lot of money starting out and might also reduce the amount we're earning," you're thinking. "Well, duh" (as your kid will eventually say way too often). Besides, you're undoubtedly confident that while other kids will continue costing their parents a lot of money, once yours are no longer babies, you're going to take a no-nonsense attitude with them and keep your finances under control. Good for you, but be prepared for your kids to take a "no non-cents" attitude about their leisure time, wanting to fill it with lots of "yes cents" (and dollars), toys, activities, take-out food, and the like. In other words, kids flock to money like bees to honey, and you need to know just how much and how often they'll be stinging your wallet.

Children are from "Mores" and Parents are from (D)Earth

By the age of three, your lovable little bundle might be as unrecognizable as a TV space alien – apropos because research shows that's when children already recognize 100 product logos. In fact, "The War of the Worlds" (Planet Want vs. Planet Wallet) costs American parents almost $200 billion of child-influenced spending annually for their kids under 12; that's in addition to the more than $25 billion those youngsters spend directly.

The good news, according to a Rand Institute study, is that teens have less influence on family spending – "only" $150 billion annually. But Teenage Research Unlimited delivers the bad news that teens themselves spend $200 billion annually of money they've earned or received as allowances or gifts – and that amount has been doubling every 10 years.

1 • Born to Burn Cash

What the Experts Say about this Level of Spending and Children

- **Children learn from the example** of baby-boomer parents who don't set limits on their own habits of indulgence.

- **Even parents who show restraint fail to convey that message** to kids by using a combination of cash-less transactions with credit cards and magical withdrawals from ATMs.

- **Kids are left without an understanding** that there's a finite supply of family money to meet the endless demands being put on it. Some pre-school kids even think there is a money store where parents buy the money they need to use to buy other things.

- **In two-income families, parents often substitute money** for the time they can't give kids, and when they do spend time with kids, it's often in the most convenient parent-child interaction, shopping.

- **The average child is exposed to tens of thousands of advertisements** annually – from magazines and newspapers, the Internet, TV, telemarketers, and direct mailings. If that doesn't directly influence a wish to spend, then peer pressure from other children who have succumbed does.

- **Kids short on self-esteem may try to define themselves** through the products they purchase – especially brand-name clothing. Parents with their own self-esteem issues contribute to this by making sure that Tommy is as well-dressed as Scotty and also has the latest hand-held video game. Just like adults, many kids learn to use spending as a substitute for unmet emotional needs.

- **Changes in disciplinary style and emphasis have led parents** to be much more lax in teaching and enforcing impulse control in young children. Kids learn that parents who give in to their non-spending impulses also cave in financially.

1 • Born to Burn Cash

- **Even parents who have some success enforcing impulse control** often fail to take the next step of teaching kids delayed gratification and how to prioritize their purchases (once they're old enough to grasp the concept).

- **Most schools do not teach kids about money management**, and they actually encourage unplanned and excessive spending with endless fundraisers. After all, who buys the candy and knick-knacks if not parents? Even worse, though, kids are targeted in schools by savvy marketers. A Consumer's Union study entitled "Captive Kids: A Report on Commercial Pressures on Kids at School," noted these commercial influences in the public schools: biased educational materials produced by commercial interests; financial pressures resulting in school systems forming partnerships with businesses in exchange for needed materials that make kids a "captive audience for commercial messages"; and pervasive forms of advertising throughout school facilities, including "branded products, licensed brand goods, coupons, sweepstakes and contests, and outright advertisements."

- **Children are not taught to value their possessions.** If their negligence results in damage or loss, parents usually take the easy route of simply replacing the item – rather than making the child go without. (Or, without something else if what's been lost is an essential item such as a winter coat.)

- **Parents feel they're putting their children at a competitive disadvantage** if they don't provide them every possible enrichment opportunity, and fill their spare and vacation time with productive – and costly – activities.

- **Parents who want their children to be popular get sucked into a vicious cycle of obligatory gift exchanges** for endless birthday parties, holidays, etc.

MONEY

1 • Born to Burn Cash

Want Yes, Waste Yes

Despite everything working against them, some parents do succeed in imposing limits on what they spend on children and in helping their children limit what they spend themselves. Unfortunately, though, they're often unable to limit their children's exposure to money molesters, those financial porn purveyors who saturate the media with every conceivable form of spending solicitation. Consequently, children who are more prepared to thwart physical predators because they've learned about good touches and bad touches are nevertheless at the whim of those who prey on their inability to distinguish good spending from bad spending.

 ### How Children Go Wrong Because They Lack a Good Sense of Values – The Sense to Buy Things They Value and to Get the Best Values

- **Kids spend their dollars and cents without applying number sense.** The "mathematical innumeracy" (documented in a book by Temple professor John Allen Paulos) that plagues adults is widely prevalent in kids who have trouble understanding the application of percentages to discounts and finance charges, division to unit pricing, and general quantification of product benefits to comparison shopping.

- **Kids are too focused on their own specific demands** to appreciate the power of the general law of supply and demand. Those great new faux leather jackets they don't really need now will probably sell for half in six months.

- **Just as adult spending has been strongly influenced** by frequent-flyer programs and state lotteries, kids get addicted to lottery-like promotions that give them chances to win prizes every time they buy a product.

1 • Born to Burn Cash

- **Parents do their kids a serious disservice by simply giving** them all the money they need so that they don't have to work and can concentrate on school and other activities. Kids tend to be far more careful with money that they've earned because they learn the relative effort required for different purchase amounts.

- **Parents deepen the damage by giving kids allowances** and then either telling them exactly how every cent should be used, or giving in to demands beyond the allowance for purchases it's meant to cover. Both behaviors fail to make kids accountable for their actions with money because they don't have to live with consequences.

- **Parents also fail to be good role models for savvy spending.** A 1999 study by the Employee Benefits Research Institute showed that more than half of parents fail to use a budget for conducting their financial affairs, and a similar percentage fails to fully pay off credit-card debt from month to month.

- **Parents either don't monitor their kids' use of TV** and the Internet, or only monitor it for sex and violence. Gullible kids then take the commercial messages at face value, rather than learning to question them when parents point out obvious untruths or relate contradictory experiences.

- **Even diligent parents are helpless in the face of "stealth advertising"** in (non-toy) kids' products, "wholesome" kids' clubs, TV, movies, and magazines. In a report entitled "Selling America's Kids: Commercial Pressures on Kids of the 90s," the Consumer's Union magazine for kids, *Zillions*, documented the ways that marketers reach kids through shrewd product licensing, product placement, advertorials, celebrity sponsorships, and similarly subtle messages.

1 • Born to Burn Cash

Financial Faith Breach:
Parents Who Don't Teach

So instead of the media being the marketing message, how about Mom (and Dad) delivering the money-moxie message. According to the "2001 Parents, Youth & Money Survey" (sponsored by the Employee Benefit Research Institute and other organizations), more parents are starting to realize the need to teach their children about money management, but far too many fail. For example, only 38% of parents feel it's their responsibility alone to teach kids about money. Most think it should be shared with the schools, yet the facts show that schools rarely do it.

When parents do teach, few leave out savings, price comparisons, or information about getting a job. But more than half don't teach kids about investing, and only half teach them to track expenses or prepare a budget. And parents score only about 60% in involving kids in discussions about family finances, while 71% help kids set financial goals other than college.

Many parents realize their shortcomings – 40% responded that their children don't adequately understand finances, and only a quarter said they are very effective financial teachers. Yet, they don't compensate much by helping children learn on their own, registering less than 30% in the categories of providing educational materials, providing financial software, or encouraging learning on the Internet (or elsewhere).

Furthermore, these statistics might paint too optimistic a picture because almost two-thirds of kids report not knowing as much about financial management as they should, while 94% of kids say that they turn to their parents as a source of financial information. (Of course, we might suspect the kids were fibbing if they'd reported that only 53% turn to parents for an allowance. NOT!)

It's clear, though, that far too many parents are turning away when their kids turn to them about money. Yet those same parents will never turn away their kids' requests for money. Their children desperately need them to turn things around and help make them into money mavens.

1 • Born to Burn Cash

Parental Teaching Failings
Leave Kids Financially Ailing

But how can a money-mentor moron, or someone who thinks he is, produce a money maven? Or what about more knowledgeable parents who still fear they'll do more harm than good.

If you don't feel up to the teaching task, relax, because anything you do will probably help. So don't feel you have to master everything in this book before you get started. Do however, consult the following list to avoid common mistakes.

More than a Pocketful of Money-Teaching Mistakes Parents Commonly Make

- **Start Too Late.** You might think you have plenty of time to teach your kids about money, but it's never too early to start. (Once they're beyond the age they won't put it in their mouths when you give it to them!) After all, they start trying to influence your spending decisions as toddlers, so why not start trying to influence them as well? Even if you don't specifically deal with money to start with, you can deal with their impulsive wants with reasoning and rules – rather than just rejecting them automatically and without explanation.

- **Fail to Teach Regularly.** Once they're old enough to be taught at all, every day offers opportunities to teach informally, but too many parents overlook most of those opportunities. For example, you can take advantage of your use of money, credit cards, and checks used in purchases to explain to your child what you're doing. Also, when kids get older and are able to be taught more broadly and in depth, parents often make the mistake of waiting until there's time to have "the money talk." Instead, they could be doling out the advice in frequent bite-size chunks.

1 • Born to Burn Cash

- **Convey Money Issues Negatively.** Some parents do better at recognizing "teachable moments," yet only the negative ones. They'll sit their child down for a lecture after a nag-filled shopping expedition, loss of a valuable item at school or play, or after money was spent frivolously on an expensive purchase. Instead, they might consider sitting down with the child after a successful shopping trip in which there was little nagging. They could then, for example, talk about how pleasant it is to take a child shopping who understands the need for the family to live within its means, and follow it up with a small raise in allowance to reward the responsible behavior.

- **Fail to Tie Financial Teaching to Values Teaching.** An increasing number of parents are concerned about teaching values – some even opting to homeschool their kids to help accomplish that. Yet most parents fail to put their money teachings in the context of the values they want their children to learn, or even contradict their stated values by the way they handle money or act as financial role models. For example, some parents who emphasize the importance of hard work and dedication to reach long-term goals will nevertheless put the family in excessive debt to buy more house than they can afford rather than plan to "trade up" later. Or parents who teach kids to respect all classes of people equally might nevertheless tell a child looking for work that they "don't want you working in that kind of place."

- **Fail to Temper Kids' Expectations.** The parents of baby boomers wanted their kids to have it better than they did. In turn, the baby boomers wanted their kids to have the best, period. Many boomer children who are now becoming parents are reluctant to retreat from their parents' standards for them, but it's either necessary, healthier, or both. It's far better for kids to look forward to having it even better as an adult, rather than worrying about not having it as good.

- **Contradict Restraint Message with Give-In Actions.** An important part of financial responsibility is listening to your inner voice telling you when enough is enough. But many parents tell their children that and then give in, making it more likely that children won't grow to trust their inner voices as adults because they couldn't trust their parents' voices as kids.

1 • Born to Burn Cash

- **Fail to Wean Them from the "Bank of Mom and Dad."** Parents who act as banks to their kids are likely to be subject to a lifetime run on their assets. Instead, they should think of themselves as "angel investors" who provide the seed money for the child's development, overseeing the child's transition into an increasingly self-sufficient enterprise.

- **Fail to Connect Behavior Issues and Financial Teaching.** Some parents don't see the possible financial lesson when children steal from siblings or friends, lose or carelessly break things regularly, or secretly hoard their allowance while nagging for things. These could indicate the development of financial insecurity or stress, so parents should always treat undesirable behavior with a financial component as both a values and financial teaching opportunity.

- **Fail to Exploit Allowance As a Teaching Tool.** Parents know they're supposed to give a gradually growing allowance as kids get older and show more responsibility. Yet, many fail to cultivate that responsibility by not defining and enforcing guidelines for use of the allowance or, in contrast, fully dictating its use and not allowing children enough discretionary use of it. And, as kids get older, parents fail to expand the allowance concept to include clothing, personal-care products, and sporting-goods allowances that encourage kids to make smart purchasing decisions (instead of always wanting name-brand jeans, makeup, or sneakers).

- **Fail to Allow Kids to Learn from Money Mistakes.** As an allowance-misuse corollary, many parents fail to allow children to learn from mistakes with all their various money inflows – including earnings from chores or jobs, and cash gifts received for birthdays, holidays, or other occasions.

- **Fail to Educate Themselves Adequately.** Parents have little hope of teaching their kids the necessary financial skills if they lack them themselves. Although recent attention has been focused on youth financial illiteracy, it's a national problem that spans the entire age spectrum. 1998 and 1996 surveys by the Securities and Exchange

1 • Born to Burn Cash

Commission and Princeton Survey Research Associates, respectively, point to a substantial majority of adults falling short on investing knowledge, retirement planning, and working towards other major financial goals.

- **Fail to Go All the Way.** If you believe in abstinence education, don't be offended; I'm referring to adults' failure to go beyond the basics when they do try teaching finances to their kids. For example, most teach them how to write a check, but not how to balance a checkbook; how to track their expenses, but not how to prepare a budget; how to buy a stock, but not how to read a brokerage or mutual-fund statement; how to get a credit card, but not how to responsibly use it; how to shop for a car, but not how to determine if you're really being offered a good or fair deal; and how to understand their paychecks, but not how to prepare a 1040EZ tax return. Let's be clear, your child's intimate familiarity with finances is not something that should wait until marriage.

- **Fail to Get to First Base.** Many parents don't feel competent to go that far, but they at least owe their children enough financial knowledge to begin successful independent living. In the final chapter on financial literacy, we'll define just what that means.

- **Fail to Involve Kids in Family Finances.** Parents would probably find it much easier to teach kids what they need to know if they started involving them in family financial meetings from the time they first have basic arithmetic skills. Then children wouldn't get the message that financial subjects are taboo, and their natural curiosity would be unleashed in a flurry of questions. Think of the possibilities: instead of asking why the sky is blue, they'll be asking why a budget is in the red, and perhaps they'll even offer suggestions to help put it in the black.

- **Leave Kids Feeling Financially Overwhelmed.** For some parents, it's not that they regard finances as adult only, it's that dealing with finances makes them feel angry, frustrated, and incompetent – so involving their kids seems out of the question. That attitude, though, is clearly picked up by kids and could very well stay with them the rest of their lives. By your attainment of financial control, and showing it, your kids will be much more confident that they'll be able to as well.

1 • Born to Burn Cash

- **Portray "Wealthiness" as Next to Godliness.** For many people, that undesirable feeling of financial frustration that can be conveyed to kids stems from a real struggle to make ends meet. For too many others, however, it's because they can't live the lavish lifestyle they want while remaining solvent. Nevertheless, the "wannabe wealthy" hide that frustration and instead project the American Dream image of "you can have anything you want" to their kids, sending the clear message that living within one's means is demeaning. It's no wonder that Americans bought into the "spend our way out of the September 11th tragedy" campaign, which will undoubtedly lead to financial tragedy for kids who have been inculcated with unrealistic expectations.

- **Unwittingly Pass on Misguided Money Values.** A 2001 article by Jane Rosen-Grandon, a PhD marriage and family counselor, cites how children are influenced by their parents' attitudes and values, and how parents in turn were influenced by their parents. The problem is that as parents, we might very well be passing on financial values that were appropriate in the mid-20th-century, but out of place today. She also says that children tend to "inherit" the particular ways we worry about money. To counteract all this, she suggests that parents talk to each other about how they want their children to think about and deal with money as a prerequisite to communicating with them about it.

What Type Are You?

Psychologist Dr. Kathleen Burney has researched financial behavior for almost 20 years. She has developed a classification scheme to help people understand their 'money types,' now widely used by financial advisors. Using her Money Max™ questionnaires, couples can determine their types and the characteristics that go with them, allowing them to better understand each other and why each approaches money differently. Check out: **www.kathleenburney.com**.

We all should recognize ourselves as guilty of being remiss in meeting at least some financial education responsibilities. But don't allow this talk of failure make you feel like a failure. Instead, build on everything you've done right as a parent and use this as an opportunity to raise your parenting grade even higher. And if that doesn't motivate you, be prepared to respond to the state of youth financial emergency being declared in this chapter's final section.

1 • Born to Burn Cash

Your Kids and Money: Make Change(s) Now

No, of course you're not the "average" American family. But let's take a look at that family's financial status to see just what's at stake regarding your children's role in your family finances and the financial changes ahead of them. Start with the estimates of average non-mortgage debt – including credit card, auto loan, home equity, and parental college loans – ranging from $20,000 to $30,000. Then consider the average mortgage rapidly approaching the $100,000 watermark. Yet this family has less than a $50,000 income and total net worth (assets minus debts, including equity in the home) of less than $75,000.

The results of this record of meager savings and swollen debt includes more than 1% of home loans now in foreclosure, and a doubling, to almost 1.5 million, of annual personal bankruptcy filings in the last 10 years of "prosperity." So maybe it's good that we're unlikely to ever again attain the sustained economic growth rates associated with that prosperity during our lifetimes. On the other hand, because you're not the average family, you might have a sinking feeling now that the recession has let the air out of your economic balloon. And you'd be right, a nation full of deflated balloons means the party's over. There's no better time to clean up your family financial act.

That's why it's mandatory that you get your kids with the program, encouraging them to act as part of your family financial team, rather than against it. Furthermore, doing so will not only help keep your family afloat now, it will also reduce the chance that your child will become a financially irresponsible adult who will cause discord years from now through requests for loans or outright handouts. And don't discount the improvements you might make in how you handle your finances from the knowledge you'll acquire in preparing to get your kids involved.

1 • Born to Burn Cash

Even more importantly, you owe your children the best possible start. From an economic viewpoint, they'll benefit far more from your studious attention to their financial education than from putting yourself in debt just so that they can go to an expensive private college instead of an inexpensive public institution. My argument is supported by a recently published study by Princeton professors of 1976 college graduates who were all accepted to an equivalent set of elite private and non-elite public schools. For various reasons, some attended the elite schools and others the less selective ones. Yet 20 years later, the two groups had approximately equal incomes.

How Parents Make a Difference

Of course, no similar study has been done of the financial position of adults who did or didn't get good home financial education and experience. But survey evidence reveals promising trends for the "financially educated and experienced" kid.

 Some Promising Trends

- **Kids whose parents never discuss financial matters** with them present scored significantly lower on a financial literacy test than kids from homes where finances are at least sometimes discussed openly.

- **Kids who receive formal or parental financial education,** coupled with experiences in investing, credit card use, and other financial activities, scored better in financial literacy than those who received education alone, experience alone, or neither. The results also show that either education or experience alone provide little advantage over those who receive neither.

- **Kids who've taken financial education** courses increase their savings afterwards.

1 • Born to Burn Cash

Why Parents Must Make a Difference

Regardless of how much or little financial education immediately affects your kids, they'll definitely need as much as possible in the long-term – starting with the fact that their (life expectancy) term will be longer. That means they'll need more money during their lifetimes – especially during retirement. Yet, often the government and private enterprise are seemingly conspiring to thwart their attempts to retire comfortably.

 ### How Our Institutions – Public and Private – Stand in the Way

- **Based on current trends,** in today's dollars, the college classes of 2020 will graduate with an average student loan debt (not including parental loans) of $20,000 and credit card debt of $5,000 – not the ideal way to start independent living and prepare for family life. Meanwhile, some benefits experts and financial planners are predicting that most of their potential employers won't even provide medical insurance coverage and will transfer the total cost of benefit plans such as 401(k) administrative costs to employees.

- **Traditional employer pensions are rapidly becoming** a historical footnote, as is the notion of loyal service to one employer, and the ability to work in one career for a lifetime. Our youth must be prepared to live in a "free agent" society in which they'll have to fund their own retraining several times during their working years while floating from employer to employer, contract to contract, or from one consulting opportunity to the next. And they're more likely than ever to be running their own business. In all cases, they must be prepared to maximize their retirement contributions to various employer and self-employed plans, be nimble in transferring them to new employers' plans or conduit IRAs, and be skillful in managing them for good long-term investment return.

1 • Born to Burn Cash

- **They'll pay more than a fair share in payroll taxes** to continue providing Social Security and Medicare benefits to their parents and grandparents. Yet it's unlikely that those programs will be nearly as generous to them when the time comes (if they still exist at all).

- **Finances have become much more complex** than they were 25 years ago – when 401(k)s, cash-balance pensions, infinite mortgage choices, home equity lines of credit, publicly accessible IPOs, Real Estate Investment Trusts, mortgage-backed securities, and numerous other financial opportunities and instruments didn't exist. Just as computer technology has progressed exponentially, the financial world appears to be getting more complex at a similar pace. Our kids will be dealing with hundreds of financial products and concepts we've never heard of, and (seemingly) infinitely more predatory scams and loaded (against them) "deals" intended to part them from their money. It will take specific, in-depth financial education, not just good logical thinking, to cope with that level of complexity.

If all that isn't challenging enough, our kids will likely be victims of real and dubious progress that is setting the stage to raise their cost of living beyond normal inflation. Globalization is bringing even the poorest parts of the world a taste of indulgent living now only enjoyed by a small fraction of the world's population, and once at the table, developing countries won't want to leave until they're served. That means greatly increased demand for the world's finite supplies of energy and water, among many other scarce resources – which will surely cause spikes in their prices.

Hopefully, technological advancements will eventually allow an unlimited supply of those scarce resources, but it might not happen soon enough to help the next generation or two. Meanwhile, because our technology has left behind some nasty waste products, our children will also be paying heavily to clean up behind us. The people who solve these problems will have to be more highly educated than ever, further driving up the cost of higher education for your children and their children. And the environmental damage done by all this technological progress is a major factor in rising medical costs, which will surely continue to outpace inflation.

1 • Born to Burn Cash

So, unless our children aggressively take every possible countermeasure, they might well not be able to live as well as we do. Just as all of us will do well if we start better conserving the world's scarce resources, so must our children start conserving their cash in the form of saving and investing. The earlier they start, the longer the time horizon they'll have for that money to grow and offset leaps in living costs. Yesterday isn't too soon to help them start managing their money better, and today isn't too late.

Finally, your children might respond to global challenges by wanting to do more service to society than any generation before, and thereby willingly accept a lower standard of living. If so, it will be even more important to become financially savvy, both to be able to live on a shoestring, and possibly to donate a significant portion of modest assets as seed money to help others realize the dream of rising from poverty. That's their choice, but it's up to you as a parent-educator to make that option possible.

Chapter Two

Earn Baby, Earn:
Financial Preparation
for Parenthood

Happy Days. May many await you once you have children (or continue to raise the ones you have).

But let's get real, especially if your idea of parenting comes from watching reruns of that TV classic. The low-maintenance, perfect-kid Ron Howard of *Happy Days* has grown into a Hollywood heavyweight who's now as high-maintenance and hair-challenged as today's newborn babies. And if your future teenager should wax nostalgic and imitate Howard's *American Graffiti* automobile antics, you'll end up paying $5,000 annually just to provide him car insurance. In other words, without realistic planning, the financial challenges of parenting today could quickly take you from *Happy Days* reverie to Happy Farm reality.

As Chapter 1 made loud and clear, parental happy days are indeed expensive days, but don't despair. This chapter kicks off our quest to cash in on parenting pleasure without running out of cash.

A Parent's Guide to

MONEY

2 • Earn Baby, Earn

Correct Your Preconceiving Money Notions

If you're like most of today's couples, you'll start experiencing that pleasure long before childbirth. But to make sure it lasts, carve a little time into those carefree-couple days to make thorough financial preparations for parenthood. Expect some pain your first time – when first confronting the costs of diapers, daycare, and 101 other intimate dollar details. You'll be glad you lost your economic innocence when you realize there's no time to waste in starting to score enough cash to cover costs you'd never have otherwise anticipated.

Before we cover those specific costs, and the more complex financial dynamics you'll be dealing with as new parents, let's establish this given: having a baby and raising it to adulthood almost always costs more in time, energy, effort, and money than even prepared parents-to-be expect while they're expecting. And that's true whether a couple plans to continue earning two full incomes, have one spouse split time between primary parenting and part-time work, or have one spouse fully devoted to parenting. Here's why you should expect the unexpected.

What's the FMLA?

In 1993, against strong opposition of the business community, the President signed the Family and Medical Leave Act. It's intended to remedy a problem with parents being able to take unpaid leave from work for at least a few months after having a child without losing their jobs. In addition, the act provided the opportunity for anyone wanting to take time off due to a family member's serious health-related problem. The act has proven useful in providing parents a better opportunity to bond with their newborn. However, the act fails to cover millions of workers in companies that employ less than 50 people.

26

2 • Earn Baby, Earn

Expect the Unexpected

- Despite the 1993 federal Family and Medical Leave Act (FMLA), mothers are returning to work earlier than ever; a Census Bureau report shows that more than 50% of working women resume work within six months of giving birth. Meanwhile, fathers are more talk than action in taking advantage of FMLA provisions; 75% of men surveyed by the Conference Board feel a sense of risk about using FMLA for parenting time-off. Although under-use of the FMLA is largely attributable to career concerns of both men and women, it's also an indication that once spouses are accustomed to living on that income, it's hard to let it go.

- **Telecommuting might not turn out to be the panacea** on which you're counting. Technology does make telecommuting highly feasible, but reports of its explosive growth are over-hyped. Although about 9 million Americans telecommute at least once a week, many companies continue to shun telecommuting due to concerns about data security, state tax laws when telecommuting from out of state, Occupational Safety & Health Administration and Americans with Disabilities Act rules and regulations, and union resistance. Furthermore, even where it exists, many managers distrust telecommuters, so new parents planning to work from home for more than a few months often get negative "vibes" from their management. They frequently modify their optimistic plans due to that and the feeling that they are out of the loop of informal office communication.

- **If anything, telecommuting is leading to less at-home involvement** with children because it's being used more as a temporary bridge for continuing work even in the first weeks after birth while the mother recovers as quickly as possible and rushes her return to the office. A 2000 Department of Labor Study of the FMLA found that for about 25% of those taking a leave, the decision to return to work was affected by perceived pressure from the employer.

2 • Earn Baby, Earn

- **Working at home with a baby** or younger children is usually either insufficiently efficient or too efficient. Some parents end up spending more time than they should be during the work day with the children, even with an in-house babysitter, just because they're there, tuned into what's going on, and more accessible. Or they find that being logged in all the time makes it hard to pull away from work at all – a sort of double standard in which they overdo it in reaction to suspicions that they're slacking.

- **Working part-time often doesn't work out** as planned because parents find they can't get enough done if they stick strictly to their part-time schedules, thus often working close to full-time while still being paid part-time. Or they get less job satisfaction or fewer opportunities for advancement because they're not taken as seriously as the full-time workers on staff.

- **When one parent stays home, the highly touted savings** – such as lower clothing and clothes-cleaning bills, fewer lunches out, and less commuting often fail to materialize. That can result from the extra time with children getting filled with more cost-incurring activities or extra fatigue resulting in far more take-out suppers than expected.

- **The marriages of new parents in two-job families** are definitely stressed. In *When Partners Become Parents: The Big Life Change for Couples*, two University of California (Berkeley) psychologists give a detailed accounting of their research on how fatigue, lack of support systems, job and other major changes, and other factors all make it a challenge to keep things together after childbirth.

- **You could become the victim of increasing activism** against family-friendly government and employer policies by singles or marrieds without children. Supported by organizations such as nokidding.com and articles and books such as *The Baby Boon: How Family-Friendly America Cheats the Childless*, childless activists argue that benefits are tilted towards those with children. They've garnered enough publicity to have some employers considering a jump off the family-friendly-benefits bandwagon, or at least a need to pull in the reins.

2 • Earn Baby, Earn

- **Especially when babies aren't planned,** some new parents feel unnecessarily compelled to become a homeowner for both the space and supposed tax and other financial advantages. However, any possible tax advantages can be outweighed by significant fix-up, remodeling, and maintenance costs for the type of home that first-time buyers can afford. It's important to do a careful analysis of the cost of buying immediately versus continuing to rent and buying when you're more established as new parents and have a better handle on your finances.

Get in (Family) Money Style

It will prove challenging enough to deal with the unexpected work-related and other external obstacles that might detour you on your path to mastering new-parent finances. But you must also be prepared to steer clear of internal personal and marital road hazards such as those stemming from the ways you and your spouse were raised. You might be unaware of these influences or think you've already explored these issues with your spouse during and before your marriage. But the reality of parenthood will raise deep-seated aspects of both of your upbringings to the surface, and expose hidden attitudes and insecurities about family living. Let's look at how these discoveries will shine a new light on the differing family-oriented financial styles of you and your spouse.

Your Parents' Money Management

Your parents might not have deliberately taught you about money, and if they did, you might not have paid much attention. But they taught you about money just the same by their behavior regarding it. If they fought about it, you certainly knew, and maybe you even knew why they were fighting. By observing who won the fights, you've probably been influenced in your beliefs concerning who should control your own family's money. If you were shouted down, ignored, or immediately acceded to in your requests for money, you might end up interacting with your own child the same way. If your parents always seemed stressed about money, you're more likely to focus on money's importance in your own family. This is particularly true if your parents divorced and you know that money played a big role in that (and in your life after the divorce).

2 • Earn Baby, Earn

Of course, parental influence could have been positive as well, yet even that can lead to trouble if your spouse's experience wasn't positive (or vice versa), leading the "happy money" spouse to assert moral authority in decisions about money management. Regardless of the specific parental influences, however, you must recognize that they're there – as do the 50% of respondents in a Lutheran Brotherhood Survey who said their parents were the biggest influence on their money management.

Your Pre-Parenthood Money Management

Ok, now you have reason to blame your parents for your financial foibles, but do you really want to have your kids someday blame you the same way? To avoid that, you must not only avoid repeating their money mistakes as parents, but also avoid continuing your own faulty money management patterns as "pre-parents." And even if you haven't made mistakes, you will if you and your spouse are not on the same "baby makes three" strategy page. Start with a reality check: two out of three spouses argue about money, and although that statistic isn't broken down by childless versus those with children, you can safely bet that a smaller percentage argue before children than after.

 Eight Questions for Spouses

- **Is money regarded as a precious commodity** or is it taken for granted?

- **Should money be a reward**, a punishment, a means to show love, or a means of withholding love?

- **Should money be jointly and equally managed** or should one parent be in charge? And should one spouse be the main provider around whose job the family revolves, or are both spouses' roles in the workforce important for both monetary and psychic reasons?

- **Did you or spouse accept financial** help from parents as an adult before, or even during, your marriage and do your beliefs differ on that?

- **What are your overall attitudes about money?** Do you see it as a positive thing that helps enhance life, or as a negative thing because you're always worried about not having enough? Does making a money mistake make you angry or depressed, or can you shrug it off and go on from there?

2 • Earn Baby, Earn

- **What do each of you think about major purchases?** Do you buy only when you have the money to pay for it, or is buying on credit against future earnings okay?

- **Are you all-for-one and one-for-all about money** or "his versus hers" in terms of allocation between yourselves and disclosures about "your own" money?

- **Do you have strong beliefs about how money should be used** regarding personal indulgence versus generosity with friends, causes, and charities? Do different religious beliefs underpin these differences?

If you're honest in exploring these areas, you'll almost certainly find significant differences with your spouse. As Robert Louis Stevenson said, "Marriage is one long conversation, checkered with disputes."

Olivia Mellan, a psychotherapist specializing in money issues, agrees with Stevenson. When it comes to money, Mellan says that opposites attract. And if "sames" marry, she believes that one will become different to create a balance in the relationship, and that it is usually necessary for one spouse to emerge as the dominant decision maker. Mellan frames her findings in terms of paired-opposite money personality combinations that are most often found in couples. Her book, *Money Harmony: Resolving Money Conflicts in Your Life and Relationships*, covers them in detail, but here's the short course with each of the six pairs identified and briefly (whimsically) described.

 ## *Six Money-Personality Combinations*

- **Hoarder versus Spender:** Or lockbox versus loosey-goosey.

- **Worrier versus Avoider:** Or what you know can hurt you, versus what you don't know can't hurt you.

- **Money Monk versus Money Amasser:** Or go for only the money you truly need to live on, versus go for the gold.

- **Planner versus Dreamer:** Or reach financial goals by the perspiration of carefully structured workouts, or by meditating.

2 • Earn Baby, Earn

- **Risk Takers versus Risk Avoiders:** Or no pain, no gain versus stay out of the rain and stay dry.

- **Money Merger versus Money Separatist:** Or united we stand together versus divided we also stand, apart.

Whether you subscribe to her classifications or not, it's critical that each spouse knows where the other is coming from financially. By each filling out the questionnaire on page 233 in Appendix A, provided courtesy of the Iowa State University Extension Service, you'll be able to compare responses and emerge with a much better understanding of your "money-in-marriage" dynamic. (Besides, it beats sitting around waiting for labor to start.)

Influence of Others

Consider yourself lucky if this close examination of marital money influences hasn't driven you to drink. But even if you're an avowed teetotaler, you'll surely admit that you're sometimes guilty of driving (family financial decisions) while under the influence (of others). Go ahead and deny that you don't spend more than you intended when you're out with other couples who empty their wallets, or in other situations act like the big spender to curry favor or impress friends and co-workers. And gender stereotypes and husband/wife roles haven't changed all that much financially. What husband of a wife from "comfortable" circumstances doesn't feel compelled to show that she's even better off now, and what wife of a husband from a modest-means family doesn't feel compelled to demonstrate that she's capable of frugality if needed?

To better understand how you're influenced in ways you might not be aware of, some experts advise writing a "money autobiography" or keeping a "money journal." Both are ways of documenting your use of money and allowing self-reflection on your motivations and influences.

You might view these exercises as flaky byproducts of pop psychology and the whole late 1980s frugality movement. But before you dismiss them, consider a 1997 article by Jane Katz, "The Joy of Consumption" in *The Federal Reserve Bank of Boston Regional Review*. The article traces the historical evolution (or mutation) of consumption from its origins in meeting basic needs to its use by the wealthy as a symbol of their status to its current use across the economic strata as a means

2 • Earn Baby, Earn

to "create identity and a mode of personal expression." In that way, consumption becomes a means of influencing others' opinions of ourselves, which Katz illustrates by citing the statistic that a professional family spends an average three to eight times as much as an unskilled-labor family does on "visible" living room and dining room furniture, but only one and a half times as much on "hidden" bedroom furniture and linens.

Katz's most convincing argument is that we spend "so we can participate in activities that make us members of our community," citing data about the "basic needs" of various population classes. In every group over the last 50 years, the cost to meet our constantly upgraded "needs" has multiplied much faster than the rate of inflation, making us creatures of social habits as much as living necessities. Knowing that is crucial in creating and nurturing your children's lives, because their well-being might require going against society's social grain in favor of your family's fabric.

Starting early is important, because it might prove impossible once your children arrive. Yet another great Lutheran Brotherhood survey revealed that more than one-third of kids say it's important to have what other kids have and almost two out of five parents agreed. No wonder that kids also responded that money matters are stressful, feel peer pressure to keep up with other kids, and are significantly influenced by advertising.

Building a No-Check-Bouncing Baby Budget

Before any peer pressure, however, you'll have to deal with "dia-pe(e)r pressure" – the pressure to deal with immediate financial changes caused by your diaper-wearing addition. So sit down with your spouse now, while you still have time to sit and are able to communicate without distractions, and reexamine your whole approach to finances. Tighten your budget belt to pay off any credit-card debt before the birth, because you'll surely have problems doing it afterwards. This more frugal approach will pay off big time once your child is old enough to start wanting things and becomes aware of the extent to which you indulge. If current trends hold up, by the time your child is a teen, you'll be giving her $5,000 annually for discretionary spending, but if you establish your own family trend, that amount should be much less.

2 • Earn Baby, Earn

Budget? What's That?

A majority of couples planning to have children have never lived with a budget. If you're among them, before trying to build a baby budget, get some experience living with a pre-baby budget. Here's one way of doing it:

1) **Gather your detailed spending records** (receipts, check stubs, credit-card statements, etc. from the last year, or start compiling them now (and forevermore) if you don't have good records.

2) **Divide your expenses into categories,** such as mortgage or rent, groceries, dining out or takeout, insurance, entertainment, medical uncovered by insurance, utilities, etc.

3) **Divide each category into scheduled fixed mandatory expenses** (e.g. mortgage and insurance), scheduled variable mandatory expenses (e.g. electric bill), unscheduled mandatory expenses (e.g. car repair), scheduled discretionary expenses (e.g. investments and monthly health club payment), and unscheduled discretionary expenses (e.g. weekend getaway). These expenses should include all credit-card charges (even if not paid) and all non-tax deductions you're currently having taken from your paycheck for insurance, investments, etc.

4) **Determine your combined annual GROSS income** (assuming no taxes or other deductions). Then determine the annual taxes (federal, state, property and other local, social security) you'll owe on that amount assuming the standard deduction. Subtract these taxes from the gross and divide by 12 to give you your monthly "budgetable" income.

5) **Using the information you've gathered** in Items 1 thru 3 as a starting point, set up a monthly budget that matches the amount you determined in Item 4. Begin with your mandatory expenses, and include discretionary expenses, starting with highest-priority, until you run out of money. For unscheduled expenses, or scheduled expenses that aren't monthly, determine the annual amount and divide by 12.

6) **The good news is that you're not actually out of money.** Recalculate the taxes you'll owe based on the actual deductions you can take based on this budget (e.g. include charitable contributions, mortgage interest, property taxes, etc.) Determine the difference between the recalculated tax and the original tax and divide that difference by 12. You can now add that much monthly to your budgetable "income" and increase the spending in your budget accordingly.

This budget is meaningless unless you stick to it. Obviously, you can't follow it exactly because your unscheduled expenses won't occur uniformly throughout the year. If necessary, you'll dip into savings if they're running ahead of your budget, but then be sure to replace those savings later with the "under-runs" on those expenses that occur later in the year.

2 • Earn Baby, Earn

If you don't like this approach (or even if you do!), here are some resources where you can learn more about budgeting, find out about books and software that you can use to build a budget, and even print a paper budget or download a budgeting program:

- **How to Make a Budget** (great lesson with worksheets and sample budget) – www.themint.org/documents/make_a_budget.htm

- **How to Budget** (Motley Fool) – www.fool.com/foolu/askfoolu/2002/askfoolu020327.htm

- **Budget Your Way to Financial Freedom** (MoneyCentral) – http://moneycentral.msn.com/articles/smartbuy/debt/1328.asp

- **How to Budget** (Bankrate.com) – www.bankrate.com/brm/news/advice/20000511b.asp?prodtype=biz

- **Kiplinger Balance Your Budget** (including Online Budget Worksheet) – www.kiplinger.com/managing/cash/budget/

- **Budget Central** (web site for the book, **Budget Yes!**) – www.tuliptreepress.com/default.htm

Speaking of taxes, be aware that you'll be gaining an additional exemption that will allow you to deduct an extra $2,900 from your taxable income, and a child credit of $600 subtracted from your tax liability (both subject to phase-out the higher your income). Consequently, you can adjust your withholding to get more take-home pay instead of giving Uncle Sam a no-interest loan that he repays at tax time.

You might even save on more than taxes. As harried and protective (especially first time) parents, you'll have less energy and desire to dine out, or go to concerts or movies – particularly when you discover that many early-teen babysitters now command almost minimum wage. And the logistics of arranging vacations or weekend getaways with an infant might inhibit your interest in those things, too. Regarding cost control of these often hefty entertainment and leisure indulgences, fatigue and family orientation might both prove faithful financial friends.

Now that you've done this budget preparatory work, let's take a closer look at the fundamental costs during pregnancy and in your baby's first year – costs that include not only specific baby items but other items and services needed because of becoming a family.

2 • Earn Baby, Earn

Maternity, Baby, and Household Expenses

Sure, the first few months after discovering you're expecting are both carefree and extra-expense free while you both are swelling with pride. But then the wife will keep swelling, which means maternity clothes, a potentially huge expense if she works in a button-down business-dress office. (Meanwhile, the husband might need a new wardrobe too if he sweats off 20 nervous pounds.)

Then there are the pre-birth baby-preparation expenses, such as decorating and equipping a nursery, car seats (moving them from car to car is a major pain in the behind, and you'll already be hurting close to there), a breast pump (if you go that route and hubby intends to be a full partner), and a chest-or-back baby carrying device.

Speaking of those cars, you'll quickly realize that the baby takes up one more seat, but the baby's stuff takes up two. And even if the car you have is big enough for all that, you might discover it's not safe enough when you find yourself reading *Consumer Reports* for the first time. So be prepared to budget for a true family vehicle, and throw in a little extra for the darkened windows so none of your still-unencumbered acquaintances see you driving it.

Next consider where you'll be parking that new car. It's tempting to forsake the apartment-complex parking space of the tiny condo driveway in favor of an honest-to-goodness "real" house. That kind of thinking can be real trouble, though, unless you've carefully saved and planned.

Therefore, don't make the mistake of letting a real-estate broker become your financial planner by delivering the good news that you easily qualify for a mortgage. She hasn't included the bare minimum $10,000 it's estimated that middle-class families spend for baby stuff alone in their child's first year, the car you might delay buying until after you're in the house, or the maintenance and fix-up costs that are typically ignored until they have to be paid when the heat stops working or the roof starts leaking. Nor has she considered how a modest amount of credit-card debt can combine with a careless management of a tighter budget to balloon into a bloated balance that sucks up every formerly available dollar. Suddenly, those mortgage payments that seemed so manageable are about as comfortable as size-too-small pre-pregnancy jeans on mommy-to-be in her eighth month. Sure there's the potential tax break from writing off mortgage interest, but your budget might break before your first new-home tax filing.

2 • Earn Baby, Earn

If you can afford a house, you should certainly care about resale value, but don't strain to get the most expensive house. It will put severe immediate pressure on your finances, and also the continuing "keep up with the Joneses" pressure of "fitting in" by living the way your more affluent neighbors do.

If you already have a home, you might not think this applies to you. But it does, particularly if you're thinking that refinancing into a larger mortgage or taking a $20,000 home equity loan can help you add a room and cover some of your other baby expenses. The net effect on your budget could be similar to buying a new home because as a new homeowner you only had to immediately cover the difference between your former rent and the mortgage.

Whether you buy a new home, add to an existing one, or stay where you are, the inside will look as though you're living in a different place – filled to the brim with maternity and baby clothes, and scores of baby-related products. The comprehensive budget worksheet on page 227 in Appendix A, provided courtesy of an excellent educational program for unwed teenage mothers in Idaho, should give you a pretty good idea of what the most inexpensive forms of all the basics are going to cost you. You should do your own price-shopping to come up with what your actual costs will be for the same items of your desired degree of quality/luxury in your region. (The prices shown are a few years old, based on discount-store comparisons in Idaho.) Finally, ignore the items for pre-natal care and hospital stay, which we'll cover separately later in this section.

The figure you came up with should cover the bulk of your expenses, but the worksheet didn't include the following items, which you should price and add in if they apply to your situation.

Additional Costs to Include in the Reckoning

- Maternity Clothes
- Cloth Baby Carrier (e.g. Snugli)
- Frame Baby Backpack
- Baby Rocker Seat
- Baby Bouncy Seat
- Baby Walker (although many child-development specialists disapprove)
- Vinyl-Cushion Baby Carrier with handle
- Camcorder
- Digital Camera
- Birth Announcements

2 • Earn Baby, Earn

The Rich Are Different. Yeah, They Spend More for Baby

If all these expenses discourage you, take heart in the bargains you'll be getting compared to Elizabeth Hurley, whose layette purchases were recently reported in the April 22, 2002 issue of *Us* magazine. Here are a few:

- Gucci bottle carrier $186
- Blueberry cashmere blanket $375
- Blueberry cashmere teddy bear $295
- Simon Horn changing unit $1,860
- Toy box $709
- Gucci baby slippers $135

If you're thinking that this is more than you bargained for, you're probably also thinking about how you can cut these costs. Your first step should be to not confuse the true pride of becoming parents with the false pride of giving your baby everything and the best of everything. Really, your baby needs love more than luxury and quantity. That might not be obvious now, but ask other parents about what happened the first time they bought their toddlers toys in a box and they ended up playing more with the boxes than the toys. Once you determine what you really need, think used but clean, and you'll open a world of possibilities for getting valuable stuff either free or at much lower cost – and take heart in the possibility that much of what you buy can be used for subsequent babies.

Start with friends and family who are done having babies and might very well have a lot of stuff that they would offer if they didn't think you'd be offended. Make it easy on them by making the first move and asking. Once you're done collecting free equipment and clothing, start scouring your local community's classifieds and you're sure to find several ads offering cribs and other items for less than half of their discounted new prices. After all that, you'll still need to buy some things new, but if you don't wait until the last minute and take time doing price comparisons, you should achieve significant savings on the bigger items from stores and on the smaller items from mail-order or Internet catalogs. Finally, join a buying club such as Costco or Sam's to take advantage of big discounts on bulk purchases of diapers, baby goods, and other personal-care baby products.

2 • Earn Baby, Earn

Medical, Childcare, and Other Expenses

Your shopping skills will also be critical in saving money while fully meeting your needs for medical and other insurance, childcare, and other services necessitated by your new parental status.

Medical and Other Services: What to Buy and How to Buy It

- **Medical: Pre-Natal Care.** The physician visits should be covered by your health insurance (usually subject to a deductible and co-insurance) or managed-cared provider (nominal flat co-pay), possibly including the pre-natal vitamins. The hospital where you'll give birth usually provides low-cost birthing classes.

- **Medical: Delivery and Hospital Stay.** Because of considerable variation in policies, it's worth taking time before getting pregnant to look at the coverage available to you and your spouse, and possibly switch if one policy covers this much better than the other. (Review your plan documents and check on co-worker's experiences. Also, just be sure that a pre-existing conditions clause won't void coverage if you switch, and be sure to notify the insuring employer when the baby is born.)

Physician charges for the delivery and follow-up, and the hospital pediatric visits, are usually covered on the same basis as pre-natal physician charges. However, the hospital charges vary widely by policy. Some pay everything, but only up to a "reasonable and customary" charge, while others handle it like physician charges with co-insurance. Managed care providers usually cost you very little out of pocket, but beware if you have complications that could require special treatments or other specialists. But also be aware that standard insurance carriers have become very stingy about coverage, usually mandating maximum two-day hospital stays for normal delivery and three days for Cesarean; your doctor will have to move heaven and earth to get them to cover longer stays if she deems the mother not ready to leave. Even your baby might have to leave sooner than desirable for proper screening of potential jaundice, a fairly common after-birth complication that isn't serious if it's appropriately treated. That makes it imperative that you do quick post-natal follow-up with your first out-of-hospital pediatric visit, because your child might very well have to be re-admitted with a high bilirubin count for treatment under the lights.

- **Medical: Post-Natal Pediatric Visits.** Managed Care usually provides the best coverage, with generous frequency of visits and small co-pays. Standard insurance often doesn't cover well-baby visits at all, so considering price when shopping for a pediatrician could be important. If your baby is sick, however, standard insurance kicks in normally (with deductibles and co-insurance) and is often better, because it's easier to get specialist care more quickly if needed. Not to alarm you, but so many different things can afflict a baby, and as a new parent, you'll probably have little clue as to what any of them are. Avoiding managed care so that you can avoid a gatekeeper doctor can help you get the best care possible and could easily outweigh non-coverage of well-baby care.

- **Employer Medical Reimbursement Account.** This isn't an expense, but a way to save on uncovered medical expenses (deductibles, co-insurance, and co-payments) for your baby and you and your spouse as well. Look into whether your employer has a medical reimbursement account that will allow you to have money deducted from your paycheck on a pre-tax basis. You can then later have it reimbursed when you submit your documentation of uncovered expenses to the plan administrator. If you're in the 27% tax bracket, putting $2,000 in such an account will save you $540 annually. Just be sure you don't put too much in because anything exceeding your actual expenses in a given year will be forfeited.

2 • Earn Baby, Earn

Life and Disability Insurance

When it's just the two of you, income-replacement insurance isn't a necessity if you both have good jobs and don't have a mortgage, high rent, or excessive debt. But once baby makes three, it's crucial to have disability and life insurance to offset the lost income or parenting services of a spouse who becomes disabled or dies. Chances are that you have minimal life insurance equal to your salary from your employer, but that isn't enough. The amount you should carry must cover what existing assets and the remaining income won't for your children until adulthood. In addition, it should cover existing liabilities, college for the kids, the extra expenses for childcare that single parenting necessitates, final funeral and burial expenses, medical treatments, debts and taxes, estate administration and probate, upgraded insurance for the surviving breadwinner, expenses for the adjustment period (for example, grief counseling, unpaid leave, inter-family travel), spousal retraining or education, and the portion of needed retirement income that your spouse won't be able to accumulate. Furthermore, life insurance should not be restricted to covering the breadwinner(s). If the spouse who dies was not a fulltime earner, that person's policy should cover the cost of replacing the childcare and household-maintenance services that will now be done by hired help.

2 • Earn Baby, Earn

How Much Insurance Does a Parent Need?

Here are a couple of calculators to determine how much life insurance each of you should carry:

- **MSN Money/CNBC Life Insurance Needs Estimator** –
  http://moneycentral.msn.com/investor/calcs/n_life/main.asp

- **Kiplinger/Finacenter: How Much Life Insurance Do I Need** –
  www.calcbuilder.com/cgi-bin/calcs/INS1.cgi/Kiplinger

You'd expect that this type of protection doesn't come cheap, but you might be surprised at how inexpensive it is when you're young and healthy and buy the term form of life insurance, which amounts to "renting" coverage for a specific time. After that time, if you haven't died, you get nothing back for all that you paid. That might sound like a bad deal versus having your premiums for "permanent" life insurance build up cash value that you can always get back, dead or alive. But as a young parent, you'll pay up to 10 times as much for cash value, making it prohibitively expensive. However, the cost of term rises as you get older while the premium for permanent insurance remains level for most young parents. In addition, permanent insurance protection is just that, as long as you continue paying your premiums, even should your health turn sharply south. With term, you have to renew and could be refused if your health has changed, but you can offset that by paying somewhat more for a renewable term over a 10- or 20-year time period.

On balance, most young parents should buy term insurance, particularly because they don't need protection forever, only as long as dependents have needs they can't meet on their own. And if you feel comfortable doing your own research, you don't need to buy it through agents, who will often try to sell you permanent insurance regardless of your circumstances. Many quality online or toll-free call-in providers offer very attractive rates, but the key is to research the companies and make sure they're financially solid. To do this, consult a service such as AM Best to find companies whose ratings are A or better. If you feel more comfortable with an agent, you can find good ones who will truly try to meet your needs and financial circumstances with term insurance where appropriate. The extra 10 to 20 per cent premium might be worth your peace of mind.

Ironically, most young couples know to look for life insurance, yet before the age of 65, they're six times more likely to have an extended or permanent loss of income due to disability than they are to die. Nevertheless, through ignorance or

2 • Earn Baby, Earn

willingness to gamble, they don't protect against being one of the 1 in 20 working-age people at any given time who are currently unable to work due to severe disability. They've heard that long-term disability insurance is expensive, and they're right. But if they looked into it more closely, they'd realize ways to reduce the cost substantially – including lower payouts, longer waiting periods before it kicks in, and shorter periods during which it pays benefits. Remember, disability insurance is a hedge against income-loss disaster, and it's truly disastrous to lose an income for a few years while raising a child.

Childcare Costs and Tax Offsets

Much like choosing the lowest bidder to build a bridge, it's also potentially disastrous to pick a childcare provider based on cost, so it's important to know what quality care goes for in your area. Of course, the best way to find that out is to do some serious shopping by visiting centers that have good reputations. But for planning purposes, you can get a rough idea by looking at the average cost of childcare in your state for urban areas and rural areas, and perhaps adjusting that 20% upward for the quality rate.

You can do that by referring to an outstanding report prepared by the national non-profit Children's Defense Fund. Those annual urban-area averages for institutional (childcare center) care of a one-year-old in the major urban area in each state range from the $4,000s in some Southern and sparsely-populated states to an astounding almost $13,000 in Boston, Massachusetts. The most common average ranges from $6,000 to $8,000. The meager good news is that the average institutional costs across each state are about 25% less because rural care is less expensive, and the average costs of urban in-home care is 15 to 30% less. Be careful, though, because the quality of in-home care is far more variable from provider to provider, and in-home providers tend to have high turnover. (The turnover among institutional daycare workers is also high, but at least the daycare center doesn't usually quit abruptly the day before a mandatory major business meeting.)

This report is valuable reading, so even if you're (World Wide) web-shy, now's the time to be bold and log in to www.childrensdefense.org/head-resources.htm. Scroll down to "The High Cost of Child Care Puts Quality Care Out of Reach for Many Families" – you'll need Acrobat Reader to view the file. As an aside, if you're just plain shy, being pregnant and having a baby should soon cure that because total strangers will start asking you intimate details about your condition.

2 • Earn Baby, Earn

The good news for everyone is that childcare is cheaper than it seems if your provider has a federal tax ID (but be sure to pay the 'nanny' tax, expecially if you plan to go into politics). Then you can either claim the IRS childcare credit or take advantage of an IRS-approved pre-tax payment of childcare costs if your employer has a dependent-care reimbursement account (similar to the healthcare reimbursement account mentioned earlier.) Higher income couples are better off with the employer approach, typically allowing up to $5,000 "set-aside" account per year by which your employer reduces your salary, later reimbursing you when you present the childcare bills you've paid. Meanwhile, you're not paying taxes on those set-aside earnings, which saves you an amount totaling your tax-bracket percentage times the amount set aside. Thus, if you set aside $5,000 and are in the 27% tax bracket, this maximum amount would save you $1,350 annually in taxes. This compares to the $480 maximum that most taxpayers can get as a credit if they don't use a dependent care account.

Don't confuse the childcare credit with the $600 child credit that all parents get, even if they let their one-year-olds roam the streets alone while they work. Of course, the child credit won't begin to cover bail when that low-cost childcare method is discovered by the authorities.

Calculating Total Child-Rearing Expenses

Here are a few more resources to help you calculate how your budget will change when you have a baby, or what it will cost overall to raise a child:

- **How Much Will It Cost to Raise a Child** (FinanCenter) – http://partners.financenter.com/financecenter/calculate/us-eng/budget07.fcs

- **What Is the Cost of Raising a Child** (Bankrate) – www.bankrate.com/brm/calc/raiseChild.asp?nav=budget&page=calc_home

- **The Cost of Raising Children** (MoneyCentral) – http://moneycentral.msn.com/articles/family/kids/tlkidscost.asp

- **Cost of Raising a Millenium Baby** (Kiplinger) – www.kiplinger.com/features/archives/2000/July/managing/baby1.html

- **Your Little Tax Break** (Parenting) – www.parenting.com/parenting/family_finance/budget/

2 • Earn Baby, Earn

Juggle Work and Childcare

Perhaps you're thinking that childcare is not an expense you'll have to budget for, because you're adamant that one of you will be a stay-at-home parent. If so, feel free to skip this section. But stay with me in case you're still on the work versus parenting fence, or open to the possibility that adverse circumstances such as divorce, widow(er)hood, and other financial struggles could ultimately thrust you back into the workforce. After all, parenthood is a circus. You might as well learn to juggle.

Working Out: Both Working

Let's start with the vast majority of couples who will both continue employment after some amount of family leave (maternity or paternity), although one might opt for part-time status. They must address issues involving length of leave, choice of childcare and how to handle a child's need to be home due to illness if using institutional daycare, whether to stay with the same employer and whether to maintain an aggressive career path, and whether to opt for flexible job arrangements such as part-time, job-sharing, telecommuting, or part-time telecommuting. (Now be honest, did you ever think you'd have so much addressing to do after as little as one time undressing?)

Taking Family Leave of Your Cents(es): A Rough Road Back to Work

As soon as you're either planning to become pregnant or make the surprise discovery you are, it's time to check out your employer's leave policy and understand the provisions of the Family and Medical Leave Act (FMLA) that apply to new parents. If you work for a large company, you probably will get four to six weeks of paid leave, during which all your benefits will remain intact, including contributions to retirement plans, just as though you were working or were recovering from major surgery.

However, most small employers, and even some larger ones, don't pay for any leave other than the several days surrounding the birth. Nevertheless, companies that employ more than 50 people are required to comply with the FMLA (and 15 states whose laws apply in certain circumstances to various numbers of employees under 50). They must allow up to 12 weeks of unpaid leave, guaranteeing your job, or one equivalent in pay, upon your return.

2 • Earn Baby, Earn

During the leave they continue to pay whatever portion of your health insurance premium they normally pay, and allow you to cover the rest – thus keeping your insurance intact. They must also maintain your status in other benefit programs, such as pension, employee stock purchase account, and 401(k) plan. Your status in these plans is essentially frozen in time, and is unfrozen when you go back on the payroll. Thus, to calculate the economic impact, you must take into account loss of buildup in these plans while you're not working.

All bets are off, though, if you go beyond the 12 weeks, unless you live in Puerto Rico, D.C. or one of six states (California, Connecticut, Louisiana, Oregon, Rhode Island, and Tennessee) whose own FMLA-type laws allow more than 12 weeks. Don't count on extending it with vacation, because the FMLA rules allow companies to make you take all accumulated vacation and sick days as part of the 12 weeks, limiting your unpaid leave to what's left. Some companies provide an FMLA-like unpaid extension, but with rules that might be more restrictive and less favorable. For example, they might not guarantee the same job, an equivalent job, or any job at all – basing the form of your reinstatement on whether and where they have a place for you. And in companies that don't provide an extension, you're out of a job if you don't return within the 12 weeks, unless your application for special consideration is approved.

When Mommy and Daddy Are Dirty Workplace Words

Compared to the way things were when women first entered professional workplaces in large numbers 30 years ago, the FMLA's very existence is almost miraculous. But it comes with as many unofficial strings as those holding the tags on a new dress. In many work environments, men meet open hostility if they request accommodations for more family time, such as less travel or fewer evening and weekend client meetings. Studies show they definitely fear the often unspoken threat that taking a major step such as requesting FMLA will send their work lives on a bumpy, unpaved country-road detour that never rejoins the career expressway – the dreaded "Daddy Track." Oddly, too, they apparently must fight their own biology, which drives them to be breadwinners to the extent shown in another study: men worked an average of 58 more hours in the year following the birth of a child.

2 • Earn Baby, Earn

It's different for women, whose change in status is subtler because they're usually expected to want some leave. Nevertheless, if they're on the fast track before childbirth and stay out much beyond medical necessity, they're often switched to the "mommy track" in management's perception. Some women respond by outdoing the "breadwinner-biology" work habits of new fathers and return to work as soon as paid leave (if any) expires, then putting in even more hours than ever. But studies show that work-family conflicts catch up with some of them, perhaps accounting for the increasing exodus of executive-material women from corporations into their own entrepreneurial businesses. There they work even harder, but at least have some control over coordinating work and family issues.

Many women, however, welcome the "mommy track" – a term first used in a 1987 *Harvard Business Review* article by recently deceased, Felice Shwartz, founder of the influential Catalyst non-profit organization that strongly advocates for women in the workplace. Shwartz was the subject of much feminist ire for suggesting that there's nothing wrong with highly industrious women wanting more work and family balance, and such women were better off being recognized for being talented, exceptional workers who should be allowed to thrive and advance (more slowly, perhaps) without using the fast track that required sacrificing family for their work.

Flexing Your Job Arrangement Muscles

With the mommy track genie out of the bottle, and the booming 90s economy, the push for more workplace flexibility has resulted in unprecedented opportunities for new parents, particularly mothers, to make flexible work arrangements. Various studies indicate that 50 to 75 percent of all employers offer some sort of flexible work arrangements that might include regular or partial telecommuting or working at home, flexible day schedules, compressed work weeks, off-shift work, job sharing, and part-time arrangements. One study by Catalyst showed that 27 of the 70 companies it surveyed had at least 100 employees using flexible arrangements.

2 • Earn Baby, Earn

This data indicates that if you're thinking about such an arrangement, the precedent has been solidly established. However, be prepared to negotiate an arrangement, because most companies handle these situations on a case-by-case basis. You can get help from organizations such as for-profit WorkOptions Inc. (www.workoptions.com), which markets the "Flex Success Proposal Blueprint," and the non-profit University of Michigan Work/Life Resource Center (www.umich.edu/~hraa/worklife/worklife.htm).

In negotiating an arrangement, make sure that you consider the effect on your benefits in addition to your pay, should you be asking for anything less than full working hours. Any loss of benefits must be considered in assessing the financial impact of an alternate arrangement. Even if you will be working full-time, try to make an arrangement that will provide enough interaction with key co-workers and managers so that you can keep your career on track. The Catalyst study showed that more than half the women interviewed had been promoted while in a flexible work arrangement. Although you might not have advancement aspirations, you must still treat flex-work in a fully professional manner if you hope to keep the respect of your peers and possibly even keep your job in these times of higher unemployment.

The Two-for-One Not So Special: Two Earners Versus Stay-Home Spouse

To heck with flex-work, you say, because you're planning to be unemployed. Unless you're adamant, however, you should do a thorough evaluation comparing the financial and lifestyle impacts of working versus staying at home after your baby is born. If you're already a careful steward of your family's finances, you'll have a big advantage making it work. But keep in mind that in a few short years, the situation has gone from employers begging for good skilled and educated help to skilled and educated professionals begging for jobs. If the working spouse should lose the job, the non-working one might be able to get one, but it will take time and will probably be at a lower-level and salary because of atrophied skills.

Chapter Three

If Piaget Had Been a Financial Planner: Kids' Developmental Money Stages

"All the world's a stage…" Many Shakespeare readers regard that as one of the Bard's most memorable lines, and we hope that after reading this chapter, many of our readers will regard "all the child's money world is a series of stages" as one of this book's most memorable messages. The message's meaning: as children mature through each of their developmental stages (a la French psychologist Jean Piaget's framework), there's a set of financial skills they should be able to master in each stage. This chapter is intended to get you thinking along those lines by examining each desired area of children's financial mastery and what you should be teaching about that area at your child's different (st)ages.

3 • Developmental Stages

Kids Discover Money

From the moment they are physically and mentally able, kids start modeling after everyone and everything they see. Naturally, parents and siblings are the main objects of attention – well, them and the TV – and one of the things they quickly notice is the frequent appearance of little green pieces of paper and small, shiny round pieces of metal. As a parent, your first instinct will be to combat their inquisitiveness with sufficient vigilance to keep those mystery objects out of their mouths (giving new expression to that movie line, "I won't touch that money; it's dirty!"). But don't be too zealous, because once you've got their attention on money, start teaching them about it.

Money's Relation to Things

In elementary school science, children learn that the world revolves around the sun. They're told the sun is a mass of incredibly hot gas located somewhere in the vicinity of 'the almighty' the world's people have been taught to worship. But at the same time they're learning something seemingly contradictory – that the world's beautiful people have an incredible good time (a 'gas,' really) worshipping the sun, while their lives revolve around another almighty – the almighty dollar.

Adults don't find this contradiction troubling because they take it for granted that everyone aspires to live beautiful people's lives – even those who aren't big spenders and don't act as though they're money obsessed. So they don't think about the effect on kids who see that most places adults go, they have to spend money. They're not even aware how often they whip out credit cards at stores without even thinking about it, exchange a "twenty" for a small bag of food and drop the change in the car door pocket, or give the pizza delivery guy a $20 and say, "keep the change." It never occurs to them that children might form deep, lasting impressions from continued observation of these routine, oft-repeated actions. But kids do notice, and what they're witnessing has a definite impact on their perception of the role and value of money.

3 • Developmental Stages

Young Entrepreneurs to Inspire Your Children

- **Three college students of age 21** started their own financial website and have now become a very successful business.

- **A 15-year-old girl** opened her own horse resort where she trains horses, teaches lessons, boards horses, and guides riding and fishing trips.

- **A 17-year-old girl** started her own clothing company with clothes she makes herself.

Telling your kids about how young kids can start their own business and make money can get their creative juices flowing and they might think of some ideas of their own. The important thing is to get kids to try some ideas out. Whether they work or not, it's good preparation for adult entrepreneurial endeavors when they're older.

Find More Examples of Young Entrepreneurs Online at **www.youngbiz.com**

This discovery of the money basics should last through the kindergarten years. During this stage, children need to learn what money does, how much it is worth, the different types, and how to make change. At about the time they turn six and start the first grade, they should understand these basic concepts of money. This is good timing because it is at this time that they will be exposed to their peer's toys and belongings and will begin asking for more and more things.

A helpful way to learn about money and making change is to make them aware of how money is made through a trip to one of the U.S. mints when you're on vacation. Failing that, you can bring the mint into your home through your computer and web connection (www.usmint.gov/kids/). There they can learn the history of pennies, nickels, dimes, quarters, and various dollar denominations, such as what they've been made of and what famous Americans' faces have been engraved or printed on them

But don't forget play money. Games such as Monopoly or simply playing store are fun ways for your child to learn about dollars and change. Here's a teachers' web site with a bunch of great online money games: www.busyteac erscafe.com/teacherlinks/math/money_links

3 • Developmental Stages

Kids Acquire Money Basics

Playing money games should provide your kids a whale of a good time, so perhaps you can be effective in teaching them that money is a lot like Moby Dick. Just as Captain Ahab chased that ubiquitous whale to the far ends of the earth, kids soon discover that money is ubiquitous; it's on everyone's minds everywhere and they're all chasing it.

Money's Use in Almost All Aspects of Our Lives

Because money's influence is so pervasive, your challenge is to show your kids it doesn't have to be that way. Think of things to do and places to go that don't involve money, because it won't be long before young kids begin to notice that almost everything they want to have or do will involve money. Just as Madison Avenue is so effective in selling us on living our lives based on things that cost money, you must be the Main Street who is just as effective in selling your kids on living in ways that don't break the bank. Start early by not indulging them in everything they want. Show them as well that there are fun things to do that don't depend on lots of money, such as having a picnic, and playing in the park instead of going to amusement parks where rides and games are very expensive.

Many times, kids will learn first that when they go to stores, things cost money. They may have not yet realized, however, that the things at your house or the things that you give them cost money. These items have always been there or just "appear out of nowhere." When they write on the wall or drop a plate, they may not comprehend that replacing breakages and doing repairs things cost money as well. It is important that your kids learn at this time that everything from the pen they lost at school to the clothes they rip to their after-school activities cost money – before they think you can get them everything they want.

3 • Developmental Stages

Our Currency, Others, and Non-Currency Forms of Money

Even if your kids never see you taking out a wallet or opening a purse, they should be aware of the money around them. Teach them that when you drive them somewhere the car is using up gas, which costs money. It's also putting wear and tear on the car, which will eventually cost money because the more you drive it, the more you need someone to do things to it that will keep it riding well, and the more it wears the tires so that you have to buy new ones.

Your kids should also learn that money does not exist only in the form of coins and bills, and that our coins and bills are not the only types. Teach them that houses, cars, expensive jewelry, artwork, stocks, etc. are also worth money. Also explain that in other countries, money comes in other forms, is worth different amounts, people make different amounts of money, and things you buy cost different amounts than they do here. For example in Spring, 2002, 100 Euros (used in parts of Europe) was equal to 91.71 U.S. dollars, but if you go somewhere where Euros are used, you can transfer your American money into Euros.

Learn All About the World of Money at
EconEdLink "On The Money"
www.econedlink.org/lessons/index.cfm?lesson=EM169

Money, Happiness, and Sadness

Of course, the best way to learn about the Euro is a trip to where it's used – but that takes money. Money is a powerful thing; it can change lives for better or for worse. For the most part, having money makes people feel good. Especially in large quantities, it makes them feel rich, and powerful, like they can do or have anything they want. Our society paints this picture for us in numerous ways, perhaps most effectively in the commercials and advertisements that encourage us to buy more and more and TV shows that appeal to our greed and portray money as a source of happiness.

3 • Developmental Stages

Many shows and movies take the importance of money to disturbing extremes – with constant emphasis on murder and mayhem related to money. Obviously, you do not want your kids to end up this way. While money is an important matter, and should be taken seriously, it is also important to show your kids that money is not so important that it rules your life, and that your outlook on life is not primarily based on how much you have in your bank account. When they're old enough, talk to your kids about the Great Depression (or encourage them to research it on their own) when bank runs and the stock-market collapse left people penniless and some responded by jumping out of skyscrapers and plummeting to their deaths. Situations are not usually so extreme, but this example shows how important money is in our society. The effect of money on you will be reflected in your children. It's not a bad thing to be happy about a raise or payday, but it is important to emphasize the achievement of getting a promotion or otherwise getting a big raise or bonus, rather than the amount of money itself.

You also can't help exhibiting some sadness or anger when you have money problems, but when kids are exposed to too many adult fights about money and bills, it can't help but sour their money attitudes. Furthermore, when parents lose or suffer big investment losses, making them stressed and uptight, children might start viewing "money shorts" as a disease as serious as cancer. So watch how you react to money adversity, because you don't want your children to view money as so important that it's the deciding factor for happiness or sadness.

A good way to get a lesson across about money not "being everything" (besides integrating these values into your own lifestyle) are educational and value-teaching television shows for younger children. For example, *Arthur* (on PBS), featured an episode in which a rich and spoiled character and a less fortunate character both found out that money was not the most important thing. This is a fun way for young kids to learn that money does not always make a person happy and the lack of money does not necessarily make a person sad.

Because money does have this power over people, it is important to teach your child the proper money manners. Teach them that money matters are personal and to be kept within the family. Unless it's a close friend and they're doing it for the purpose of being a smart consumer, one shouldn't ask others

3 • Developmental Stages

about how much money they have or how much the things they own cost, nor should children offer this information about themselves or their families, even if asked. Finally, teach them never to make fun of anyone else about how much money they have or what they spent on something and tell them never to show off about new clothes, toys, or gifts or how much money they have. These lessons might seem obvious, but if you could be a fly on the wall in a middle school or high school, you might be shocked at how much "economic classism" exists and is flaunted.

Money Transactions

Because you must do so many things with money that kids will be observing, you might as well use those transactions as educational opportunities that will have the added benefit of lessening their boredom while you wait in line. Tell them how much you're spending, why you need what you're buying, and how much you saved by shopping carefully for it. After doing this for awhile, engage them in games where they guess prices, and encourage them to "cheat" by trying to notice the prices from either reading tags on the items or noticing them on the shelves below where they were taken. In fact, once you start taking the time to give these lessons and field all their questions, the effort it takes might discourage you from some of your transactions, and you'll end up saving money!

When you use your credit card or ATM card to pay for items or get money, kids might become as desensitized to the fact you are really spending money. It is important that they understand that the money is still coming from the work you do and is simply in a non-currency form. To reinforce this point, you might play a shopping game with them at home with play money and expired ATM and credit cards. Exchange roles as the shopper and clerk and do transactions alternately with money, checks, and plastic, having the clerk always ask, "Will that be cash, charge, check, or ATM"? You can set up your computer to print out something that looks like a cash receipt or credit-card slip, and you can give them "play IDs" that they must show when cashing checks. When they're older, enhance the game when you're the clerk by occasionally making a mistake and charging the wrong amount, giving them the wrong change, or forgetting to return their card to see if they catch you at it. You're not just playing a game with them; these things really happen and shoppers need to be alert.

3 • Developmental Stages

Kids' First Financial Responsibilities

Piggy Banks

That lesson in alertness will serve kids well when they have to take responsibility for their own money, starting with their normal first responsibility, a piggy bank. When you give your youngest child spare change and supervise its deposit into the piggy bank, stress the importance of making sure it doesn't get lost when it's taken out to be counted. When children are younger, the responsibility should not include larger gifts. Tell your child that you're sharing money responsibility with him by putting that money in a bank account for him. When your child gets older, though, have her take gift responsibility temporarily by telling her to keep the money in a safe place until you have time to take it to the bank. When you do visit the bank and make the deposit, bring her along so that it seems like the responsibility is completely hers.

Allowance

Add to your child's responsibility at about age four by starting a small allowance that your child can either save or spend on small unnecessary things such as candy bars or the kinds of inexpensive toys that are given as kid prizes at carnivals. He'll now have to make decisions about what part of it to save and what to spend, knowing that once it's spent, he won't get more until the next time allowance is given (the same time each week). When he does spend, he'll also have the responsibility of hanging onto it in a pocket or change purse from the time it's removed from the piggy bank until it's spent.

You can reinforce the allowance responsibility lesson by how, when, and where you give it. You could make it your child's responsibility to remind you and not give it unless reminded. Or if that seems too harsh, you can give a slight bonus if your child reminds you on time. Always give it in the same place in the house, as far as possible from the piggy bank. That makes your child take the increased responsibility of either immediately taking it and putting it in the piggy bank, or keeping it in a safe place until she goes back to her room and puts it in the bank. If she loses it, tough luck. Point out that money doesn't have its owner's name on it, so even impeccably honest people don't know who owns money that they find. A few might try to find who lost it, but because many people would lie and say it's theirs, most finders will just keep it and you're out of luck then, too.

3 • Developmental Stages

What Does a Dollar Do All Day?

To emphasize this point about money ownership, while strengthening your child's creative and writing skills and sense of how the life of money relates to our lives, challenge her to make up a story about a week in the life of a dollar bill. Ask her to explain how it passed from person to person to store to person, etc. – including interesting things that happened to the people while they had the dollar bill. Tell her in advance that you'll give her a small monetary reward for doing the story and an even bigger one if it's really good. You might even sneak in a lesson about hygiene by emphasizing all the different people who've handled the dollar, and what kinds of places they kept it, and what they might have been doing with their hands right before handling it.

As a final reinforcement to the importance of safeguarding money, tell your child about the real, but bizarre things that can happen to money when people are careless. It's been known to be eaten by pets at home and by animals in zoos and elsewhere where it's blown after someone has dropped it. Animals have even eaten garments or shoes in which people have left money. Sometimes, "laundering it" is an offer that non-Mafia mothers (and fathers) can't refuse because they don't turn pockets inside out before the wash. And although money doesn't really burn a hole in the pocket of people who are compulsive spenders, it's been know to be burnt when it accidentally finds its way onto a stove burner or into the oven.

Beyond Simple Allowances

As each year passes, allowance should be raised, but so should parents' expectations of what children are expected to do around the house in return, and what expenses the allowance is meant to cover. Parents should encourage saving, and help children open a bank account to earn interest on the money that they're saving. Although you want to reward saving, don't let that sway you if your child does a good job of saving but fails to do what you agreed in order to receive the allowance; don't give it when children don't live up to their end of the bargain.

Also encourage your child to use some of the allowance to give to charity, and reward that behavior with a small allowance bonus that's less than the amount given. You're paralleling the way Uncle Sam rewards taxpayers with a tax deduction when they give to charity. Encourage kids to do volunteer work for charities as well, partly as a way to give them a sense of how charitable donations are used, but don't make them feel they have to volunteer. Either

3 • Developmental Stages

way, you should tell them about the types of charities that exist and what they are for. Children will especially sympathize with other children in need because they'll think, "What if I were in that situation? I would want someone to help me."

Also encourage older children to donate to charities for causes that interest them. For example, if they're very interested in animals, they might enjoy donating to the animal shelter or wild animal rescues. Be sure to tell them about charities that you support as well so they'll understand it's something to continue to do all of your life. For a further lesson in the value of money, when giving old clothes and toys to charity, tell your children how much the items cost originally and challenge older children to guess. This will not only help them develop consumer skills but also give them a sense of how valuable even modest charitable giving can be.

Complex Allowance Lessons

At the point when children begin to want expensive clothes and toys, give them a budget that details how much you are willing to spend on them and what categories of expenditures that covers – leaving them responsible to cover excess expenditures and non-covered categories with their allowance and earnings. For example, you buy the necessities like clothes, food, etc., but if they want the more expensive brands or extra toys and games, let them make up the difference or wait for a special occasion when they'll receive a gift. Dr. John Whitcomb, author of *Capitate Your Kids*, suggests creating a budget and a contract and making sure children follow it. You can loan your kids money, but make sure they pay you back with interest.

Learn more from Dr. Whitcomb, author of **Capitate Your Kids**, at **www.capitateyourkids.com**.

3 • Developmental Stages

Kids Joining the Family Financial Circle

Make sure your kids understand that although they get paid an allowance that covers certain chores they're always expected to do, this does not entitle them to money for everything that they are asked to do. As a part of your family, they are expected to do what you ask of them without pay – unless they are chores that entail significant work at a child's particular age (such as a five-year-old raking all the leaves on a big lawn with lots of trees) – thus justifying separate payment. And if they want more money than you can provide for extra chores, your children can rake the neighbors' lawns as well (with the side benefit of avoiding energy and noise pollution from leaf blowers).

It is important that at an early age you explain to your child your family's financial status. Don't wait too long to do this and let your child get accustomed to getting most things that he wants and keeping up with all the toys his friends have. Wait too long and you'll have a difficult time getting children to understand that you can't (or won't) afford the things they ask for – especially as they get older and want increasingly more expensive things. And when they're old enough to understand, explain about the possibility that you could lose your job and, therefore, your paycheck. It's important to save and spend wisely, even when times are good and you can afford to spend more. Because if something bad does happen, getting through it will be easier with the extra money saved up, just like squirrels save nuts for the winter months.

Show them the family budget and let them see how much income versus how much money is spent each month or even each year. Have them help you enter in the data or even start a budget book of their own. Further teach them this lesson by keeping a record of all the things they want, but didn't get, and they'll be very surprised when they find out they would have to give up necessities in order to afford all the extra toys they want.

Check out the following online child's budget worksheets:
- www.usefcu.com/budget.htm
- www.listorganizer.com/childbudget.htm
- www.plan.ml.com/family/parents/personal.html

3 • Developmental Stages

Explain to your kids about insurance. Tell them how it pays for your house or your car if something happens. They can also help you inventory all of your valuable household items so that if something ever does happen, you can tell the insurance company exactly what is missing or broken. While helping with the inventory, they can learn exactly how much each thing is worth and how much everything together is worth. That way, they'll realize just how much money your family has, but also realize how much of that is not available for spending purposes. Also tell children about life insurance and what they should expect if something happens to both you and your spouse and you're unable to take care of them. Explain that they will go into the care of another family member or family friend, and the money from the life insurance would be given to that person to care for the children.

These discussions might make your children a bit apprehensive and feel that they have little control over what happens to them. To counteract this, don't make these discussions into the one big "if we die talk" – just as you don't want there to be the one big "sex talk." Instead, make these discussions part of a regular series of family meetings that include financial status and strategies on their agenda. When you tell your children about wills, insurance, and similar matters, listen to their concerns and reactions, and address them at a level appropriate to their ages. You'll probably learn some things that influence future revisions or refinements of your estate plan. Similarly, involve your children in discussion about vacations, car purchases, college savings, and other financial matters. They'll feel more a part of the family, and it will reinforce what you've been teaching them about spending and saving. Their input is bound to influence some of your decisions or your sense of budget priorities.

Earn and Learn

Your child's first income besides allowance will probably be some sort of entrepreneurial endeavor such as a lemonade stand, but by the time your child becomes a teenager, she'll begin to get job offers for baby-sitting and other neighborhood chores, if she hasn't already. A few years after that, she might start a real wage-paying job. From then on, college is on the horizon, and work before and during will be an important factor in how free of debt she'll be upon graduating and entering the work force.

3 • Developmental Stages

Earning

 Jobs for Kids (and the Skills They'll Need to Get Them)

- **Typing documents in a word-processing program.** (Good grammar, spelling, etc.)

- **Addressing holiday cards and gift wrapping.** (Good penmanship and sufficiently developed manual dexterity.)

- **Pet walking** and **pet-sitting.** (Strength and quickness, experience with dogs and other animals, maturity to follow instructions to the letter and remember the schedule.)

- **Baby-sitting.** (Strength, quickness, patience, experience with children, and maturity to recognize and react rapidly and appropriately to problems and emergencies.)

- **Snow shoveling/lawn mowing/car washing.** (Strength and maturity to handle dangerous power equipment.)

- **Interior painting and washing/staining wood fences and decks.** (Maturity to safely handle potentially toxic substances, ability to maintain balance on short ladders, and manual dexterity to apply paint evenly and within borders.)

- **Selling lemonade,** other drinks, or baked goods from a stand or to adults needing baked goods for the office or organizational meetings. (Sufficient maturity to practice strict cleanliness in food preparation and handling.)

- **Tutoring.** (Old enough to have sufficient subject mastery; mature enough to inspire confidence in prospective client-parents and communicate with teachers about client's performance.)

3 • Developmental Stages

Children can also usually get a paper route if they ask the newspaper for one – especially from local papers that aren't daily. But they must be old enough and mature enough to be and feel secure about going to people's homes to collect payment, and able to avoid the potential dangers when delivering in the pre-dawn hours. Most of these jobs require only modest skills and can be done by kids as young as pre-teen. They're good ways for kids to get a sense of responsibility for a job and to earn a small paycheck without the pressures of a job with an established business. Your child can also get an idea of whether business is the right field for him.

Other types of jobs can be done as non-paying internships or volunteer work. The type of job can be something your child is interested in for fun or for a possible future career. For example, she can volunteer in a hospital if she wants to be a doctor or nurse. This is a good way to prepare for a real paying job someday and to find out if the type of work is something that interests your child.

When they're old enough (14 or 15 in most states), children can do many wage jobs for businesses, although they must abide by local laws and restrictions on hours and times they can work. Wage jobs teach kids the relationship between work and wages, and the responsibility of working on a schedule, unlike the greater flexibility of neighborhood chores. Wage jobs will greatly increase a child's spending money, so it's important that parents have given their children progressively more control over their own money as they've gotten older. By the time they can get a wage job, they should have almost complete financial independence, although you might want to require that they save and invest a certain portion of their earnings since, as they get closer to college and adulthood, they'll need to start building up some reserves. A good goal is that they should be able to use the combination of money they're earning and their allowance to cover all their expenses and a certain level of investment – everything except the basics you'll still cover: three meals a day, shelter, medical care, education-related school expenses, etc.

3 • Developmental Stages

During the summer, high school kids should be expected to work almost full-time if possible. Combine summer earnings with what they make during the school year and they might make enough to have to file a tax return. Don't do it for them, but help them the first time and then make it their responsibility. Unless adults' taxes are complex, *parents* should be doing their own because it helps them stay in touch with their financial situation. To give children a better sense of this, also have them help with the family taxes, which will demonstrate how much they will realistically keep from their gross earnings when they're adults.

> Chapter 6, "Earning," has much more detailed information on pre-college neighborhood chores, wage jobs, and entrepreneurship.

Learning

At this point, it is very useful for you and your child to learn relative costs of professional training in college or graduate school, or vocational training in a technical school. Together, you should discuss how much you'll help (possibly including parent educational or home equity loans), with the rest their responsibility from either savings or student educational loans. If college is their goal, investigate tuitions and expenses at a range of in-state and out-of-state schools, financial-aid prospects, and outside scholarship opportunities. Also discuss whether it's really important that they go to an expensive elite private school for undergraduate education, versus reducing or avoiding debt, or keeping savings intact by attending a less expensive public school.

A Parent's Guide to

MONEY

3 • Developmental Stages

Web Sites to Help Plan College and Career

- **www.fbla-pbl.org/libr_main.asp?featureid=720** –
  This website has links to many different sites about career and college planning.

- **www.collegeboard.com** –
  This website has information on SAT and ACT tests and practice problems and college and scholarship information.

- **www.review.com** –
  The Princeton Review offers classes intended to help students raise their test scores (SAT, ACT etc.), and the web site also offers college searches and tips on getting into college.

- **www.finaid.org** and **www.fastweb.com** –
  These sites are reputed to provide the most comprehensive information available on financial aid and outside scholarships, respectively.

- **www.bls.gov/oco** –
  This is a handbook covering a wide variety of occupations. You can search or look through a list and find out information about training and education prerequisites, what the job entails, and salary.

- **www.headhunter.net/index.htm** and **http://jobsearch.monster.com** –
  These sites offers a career search for finding openings near where you live.

- **www.homefair.com/homefair/calc/salcalc** –
  This site compares the costs of living in different states.

3 • Developmental Stages

Managing Money In(flow)s and Out(go)s

Before children leave you to go off into the real world for the first time on their own, they need to be able to manage their money. This includes keeping a budget, managing a checking account and financial records, using ATM and credit cards, making smart consumer choices, and investing some of their savings. In today's entrepreneurial world, teens should also learn bookkeeping and how to file taxes when self-employed because of the strong possibility they could end up working for themselves.

Before college is a good time to give children their first ATM card. Starting with a card such as Visa Buxx can insure you that your child will not spend over her limit because you can put as much or as little money into the card as you want, and you can monitor spending easily. Learning to spend within a budget and managing her own checking account should be established before allowing your child to buy on credit.

A first credit card, co-signed by you, should be given when your child is still living at home with you so that they can learn the basics before they go off to college where the average college student soon finds himself in credit card debt of almost $3,000. They won't succeed in credit-card management, however, unless you've taught them to be smart consumers in increasing doses, starting before kindergarten.

To make sure your kid is a smart consumer, teach him how to research products and services he wants to buy. Compare prices and quality even on the smallest items. Compare advertising claims to your actual experience after you purchased and used the product. Warn your children about false advertising and how commercials make products look much better than they really are. Don't simply instruct them to buy the cheapest products – help them understand that better quality is worth paying more money for in the long run. On big items such as electronic equipment and cars, comparison shop for the best deals, but also look at reviews and ratings. Be sure they know how to read contracts and comprehend all of their terms before they sign them.

Chapter 4, "Spending," has much more detailed information on becoming a smart consumer.

3 • Developmental Stages

Developing Money Mastery

When he reaches the final stage of child money development, your child has gone from counting change to keeping his own checking account and using a credit card. Now it is time for the stage that many adults are still trying to master – understanding the economy and how it affects credit management, investing, and making and managing a living.

Economic Concepts

You don't have to be an economist to effectively manage your money, but you do need to know enough about how the economy works so that you'll understand its effect on credit and interest rates, and the investment climate. Here are some of the major economic concepts your child should learn at each (st)age of her development.

Children's Stages of Economic (Concept) Development

Elementary School

- **A person cannot have everything he wants.** Understanding needs versus wants and costs versus benefits of different items is necessary in order to make good purchasing decisions.

- **Banks are where people can save and earn more money,** but also where people borrow and pay money. They use what people deposit to make loans to those needing money.

- **Inflation is a rise in prices due to an excess of currency versus actual growth of the economy,** which can result from an excess of demand for goods versus manufactured supply of them.

3 • Developmental Stages

Middle School

- **Market prices** are based on the relationship between buyers and sellers. If the buyer won't buy at a certain price, the seller will have to lower the price.

- **Competition** between buyers raises prices and may lower quality in a race to produce products that are in demand. Competition between sellers lowers prices and raises quality because consumers want the most and best for their money.

- **Entrepreneur:** A person who starts her own business and takes financial risks in order to possibly someday be highly successful and make lots more money than was invested.

- **Gross Domestic Product (GDP)** is the amount of money of all goods and services produced in the economy.

- **Governments provide services to the people** (roads, health care, social security, public schools…), but in return the public pays taxes to provide for these needs.

High School

- **Interest rates are the price for borrowing money** or the premium earned for saving it. A higher interest on savings encourages more saving, while a lower one encourages spending – especially when inflation is high at the same time so that people are afraid of losing the buying power of their money. A higher borrowing interest rate does not encourage buyers while lower interest rates encourage more buyers. (After 9/11, to encourage spending, many car dealerships offered 0% APR financing.) Different interest rates apply to different types of borrowing. For example, lower rates often apply to houses and cars because of the ability of the lender to recover some of the cost of the loan if the borrower defaults (the property itself acts as collateral). Credit cards often have higher rates because they're so often used to pay for entertainment and other services that don't have much value that can be recovered (they won't accept the experience of watching the latest *Star Wars* episode as collateral).

3 • Developmental Stages

- **When the GDP increases substantially**, inflation and/or higher employment rates occur because businesses are running at capacity and expanding to meet higher consumer demand. When GDP increases modestly or not at all, inflation is usually low because of cool demand, and employment is lower because companies cut workers due to cool demand.

- **Inflation** and expectations of inflation lead to higher interest rates because people saving money demand a return that keeps the growth of their money in line with the economy – they want to keep buying power they now have. And higher interest rates for borrowing discourage *buying*, thus cooling demand (and inflation) as consumers have to pay higher credit rates, while businesses must charge more for their products because they have to pay higher rates on borrowed funds used to run the business.

- **Monetary Policy** consists of government policies that affect the amount of money and credit available due to a recession or a threat of inflation. Interest rates are raised when inflation is expected and are lowered to encourage spending when there is a recession.

Credit

Over 70% of college students have credit cards, and the average student who owns a card is about $3,000 in debt after college, many with much higher debt. That is why it is very important, before they go to college, that your kids understand how credit works, what it should be used for, and how to get the best deal on a credit card. Just as you taught them smart consumer skills, they need to research the deals and terms and comparison shop between other cards.

Tell your kids not to necessarily trust the advertisements because the rates advertised are often only for the best customers or are temporary "teaser" rates to get them hooked. Don't let them get excited over the "You are pre-approved for a credit card" mailings because they're as common as all the letters from colleges after students have taken the SAT. It's easy to mistakenly accept too many of these offers and have much higher total credit than you can handle. Even if they can handle it without going bankrupt, chances are that they'll make late payments and sully their credit records. Get a free copy of

Chapter 4, "Spending," has much more detailed information on becoming a smart consumer.

3 • Developmental Stages

your credit report and show it to your child so that he can see what such reports track. Emphasize that it's very much like a permanent record in school; the bad marks can stay in his file forever, or at least long enough to wreck his chances of getting credit he needs for houses and cars.

Investing

If your kids can absorb those credit lessons, give them credit for being ready to learn about investing. You may want to try very early on to teach them this concept by pretending to buy stocks and following them each day. You can enlist them in calculating how much money you would have made or lost if you had actually bought the stocks. Eventually, you will want to have them invest for real. Before doing this, they need to research the companies they want to buy stock in. Show them how to learn about the company and its financial trends.

When children are younger, investing in companies they've heard of is preferable because it's easier to have a sense of how good the company is, and more interesting to learn what it does and how it's doing. It's not enough to know what to invest in, though. When children get older they must also understand how profits are made from investments, including the effect of taxes on profits. They should know if they sell an investment soon after buying it, they'll pay a higher tax rate than if they keep it longer. They should also know that profits on investments can be taxable if bought normally, but tax-deferred if bought in IRA or 401(k) accounts that are usually available only to adults. The difference between tax-deferred and taxable investments can mean a big difference in the amount of money they end up making.

This has all referred to investing in a single company's stock, but there are many other kinds of investments, including several that don't involve stock – and all involving different levels of risk that you'll lose the original amount you invested. To prepare them for these different risks, you should talk to your children in general, long before they invest, about risk and safety. As they get older, you can apply these lessons to investments. For example, investing in a bank savings account is like sitting at home in your easy chair. Investing in a quality stock is

Chapter 7, "Investing," covers this in much more detail.

like driving a car on the freeway, and investing in the stock of new companies is like driving in the Daytona 500 if you're not an experienced race-car driver.

3 • Developmental Stages

Making and Managing a Living

Although your young child might have already made money from many types of neighborhood chores, and early teens from part-time wage jobs, neither really think about making a living from these efforts. With college and career planning, your kids must start to become aware of the financial consequences of their choices – both in how much it's going to cost to prepare for the career, and how well their choices will provide the type of economic lifestyle they envision. This includes comparing different places where she's likely to get a job in her chosen field, how much it's likely to pay her in those places, and how much it should cost to live where those jobs are found.

She must also look beyond just salary and be able to determine how the combined package of salary and benefits will serve to support her. If a job with a lower salary has great health insurance that's totally covered by the company, it could very well be the preferred choice over a higher-salary job with crummy insurance for which the employee must totally pay. She should also consider stock options, other insurance, pension and 401(k) investment plans, and a variety of other possible benefits that can make a smaller-salary job beat a larger salary one hands down.

There's no exact formula for quantifying benefits so that total compensation (salary plus benefits) can be compared between two jobs. But good math and computer skills will help, in order to make "guesstimates" of the total value of different offers, and to use computer tools to help in such an analysis. Encourage your child to get good at estimating because in financial planning, it comes into play in so many ways. At different stages, put those estimating skills to work on family matters so he'll get the hang of it, such as how much will it cost to paint the house, get new carpeting, take a family trip to Disney World, etc. Ultimately, you can show your child what you make and what your benefits are and have him estimate the total value of your compensation.

Let's end this discussion of financial estimates and tools, and this chapter, with what this book is all about, getting to the point where your child is able to live independently as an adult in the manner he desires. To get an idea of whether this is likely, follow the link for a helpful way of estimating how much he'll need to earn in order to afford his desired lifestyle.

> **What It Costs to Be an Adult: A Lesson for Junior –**
> www.jumpstart.org/madmoney/pgv_money_rc_main.html

Chapter Four

Spending

Whether you have children or are awaiting a birth, your mind is undoubt-edly stuffed with the contents of endless books on child development and raising children, so the last thing you want is even more. But bear with us as we spend a few moments applying that material to your child's growth into a spender – hopefully not one who thinks money grows in ATMs.

4 • Spending

Needs, Wants, and Wishes:
Your Little Consumer Grows Up

It starts in earliest infancy, when we're told to always attend to them when they cry, that doing so won't spoil them. That's because they're crying out of needs such as food, warmth, wanting to remedy the discomfort of a wet diaper, or wanting comfort when they're scared of being alone. As they grow into pre-verbal infancy, however, crying for needs diminishes a bit, but crying for wants begins. They want to be in the crib if they're out, out if they're in, held if they're on the floor, put down if they're being held, paid attention to if they're being ignored, and left on their own if they're feeling smothered, and being given every single thing they see to shake, lick, and otherwise examine. Then, we're told to try to always respond to needs, but only sometimes to wants

Parents can become understandably frustrated when this phase begins, just when they thought they'd be getting an occasional break to relax. Fortunately, experts tell them that they no longer have to respond to every cry, just to all of the true needs and only some of the wants. And they learn that babies have a language of crying that enables parents to distinguish between need and want cries. Soon, though, some of the crying is replaced by baby's gestures, pointing to things that are needed – or is that wanted?! That phase is quickly followed by baby's first words; WANT to guess what one of them is?

"Want. Want that. I want that. I want that now!"

In many cases, they don't yet know how to say the item they want, but they know how to combine "want" and pointing to make it clear. Yet when they truly need something, they usually don't yet know the word need, instead just naming what they need: banana, water, juice, bear, blanket, diaper (change). Then, as with crying, they start saying want about everything – and it's up to you to figure out (or decide!) whether that's a need or a want.

How you handle all that ambiguity about early needs and wants goes a long way toward determining how well-adjusted your child becomes. So it's not surprising that in your child's early introductions to the commercial world, your handling of need versus want will be a major factor in what kind of spender your child becomes. Just as with infancy, your goal is to satisfy all your child's needs while she can't herself, increasingly teaching her to participate in satisfying them, and making it clear that your job is to make sure her needs are sat-

4 • Spending

isfied by you now and by her later. You'll also satisfy a reasonable share of her wants, because you don't want her to just survive, but to thrive. The trick is to know how far to go with wants so that your child does strive to thrive, but doesn't start a pattern of indulgence that culminates in a never-ending quest for satiation.

It will be a long time until you can even attempt to explain this to your child, but you don't have to wait to teach your toddler "enough" or "just one thing" or other words of limitation. And toddlers are capable of understanding tradeoffs: "If you want that candy, then you can't have that donut; if you want that ball, then you can't have that miniature truck." When they get older, you can start to explain that even needs are tradeoffs for wants. "If we buy you those sneakers, then we can't afford to send you on the trip to the zoo with the rest of your class, and you won't be able to do the project about animals. If you want those designer jeans, you'll have to take sandwiches from home on the days that they sell pizza in school." The sooner you start verbalizing these choices with concrete examples, the sooner your child will be on the road to developing the spending discipline that comes from an appreciation of needs, wants, and their tradeoffs. And once you start, don't ever stop, even when your child says, "I get it already, Dad" – and he really does! In other words, disciplined spending is about learning not to have too much of a good thing, yet you can never *do* too much of a good thing by constantly teaching spending discipline.

 ### *Spend Some Time Helping Your Children 'Get' Spending*

- **Introduce your child to money** as soon as he's old enough to understand that you use it to buy things. Help him learn the different types of paper currency and coins and the order of their value. When your child starts doing simple arithmetic, teach equivalency, such as 5 pennies makes a nickel, 5 nickels a quarter, 4 quarters a dollar. Next, teach how to make change, and then find pictures and advertisements of various items and show your child how you would buy that item with a certain number and type of coins and dollars. To help you accomplish this, look online for information, activities, and games.

4 • Spending

A Few Games and Activities to Find Online

- **U.S. Mint Kids' Section –**
  www.usmint.gov/kids/

- **Cash Register Game –**
  www.funbrain.com/cashreg/

- **A.G. Edwards Money-Counting Games –**
  www.agedwards.com

- **Money Flashcards –**
  www.aplusmath.com/cgi-bin/flashcards/money

- **Change for a Dollar –**
  www.teachnet.com/lesson/math/293changedollar.html

- **You Can Buy Anything You Want –**
  www.wallowa.k12.or.us

- Take a page from a California CPA firm's educational program for grade-schoolers called $KidsAccounts. Teach your child that money is used in one of four ways: "spending, saving for a rainy day, saving for a sunny day, and sharing/giving." (Save explaining the IRS until later.)

- Start your child on an allowance as soon as she's mastered understanding the value of money and its various uses. Recognize the "Allow" in allowance as your command to not interfere with your child's use of it, but only to counsel its use and help him plan for both immediate and future goals. Allowance is a crucial first step to your child's understanding the cause and effect in spending choices, and will be covered in more detail in Chapter 5 on saving. Meanwhile, help your kid learn more about managing allowance by checking out this interesting web site for kids: www.bigchange.com. This download form tracks allowance. www.makingallowances.com/pdf/tracker.pdf (You'll need the free Acrobat Reader to view this).

- Play the Give It Up game, a creation of the Wise Pockets web site. It involves having your child go on a scouting expedition with you in a toy store picking out five low-priced items he wants and then going home and doing a set of discussion, writing, and drawing activities that help your child "give up" all but one of them. They include

4 • Spending

helping your child to determine the pluses and minuses of each item, ranking them in order of preference, selecting the one he wants to keep, and discussing how in real life you have a limited amount of money and must constantly make such choices. Go to www.umsl.edu/~wpockets to see everything at this site and then www.umsl.edu/~wpockets/treehouse/spending/spend2/Give_It_Up/give_it_up.html. The site includes several other spending activities such as Halt-Plot-Do-Review (to avoid impulse buying), Penny Pushing (for younger children to make spending choices), and Coupons: Your Money or Your Time.

- **Make up a home improvement project** such as redecorating your child's room and enlist her help in developing a list of possibilities involving painting or wall-covering, window treatments, furniture, carpeting, lighting, etc. Set a spending limit and help your child decide what choices she'd make (involving many tradeoffs). That's a short description of "Money Math: Lessons for Life" game developed by Mary C. Suiter and Sarapage McCorkle of the Center for Entrepreneurship & Economic Education, University of Missouri-St. Louis. Download it at www.publicdebt.treas.gov/mar/marposte.htm

- **Jointly develop a budget,** possibly using one of these online guides: www.momsbudget.com/childrensbudget.shtml, and www.makingallowances.com/pdf/kidsbudgetplanner.pdf

- **Play one of the following board games**: The Game of Life, Payday, The Allowance Game, Monopoly, and Monopoly, Jr.

- Play one of the following spending activities and games to learn the value of money, etc.
  Check It Out –
     www.mpt.org/senseanddollars/games/checkitout/home.html
  Teen purchasing (Download form) –
     www.makingallowances.com/pdf/teenpurc.pdf
  Purchase Plotter (Download form) –
     www.makingallowances.com/pdf/wisepurc.pdf
     www.fleetkids.com/ (Several games)

4 • Spending

Become a Smart Consumer (By Paying Attention to Infomercials)

The chances that your child fully ever gets the idea are slim; after all, do we fully get the concept of safe spending? If we did, companies wouldn't spend $2,000 annually per household saturating every possible media outlet, every public bus, and every NASCAR driver's jumpsuit with advertising. We can no more ignore these messages than we can sunlight. But just as sunglasses filter sunlight, we can filter advertising to understand its shades of meaning.

To start getting your children out from under the spell of advertising, you might find it helpful to think about it in the language of needs, wants, and (increasingly) wishes. With some effort, it's not hard to teach kids how to evaluate advertising claims for the things they need (even if they don't want them), such as toothpaste. We can explain that perhaps one brand makes teeth whiter, and another has a clean, fresh taste, but the purpose of toothpaste is to actually clean teeth and gums. If it does that effectively, our mouths will have the clean, fresh smell that one toothpaste implies will result from "clean, fresh taste," and our naturally white teeth will maintain their whiteness and not lose it from an abrasive that can eventually wear whiteness away.

But what about advertising that's as much about increasing our urgency to satisfy existing wants *and* create new ones? Kids love gadgets, so while the superiority of more expensive disposable power toothbrushes is debatable, their attraction isn't. A toothbrush that has the logo of a favorite TV character becomes a must-have item. That could lead to a discussion with your child of how by observing him, you, just like advertisers, are able to figure out things he wants, and things he might want if he knew about them. You can then ask your child to make the same guesses about your wants. To pull these insights together, you can then explain how the people making these products have ways of "watching" us to figure out what we want and they package their products and advertise them accordingly.

That leaves wishes, and what kid doesn't wish she could skip brushing her teeth? You might try an experiment and tell your kid about a new power toothbrush that has been invented that works with a laser beam. You simply open your mouth and hold it in front of you. The toothbrush features a specially designed mirror that helps you point the laser at all your teeth and clean them. You don't have to use toothbrushes and water, so there's no mess, and the whole process takes less than a minute.

After she's sufficiently enthused, break the news that no such toothbrush exists. Ask her why she was so happy to learn about the wondrous new device. Now, switch on the TV and tune in to an infomercial – there's always one on somewhere these days – you may even find one promoting any of the numerous products for whitening teeth. The actual product isn't important – acne cures, get rich quick schemes, miracle weight loss aids, whatever. Then ask your child if she thinks these claims are true. Point out that advertisers know that we wish for magical devices and simple ways to make our lives better, and that we're letting them steal from us when we just believe their claims and buy the miracle products and services they're selling.

With that accomplished, your child is ready for more sophistication, the subtle ways that advertisers influence our wants and tap into our wishes. Start by returning to the toothpaste ad, in which the standard characters are impossibly handsome and beautiful men and women. You can then explain how the advertisement attempts to cover needs, wants, and wishes, all at once. You **need** to get your teeth clean, you **want** the product that will make your teeth look their best, and, when you're a little older, you might **wish** that you could date the most beautiful or handsome people. That wish has nothing to do with the effectiveness of toothpaste, but many people decide to buy a particular brand because of the strength of the wish. Advertisers use the same techniques to sell soda, snack food, clothes, cars, and just about everything else.

You'll find that young children are fascinated with being let in on secrets of the world that they thought only adults know. (We emphasize young because when they're older, they're sure adults don't know anything, and they sure aren't going to let you in on the secrets of the world they know.) So it's the perfect time to use the advertising on TV as a far more powerful educational experience than they'll ever get from even high quality shows such as *Sesame Street*. Think about how analyzing advertising calls into play verbal skills such as reading and comprehension, and mathematical concepts such as less, more, and how much – not to mention all the social science and psychology associated with how people are influenced and the harder physical sciences involved in what is really possible and not possible.

4 • Spending

As your kids get older, you can add written advertising into the mix of marketing strategies you'll help them understand and defend themselves against. "Wait a second," you might be thinking, "won't I be playing right into the hands of advertisers by encouraging my kids to be exposed to their creative efforts?" Well, yes and no. If you don't do your own "advertising" about consumerism to follow up what they see, then you'll be sending your kid farther along the path toward adult bankruptcy. But if you add a heavy dose of interesting and fun learning about what they're seeing, you'll become the advertisers' worst nightmare, and probably guarantee that your kids will be able to afford bringing your future grandkids frequently to visit.

11 Quick and Easy Ways to Teach Your Kids How to Read Between the Lines of Advertising Claims, Investigate Product/Service Quality, Analyze Choices by Including Total Cost of Ownership, and Consider All Costs in Comparison Shopping

- **When you take them to the grocery store**, show them choices between products and explain why you're making the choices you do. Also explain how you like certain fruits and vegetables but are not buying them now because they're out of season and therefore cost too much. Play a game in which you tell them you can only spend a certain amount of money on this shopping trip, and show them how to use a calculator to estimate the total. Then purposely fill your grocery cart so that the tab will exceed your budget, and enlist their help in deciding what to put back so that you stay within the spending limit. Be careful you don't leave the store with a cart full of candy bars, ice cream, and nacho flavored crackers (or perhaps you don't want to leave without them!).

4 • Spending

- **Let your children buy a few heavily advertised things** that you fear might not be good choices, and use a VCR to tape the commercials that advertise them. When the items break or otherwise don't live up to expectations, show your child the recordings you made and compare the advertiser's claims with your child's actual experience with the product. For a simpler approach, the next time you splurge on fast-food, bring along magazine advertisements featuring pictures of fast-food items and compare the pictures to the food you actually purchased.

- **Counteract the forces** that lead your child to become a commercial victim of peer pressure by arranging with other parents to enlist their children in a circle of smart shoppers. Ask the kids to become an alert service for each other so that when one buys something that proves disappointing, the others won't repeat the mistake. That way there will be more different toys to share when they play together. And equally important, you're also teaching them a more general lesson about routinely sharing information and seeking opinions from other consumers.

- **Teach your kids how and where to get information** that helps consumers make product comparisons. For example, consider a subscription to *Zillions* magazine, Consumer Union's kids' version of *Consumer Reports*, and when at the library, show them *Consumer Reports* so that they can see how adults get the same kind of information about cars, appliances, etc. Tape consumer pieces from news programs on TV, watch them together, and discuss them. Go to Internet sites that provide this information.

Many web sites provide valuable consumer information. Here are several:

- www.stretcher.com
- www.pueblo.gsa.gov
- www.consumernet.org
- www.pricescan.com
- www.compare.net
- www.consumer.gov

- www.consumerworld.org
- www.window-shopping.com
- www.thepubliceye.com
- www.caru.org
  (Council of Better Business Bureaus)
- www.ag.ndsu.nodak.edu/otheryf

4 • Spending

- **Encourage your children** to sift through your junk mail and your local newspaper to find coupons for groceries and other products that your family needs (give them a list). As a reward for success, allow them to find coupons for one or two indulgence items you wouldn't normally buy. Explain that the reward is because they saved the family money, and help them calculate how much. But don't make the reward nearly as much as the savings, and explain that if it was, you'd be doing just what the advertisers wanted you to do when they sent the coupons.

- **Confront the issue** of promotional "extras" directly. Explain how they're often used to get you to buy products that you might not otherwise purchase because they're not things you really need, or they're not very good. Make a game out of it by asking your children to list all the products they see advertised with such extras and categorize the main products as either good or bad. As they get older, you can discuss the value of these extras and the amount of money that the company makes from selling you the main product, showing how they still make plenty of money when they "give away" the extra. Then explain how the extras are actually worth so little. Tell them that if they learn not to nag you for such products all the time, you'll occasionally reward them by giving them the dollar amount the extras are worth, and let them spend it on anything they want. (Don't worry – the amount won't be much.)

- **Make rules for your kids** about how to handle direct-market mailings and Internet spam sent directly to them, and teach them how to recognize and handle telemarketing calls to the house. This article (www.wsjclassroomedition.com/0402_onln.htm) in the *Wall Street Journal* (Classroom Edition) might help.

- **Teach your kids about discount sales**, and how to tell a real sale from one that just calls itself a sale – such as those bogus "storewide sales" some big retailers seem to have every other weekend in which they discount only the merchandise that isn't moving. Explain the concept of seasonality and why certain products go on sale at certain times (for example, leftover summer clothes in the fall; calendars, gift wrap, and related items after Christmas). Also explain how products that are

4 • Spending

replaced by newer versions are often available at much lower prices, even though the "old versions" are still useful (for example, show how new cars cost far less just before the next year's cars come out). Have them make a list of all the car dealers, furniture and department stores, and other businesses advertising on TV that seem to always be having sales that really aren't.

- **Teach older children about manufacturers' warranties**, how to use them, and how to get satisfaction from a business providing a product or service if there's a problem from the get-go, whether there's a warranty or not. Don't worry about your children seeing you a bit angry, as long as you're constructively assertive in your attempts to get satisfaction. Also teach them about fraud and scams, and the how they can recognize them, or at least "sniff" the possibility, and deal with it. The websites listed below have lots of information about fraud and consumer rights.

  www.consumerlawpage.com (Information about consumer rights)
  www.fraud.org (Non-profit with information on scams and fraud)
  www.ftc.gov (The federal government agency that educates
    consumers to combat fraud)

- **Show your kids how to calculate** whether an extended warranty is really worth the extended cost. Point out that if you feel the need to get an extended warranty for a product, maybe you don't have the confidence in its quality that you should. And add that one problem with extended warranties is that the companies who provide them sometimes go out of business and might not be there to cover your warranty.

- **Educate your kids on the costs of major family expeditions** and vacations, such as dining out at (other than fast-food) restaurants, trips to fairs and amusement parks, and trips to the Grand Canyon. Keep track of the budget and, depending on their age, explain in appropriate terms what could have been purchased with the money if it hadn't been spent on the vacation. Also review the choices you made on the trip regarding hotels, places to eat, and driving versus flying, and attractions you chose to see or bypassed. As they get older, challenge

4 • Spending

them to research the cost of a number of vacation alternatives, or to arrange a particular trip for the lowest possible cost that would still make it fun and comfortable. Offer them a "commission" for the effort of a small percentage of the amount saved by choosing a lower-cost alternative or carefully budgeting a particular planned trip. To get them started, here's one web site where they can find ideas for low-cost leisure activities: www.frugalfun.com.

If your reaction to this is that your kids would never sit still for all this financial and consumer education, or that they are too young to understand it, think about all the things your kids do and say that constantly amaze you. Tap into their almost unlimited passion for learning and being recognized for their role in the family – and you'll be surprised how positively they'll respond. But even if they don't, it's something you have to do. After all, as early toddlers, your kids are old enough to beg and whine for what they want, and to learn all kinds of things from TV and elsewhere that you don't want them learning. Therefore, they're old enough to learn about the objects of their begging and whining and alternatives to the undesirable stuff they're absorbing. The time you spend making them smart spenders will more than pay off in your ability to control family spending as they grow.

Credit (Your Kids) for their Financial Discipline

In case the message isn't clear, make sure you do a good portion of the teaching recommended so far if you don't want to gamble on your kid's future spending habits. Unfortunately, the best teaching can't eliminate the biggest gamble, the game of spending poker with Credit Cards Wild. You might think you should teach your kids to win by telling them to simply *straight flush* credit offers down the commode. However, without establishing good credit, they might never achieve (the purchase of) *a full house*. So help them look credit in the eye and win by giving it to them straight.

4 • Spending

Too Young for Credit Credentials

If you have young children, you probably think there's plenty of time to talk to them about credit. Before you know it, though, the day will come when they'll ask where the new deliveries to your house came from, and they'll be smart enough to know that the stork couldn't have carried them. So even though it's not easy, now's the time to prepare yourself to tell them about the economic equivalent of the birds and the bees: the banks and the businesses.

This isn't just another example of everything being about sex, because careless use of credit is much the same as careless sex – a way of getting pleasure now with consequences later. Furthermore, teaching credit abstinence is just as ineffective, because the impulse to get now and pay later is almost a physical need in our consumption-driven society. Therefore, you must teach your children safe credit.

Consequently, your kids must understand that there's no way to get cash (or check) free consumer gratification without the risk of credit-transmitted diseases that can be financially fatal. Finally, they must be prepared to meet their responsibilities when engaging in credit. Here's how to prepare them so that the bills they incur during life won't grow to take on a life of their own later.

First Credit Lesson

When your children are young and they watch you use credit cards for purchases, make an extended lesson out of it. At the store, tell them exactly how much the things you just bought cost, and that the card you're using let's you pay for them later. Show them the receipt so that they'll see the amount you owe written on it.

When your credit card statement comes, remind them about the time they saw you use the card. Retrieve the receipt and show your kids how it matches an item on the statement, and then do the same with some other receipts from times they weren't with you. Then show them how you're writing a check for the total of all the purchases shown on your statement. Of course, you'll be using a check to make that payment and that could be confusing to them, so explain how checks work (see Chapter 5 on saving) as a substitute for cash you have in a savings/checking account.

4 • Spending

They might still have a hard time understanding the difference between credit cards and checks, and even if they do understand, they'll wonder why you just didn't use checks for your purchase. Smile, parent, because your kid has just served as the perfect straight man for the routine you're about to perform in explaining the different reasons and ways to use credit.

Three Ways Credit is Good for You Now (and Later)

- **Convenience and Security.** Explain that you use credit cards so that you don't have to carry around a lot of cash to pay for things and you don't have to use checks, which many stores don't like to accept. Cards also save time because you can give the numbers on them to someone on the phone or type them into a computer web site and you'll be able to buy what you need instead of waiting for a check you send to get to the company selling what you want.

  Furthermore, by not carrying wads of cash, you won't lose as much money if you lose your wallet or purse (or worse). Emphasize that when you use credit this way, you know you already have enough money in the bank to pay the bills.

- **When Money Is Coming Soon.** Teach your kids that another positive way to use credit is to buy something that you know you'll have the money for very soon, and that the purchase fits into your budget. For example, you might have been planning to buy a new refrigerator (with the 100% additional capacity you'll need for each kid), and just discovered that the one you want is on a big sale that ends tomorrow. However, you won't get your paycheck until the end of the month and by using credit, you can take advantage of the sale now and then actually "pay" for the refrigerator when you pay your credit-card bill from the check you'll deposit. You can reinforce this lesson by involving them in all aspects of the transaction and showing them all the relevant receipts, statements, and checking balances when you get your paycheck.

4 • Spending

You should also teach your child that buying on credit doesn't always involve a card. Many businesses, such as book or CD clubs, send you merchandise and bill you later. They should understand that credit is an agreement between you and a business allowing you to pay later, and the better you are at keeping your end of the agreement (by paying on time), the more likely other businesses are to make the same agreement with you later.

• **When The Money to Pay for It Is Not all Coming Soon.** Explain to your child that sometimes you buy things that cost so much money that it's almost impossible to have all the money you need to pay for it right then. You and most other people buy houses that way, with the bank making you a loan of the amount you owe for the house after you paid what you could. Show them your mortgage statements to show how much money you still owe the bank for the house, and how you're paying a few hundred dollars of it each month. Then do the same thing in explaining how many people buy cars with money they borrow from a bank.

Explain that you're able to do this because the bank has checked you out and knows you'll be making money on your job(s) and that you'll be able to use part of this money each month to pay back the loans. Emphasize, though, that sometimes banks aren't as careful as they should be and let people borrow more money than they can pay back. Then the bank gets its money back by taking away the cars and houses people bought. However, strongly assure them that even if the bank wasn't careful enough, *you* were very careful to borrow less money than you knew you could pay back.

Make sure that they understand that the bank isn't doing this as a favor, but using it as a way to make money – by charging interest on the loan. A bank is a money store just like some stores are toy stores. In return for the bank giving you that money, you're paying back a lot more than what you borrowed. Compare that to the way a store sells you toys for more than it cost them to buy, making a profit on the difference. Say that this extra money is called interest, and when they're older, you'll explain more about how it works.

4 • Spending

Giving Your Kids Credit

Don't be surprised if your initial credit lessons cause your kids to start questioning every future use of credit: "Are you sure we'll have enough money to pay it back?" Take advantage of their "interest" (in more ways than one) by lending them money for something they want but don't have enough money for. Don't introduce the actual calculation of interest into this. Instead, tell them you're going to add a small amount to what they have to pay back so that they'll understand about paying back more than they borrowed because of interest (perhaps $1 for a $20 item).

When you buy the item for your child, set up a loan agreement showing how much must be paid each month and when the loan will be paid off. Instead of automatically taking the payment out of allowance, make it your child's responsibility to make the payments to you each month, and make the consequences the same as in a bank loan if he "defaults": take the item away and cut off allowance until it's paid for – just like banks repossess cars and garnish wages to close out an outstanding debt. You're not doing this to be a mean parent, but to make sure your child understands what a big responsibility it is to borrow money to buy something instead of already having saved the money to pay for it.

Fortunately, this lesson in credit departs from lessons about sex because this loan allows your kid to screw up without lifelong consequences. Because failure to pay actual loans has more serious consequences, take this opportunity to explain what they are. Also explain how the way you handle credit is measured by credit ratings and that a bad rating makes you unattractive to lenders. Explain that having clean credit is a must if you want to be able to raise a family comfortably, because otherwise you won't be able to buy a house, perhaps not even a family sized car.

4 • Spending

Old Enough to Make (Credit C)Hard Choices

By the time your child's a teenager, his view of clean credit might be having enough credit to clean out the inventory of a number of stores. So before he gets a card, you must become a card-carrying member of the American (Un) Civil (No Financial) Liberties Union. That's right, you must protect your and his rights against future creditors to keep a roof over your head and food on the table, and here's how.

Simulated Credit

Once your child is working with decimals and percentages in school, it's time to carry the simple loan scenario one step further and make a loan of $50 or so on which you charge actual interest. Don't force it on her if she chooses to delay gratification until saving for a major purchase. If she knows the loan is available then she'll probably want to undertake it at some point. When she does, set up a repayment schedule based on simple interest (see sidebar) in which the payments shrink (unlike an amortized loan with compound interest when all payments are equal).

Simple Interest

Assume your child borrows $60 and you want her to pay it back in one year at a rate of 18% annual simple interest (high, but still charged by some credit cards). Each payment will include 60/12 = $5 principal plus interest on the balance at the monthly 1.5% equivalent of the 18% annual rate. Thus, the first payment will be (.015) times 60 = 90 cents, plus $5, equals $5.90. The second payment will be (.015) times 55 = 82.5 cents, plus $5 equals $5.83 (rounded in your favor, of course!), and so on.

As each payment is made, fill out a chart showing the new balance of the loan, the monthly principal and interest, the accumulated interest paid so far, and the actual total paid so far. She'll see how the interest makes the purchase much more expensive than its face value. As teachers like to say, I'll leave it to you as an exercise to determine how to mathematically handle any skipped or late payments.

MONEY

4 • Spending

Once the loan is paid off, the next step simulates children having a credit card by loaning them an amount to make for a purchase that they pay back to you as they see fit, but with a minimum payment each month that exceeds the interest owed. (For example, if the amount was $100 and the interest rate 12% annually, that's equivalent to 1% monthly; the minimum payment would have to exceed $1, which exactly covers the interest.) You can set up a repayment schedule as with the loan, but you can also set up a worksheet to show the monthly status of the account. In this case children will see not only the substantial interest that would be owed when the balance is not rapidly repaid, but also how failure to make significant monthly payments can drag out the debt for years. To make this more realistic, you can send your children the statement by snail mail or email (but for cyber safety, don't include her Social Security number!)

In comparing loans and credit-card use, you can emphasize how credit-card vendors take double advantage of undisciplined consumers. First they make it easy to buy on impulse without feeling the immediate consequences of seeing their wallets empty, and without knowing if and when they can complete the actual purchase by fully paying it back. Second, almost no requirements are placed on the repayment schedule, thus making the cost of any purchase grow in relation to how undisciplined the consumer is. To best illustrate this, make up a hypothetical worksheet for paying back a charge. Here's what the first few months of one would look like for a "charge" of $56, with the "card" carrying 15% annual interest, and the child paying back $3 a month:

Month	Balance	Payment	Interest	Cumulative Interest
1	$53.70	$3.00	$0.70	$0.70
2	$51.36	$3.00	$0.66	$1.36
3	$48.98	$3.00	$0.62	$1.98

To explain, the first line is calculated by converting the annual 15% rate to a $15/12 = 1.25\%$ monthly rate. .0125 times $56 = $0.70 (or 70 cents), The principal repaid would then be $3.00 − $0.70 = 2.30, so the balance next month would be $56.00 − 2.30 = $53.70.

You can also use this calculator found online:
www.calcbuilder.com/cgi-bin/calcs/CRE1.cgi/FinanCenter

In reality, however, most people don't pay back the same amount each month. Suppose that your child paid back $3 the first month, $2 the second, and only $1 the third. The table would look like this, with a higher balance at the end of 3 months.

Month	Balance	Payment	Interest	Cumulative Interest
1	$53.70	$3.00	$0.70	$0.70
2	$52.36	$2.00	$0.66	$1.36
3	$52.01	$1.00	$0.65	$2.01

You won't be able to use the previous calculator, which assumes the same payment every month. Instead, use the method just explained for the $3 first month payment on the $56 charge, repeating it each month for that month's payment and balance.

These worksheets allow children to see dramatic differences in how paying back more or less per month will change the total time to pay and the amount of interest paid all together.

Getting and Managing Real Credit Cards

When children are older, but still under 18, the normal legal age for their own debt responsibility, they can get a number of charge cards that work like credit cards and are accepted by most merchants. These are a convenient way to allow your kids to shop on their own without carrying around a lot of cash, but unless they actually work like credit cards, your kids won't learn the responsible use of credit cards while you're still able to exercise some control.

Therefore, your best bet is to co-sign a credit card for them with a limited balance and give them full responsibility for managing it. You'll be risking several hundred dollars if they're totally irresponsible, but you can always pay it off and close the account when you've had enough and don't want to damage your own credit record. It's worth taking the chance, though, because it's better they be burned by a relative "candle" now, rather than a raging inferno when they can get unlimited access to credit when they turn 18.

4 • Spending

A Few Final Lessons to Teach about Credit

- **Credit card rules and rates vary widely.** They have different credit maximums, different grace periods for payment before interest is charged, and different rules about how to calculate the balance on which interest is charged. Some have variable rates that allow the creditor to change the rate as economic conditions change and others guarantee a fixed rate, some permanently switch you to a higher rate than your initial rate when you haven't had a good payment record, and some differ in the way they quote rates – meaning that two companies with identical rates *really* have different rates. It's crucial to read the lengthy fine print that spells out these rules, which you receive along with the card, and to read any inserts with your monthly statements, which sometimes contain rule changes.

- **Credit cards are far too easy for college students to obtain** – only requiring proof of full-time enrollment. Rather than helping students defend themselves against solicitation, many colleges happily accept payments from credit-card companies in exchange for the privilege of setting up shop in high-traffic areas on campus during registration – giving away enticing freebies when students sign up. In addition, students are eligible to take maximum federal Stafford Loans without showing need, and that gets them in further debt trouble when they graduate owing huge credit and loan balances.

- **Once out of college, students might find it impossible to get credit** for buying a car or a house if they've established a poor credit record (or perhaps even have to declare bankruptcy). Insurance companies now routinely charge higher premiums to policyholders with bad credit because data shows they're higher risks for accidents. In addition, some employers avoid hiring people with problem credit because they worry about how the stress will affect job performance or possibly tempt employees to commit fraud or embezzlement. Bad credit might also affect their romantic lives, as it's become more common for even young adults to check the credit records of prospective dates.

4 • Spending

Despite the problems associated with it, debt is not evil and it's unrealistic to totally avoid it. In addition to homes and cars, your children might need to borrow for a business or unanticipated but necessary major expense such as a medical emergency not fully covered by insurance. The goal is to control good debt and avoid bad debt. Be open and honest with them about your family's debts so that they'll see how you've managed it and what you're doing to improve your debt situation.

Financing Your Teenager's Wheels

Before America's age of affluence (or living as though affluent), kids didn't spend enormous amounts on consumer goods. Parents were able to get their pre-teens' attention on money matters by focusing them on how they could start saving money toward eventually buying an old used car. These days, though, kids expect parents to buy them a car – a new or recent model at that – and even parents who require junior to chip in usually limit his responsibility to paying for the insurance. Of course, that alone costs as much annually as buying a 10-year-old car.

Both ways have merits, and negatives. Saving for one's own car is a great learning experience, but it's no longer realistic for most kids to repair and maintain their own cars the way they once did. Furthermore, older cars are often less safe. So buying a newer car makes more sense, even if your child can't cover its total cost. However, you can still have your child aim for covering a substantial percentage of that cost by saving towards a specific figure, say $5,000, from a younger age, eschewing many consumer disposables in order to achieve that greater goal.

Children should also be responsible for some of the ongoing insurance, finance payments, and gas – but not so much as to significantly interfere with academics. True, your child might be able to pay the full freight by working 30 hours a week, and some do. But the negative effect on college preparation and future earning power is greater than the positive lesson of being fully self-sufficient. Instead, make your child partially responsible for the money but fully responsible for understanding these financial aspects of ownership.

4 • Spending

 ## *Use Your Family Car(s) to Teach the Lesson*

- **How do you decide what car to buy?** Talk about determining a budget, identifying the things you need in a car, and identifying what cars fall within your budget and meet those needs. Also explain that certain cars have much higher insurance rates, and might have to be avoided even if their selling prices fall within your budget.

- **How to shop for the car(s) you want,** starting with information you can get from the Internet and print publications that help determine how much you should expect to pay for a given car.

- **How to negotiate the price you'll pay,** including how you try to split the difference on the extra a private seller can get versus selling to a dealer. If buying new, explain how to arrive at a price that will still allow the dealer to make a reasonable profit but save you hundreds of dollars under the price paid by those who don't have this information. Finally, emphasize the tremendous profits dealers make with extras such as undercoating and fabric treatments, which aren't discussed until you think you've made a deal and have to talk to the dealership's business manager.

- **How to arrange financing for a car.** Dealers don't always provide the lowest-cost financing because much of the profit they make in selling cars comes from their ownership stakes in financing companies. Credit unions often offer very competitive financing rates because they run on much lower cost overhead. Finally, point out that leasing a car is actually a form of buying a part of a car and financing it. In other words, when you lease, you are buying the portion of the car that depreciates while you have the lease and that depreciation amount is what you should be negotiating, rather than the monthly payments. Explain that leasing is so complex that it gives dealers back a big advantage in negotiating that they'd lost when people become more knowledgeable about traditional car-purchase negotiations.

- **Why how much it will cost to continue owning a car** is just as important as what you pay for it. Cars with lower reliability records will require more repairs, as will older cars in general. Also, some cars are just more expensive to maintain because of poor design that makes it difficult to get easily at all the components. And fuel efficiency makes a huge difference; you pay three times more to keep an SUV in gas versus a fuel-efficient compact car such as a Toyota Corolla. With fuel prices likely to rise, these costs could make inefficient cars too expensive to own on a teenager's modest budget.

Click Here for More Finance Know-How

Bankrate.com not only provides a rich source of information on competitive financing rates around the country, it also has great personal-finance articles. See this page for links to a wide range of articles related to buying a first car:
www.bankrate.com/brm/news/lifestages.2001081c.asp?prodtype=bank

Renting and Home Ownership

It might seem premature or overdoing it to fill teenagers' heads with information about real estate that they won't be using until adulthood. But because buying a home is the biggest purchase they'll likely ever make, and is best done with a long-term savings and investing plan, it's never too soon. Furthermore, the earlier kids start learning about real estate, the earlier you can get them to take interest in what your family must continually do to maintain your home, and the money that can be saved or wasted in doing so.

You can also start using for-sale signs in your neighborhood as opportunities to talk about the real-estate market, pointing out periods when homes are moving slowly or when they are selling like hotcakes. Explain how the economy affects this, and how the way individuals maintain their homes or that the way they price them for sale affects how quickly they sell. You might get kids interested in starting to look at the real-estate section of the Sunday paper, or at real-estate listings online, too.

Once they're doing that, you can also get them to notice the rental portion of those listings, and point out different apartment complexes as you drive around town. At times, many buildings will have signs such as "3 months free rent," which you can explain as indicating a buyer's market (when apartment complexes have too many vacancies). Start talking to them about monthly rents for such units, which they'll probably relate to better than astronomical

4 • Spending

home prices. However, getting them versed in rental prices will make it easier to go back to home-purchase discussions, comparing monthly mortgage payments to rental prices and explaining how and why they differ.

When your child is old enough to look like a college student seeking an apartment, spend a Sunday responding to apartment rental ads and showing her different places and how much they cost. Tell rental agents you're not ready to make a decision, but you'd like a copy of the blank contract to review. When you get home, go over the contracts together and discuss lease terms, the cost of breaking a lease, required deposits, damage charges, renter's insurance, dealing with landlords when you have maintenance issues, and legal recourses when either landlord or renter doesn't meet their responsibilities.

It's not to soon to do this during high school because in a few years, your child might be on her own working between high school and college, or far enough along in college so she's no longer required to live in a dorm. This apartment window shopping experience will prepare her to find a better deal or avoid a big mistake. If you think it's unethical to waste a landlord's time, then give back by subsequently making it a point to keep your ears open for acquaintance's kids who might be looking to rent locally, and direct them to places that stood out to you.

More Real Estate Info Online
The Metropolitan Life web site has a good series of "Life Advice" articles that cover many topics useful for educating kids. Here's a series on renting:
www.metlife.com/Applications/Corporate/WPS/CDA/PageGenerator/0,1674,P1623,00.html

Charitable Contributions

Speaking of giving back, don't forget to consider charitable contributions as a form of spending that you should teach your kids. In fact, you might even have religious beliefs that require tithing, so it's not to soon to start your kids' giving part of their allowance once they're no longer teething. You might wonder what there is to teach, other than figuring out how much you can afford to give. But just as buying things relates to the kind of lifestyle one wants, the way one "buys help" for others is equally a part of that lifestyle, and the choices are almost infinite.

4 • Spending

Furthermore, the consumer pressures exerted by non-profit charitable organizations are starting to rival those of for-profit companies selling products. So it's easy to feel pressured into giving too much or giving to less-worthy organizations.

 ## *Not All Charities are Created Equal*

- **The more a charity advertises**, the more of its donations go to pay administrative expenses. However, substantial marketing expenses might be necessary to get ample donations when people are less generous in a recession economy. Some seemingly wonderful non-profit organizations pay huge salaries to their executives, sucking away needed funds from their true purpose. The key to determining whether a charity exists more for its cause than for its own staff's financial gain is to examine the ratio of money collected versus money spent on administrative expenses. This information is available from charitable organizations' financial reports or from web sites containing data bases about charities' finances (such as www.guidestar.org). If you can't get information from these sources, don't give because non-disclosing charities might be often hiding poor financial management or worse, outright fraud.

- **Don't base your giving on sterile financial information alone.** Getting a good feeling about an organization from direct personal involvement is the best way to have confidence your money is going to a worthy cause. After all, if it's easy and appealing to volunteer, the charity must be doing something right, and is reducing its administrative costs by using so much volunteer labor.

- **By making your child financially-savvy**, you're cultivating a future adult who will be perfect for sitting on the boards of financial organizations and helping to make spending decisions. You can further prepare your child for this by using donation techniques that allow them to influence the way their money will be spent. Look into donor-advised funds and pooled-income funds as donation vehicles to accomplish this.

- **Be wary of charity-related fraud** from organizations, especially those that make telemarketing calls or send people door to door – unless they're immediately recognizable charities such as the American Cancer

4 • Spending

Society or American Heart Association. Be careful of charities that have names similar to respected national charities, because some deliberately choose such names to perpetrate fraud. Also, avoid the heart-string tug of personal begging by people stationed with signs at major traffic junctions. Although some are legitimately needy, others aren't, and you're far better off giving to an organization that efficiently serves such people, such as a homeless shelter.

- **Before adulthood, children have more time on their hands than money,** so it's better for most of their donations to be in the form of labor, and only modest amounts in money. That's also because donations provide savings on taxes, and such savings are higher, the higher one's income. In fact, kids generally don't earn enough to get any tax savings from donations. If they feel they're not giving enough, have them earmark a savings account or investment fund for future use as a source of charitable donations and give to it until then as though they were giving directly to charity. Or have them tell you to withhold allowance and divert it to a charity as a parental contribution that does save on taxes.

More Charitable Info Online

Here's a comprehensive article on how to teach children about charitable giving, including explanations of donor-advised and pooled-income funds:
www.cof.org/newsroom/newsletters/familymatters/winter01/winter01.pdf

Children Need and Want Good Role Models

Undoubtedly, you're feeling spent and impatiently thinking that we've spent more than enough time on spending. You might also be thinking that you'll need to spend more time than you have to teach this stuff to your kids, yet you want to be the best parent possible.

Don't despair, because far more important than covering all these spending specifics is demonstrating them by example, and then reinforcing what your children are observing by talking to them about it. It's up to you to make your lessons on spending into a better way of spending time with your kids. But also make sure to save some time to cover saving, which we'll now cover in the next chapter.

Chapter Five

Saving

It's too late to save us from ourselves; we insist on starting this chapter with a movie analogy about saving.

In *Marathon Man*, the demonic Nazi medical butcher, Dr. Mengele, becomes a post-war demented dentist Christian Szell (played by Laurence Olivier) who keeps asking chair-trapped "patient" Tom Babington (Dustin Hoffman), "Is it safe?" Clueless as to Szell's meaning, Tom vacillates between "Yes, it's safe," and "No, it's not safe," and anything else he can think to say between screams as Szell drives the drill straight into his un-anaesthesized tooth roots.

Imagine instead, that the movie had been entitled *Money Man*, starring you. You're in the chair staring up at your wild-eyed drill-wielding dentist and the X-rays of your bank account that he's projected on the ceiling. Without hesitating, you repeatedly squeal "I'll do anything" in response to his question, "Will it be saved?"

5 • Saving

You probably wish you had such a dentist as a motivator whenever you look at your meager bank balance, unless you're unlike most Americans and have saved. Admit it, up until now, it hasn't been saved, so being such an anti-role-model, how can you hope to "drill" the importance of saving into your kids' heads? After all, they'll hardly develop positive savings behaviors if you must forcibly anaesthetize them, steal their coins while they're under, and stuff them into a piggy bank. So how do you save them from following in your non-saving footsteps?

There's only one way. You must start to stress the importance of saving from the first time the tooth fairy leaves money behind for an old tooth. Perhaps you can do this by augmenting the legend, and telling your kids that they should save part of that money to pay back the tooth fairy when she comes to put in the new tooth. Then you can secretly remove a bit of money from the piggy bank the night after that tooth first shows up, and count it with them the next day to prove the tooth fairy had taken it.

Okay, we're being tooth in cheek here, but it will take your creativity and persistence to captivate your child with the need for saving. In this chapter, we'll develop a philosophy that will help you to suggest some strategies that really have teeth in them, and cover the various vehicles for savings that you should consider once the piggy bank becomes a pork chop.

Saving Rewards, Philosophies, and Strategies

Start with a definition: saving is what's left over after spending (hence that chapter right before this one). Actually, though, it's that way of thinking that makes saving such a problem. Why not make spending what you do with what's left over after saving – assuming, of course, that you can cover more than basic needs with earnings (covered in Chapter 6 that follows).

Financial planners put this another way, "Pay yourself first" – a philosophy tied to the realization that some basic needs aren't month to month, but must be met over time by contributing monthly to mandatory savings. These are the things that wear out, so-called durable goods, such as cars, lawn mowers, and appliances; home maintenance items such as repainting, a new roof, and a resurfaced driveway; and YOU – necessitating hundreds or thousands of dollars for vacations that enable you to revitalize and live to fight another day.

5 • Saving

Although you might use credit to pay for the largest of these expenses over time, you still want to know that you can pay for them upfront if need be. In fact, many financial experts say that you should never buy disposable items or entertainment by using credit over time. Heeding this advice, such items should be first covered if possible in your monthly budget, and second from your savings. The real purpose of your savings then becomes a way of taking care of bigger-ticket items, unanticipated expenses such as emergency storm repairs or medical treatments uncovered by insurance, and anticipated wishes and dreams – such as the boat you'll buy if you can save enough for it.

Saving and Its Rewards

You probably know few adults who take the emergency part as seriously as they should, so forget that as a motivation for kids. Younger kids will only identify with wishes and dreams, so make sure you leave some for them to save toward by not indulging their every whim. Furthermore, the task might seem hopeless unless you can get them to think small; instead of a trip to Disney World, they can save for a stuffed version of their favorite Disney character, or a video game related to a character. After saving enough and buying it, they can then save towards a small amount to contribute to a future family trip to Disney World.

When kids grow older, their dreams get bigger. Perhaps your kid will want a motor scooter. It might take a few years to reach that goal, but one strategy might be to chart your kid's progress towards that goal in an ostentatious visual display posted on a bedroom wall. To make the goal more reachable, break it up into interim goals, and reward the attainment of those goals with a bonus contribution.

Chart That Progress!

If your child wants a motor scooter, chart her progress by taking a picture of it to a copying facility and having it blown up. Then trace it onto a huge sheet of poster board, mount it on a wall, and print the total amount it will cost in big colorful numerals above or below it. Then make a grid out of the traced scooter with horizontal and vertical lines, and make each rectangle of the grid into a $5 unit. As your child saves money, she turns it over to you and fills in the appropriate additional squares like a paint by numbers portrait. As the amount of money saved approaches the goal, the picture comes to colorful life.

MONEY

5 • Saving

Once children have successfully saved for a few small fanciful dreams and wishes, it's time for them to start saving for more mundane goals and things that you don't consider necessities but they do. These might include clothes or cosmetics that exceed the budget you've allotted, magazine subscriptions, concert tickets, and sophisticated sports or stereo equipment. As your children's allowances rise and they're more able to start earning money through neighborhood chores and babysitting, reduce the list of expenses that you automatically take care of for them by shifting items to this category. Your ultimate goal is to increase their need to use saving as a way of getting the things they both want and need.

Philosophies for Saving

It's one thing to know that it's important for your children to save, and what benefits it will provide them, but it's another to communicate that in a way that motivates them. Success depends on the extent to which *you* truly buy into saving and they see that you do, which means that you must think and act with a solid savings philosophy. Here's how to develop one without studying Aristotle.

A Non-Aristotelian Philosophy of Saving

- **De-program yourself** from the current insistence that spending is patriotic and good for the economy. Saving is actually better in the long run, providing capital for business to grow, people of modest means to buy houses, etc. It also provides more flexibility; once you spend it, you can't save it, but if you save it, you can always spend it later.

- **Saving is necessary** because of economic realities and pessimistic possibilities. It hedges against future inflation in energy, water, and other costs, because even if your paycheck can always cover your needs, your wages might not keep up with inflation. It's also necessary to compensate for disappearing pensions and employer medical coverage, future shortfalls in Social Security and Medicare, and to pay for possible career-change training several times during a typical future career.

5 • Saving

- **By saving toward a future goal**, a child begins to learn the overall importance of working towards future goals in non-financial aspects of life: college, career, marriage, family, life dreams, retirement.

- **Saving is distinct from investing** – actually a prerequisite. Investing is what you do with a portion of what you've saved. Being a good investor is useless if you're a poor saver, and being a good saver is wasted if you're a poor investor. But if you're a good saver who doesn't invest, you'll be better off than a good investor who doesn't save.

- **It's not what you earn**, it's what you save. *The Millionaire Next Door* (Stanley and Danko) documents the thousands of stealth millionaires who got there through steady savings, even though they had only middle-income jobs.

- **Savings means freedom and power.** You can do what you want for the rest of your life when you're financially independent, but you can only do what you want for a very limited time now if you live for today and get into debt.

Strategies for Saving

Knowing and believing that they have to save, however, might not be sufficiently motivating to some kids, and others will simply be unable to think long-term on their own. Kids will need as much of your help as possible in becoming self-motivated to develop savings discipline.

 ### *Tricks of the Saving Trade*

- **Get young children an attractive piggy bank** into which they can put small cash gifts and allowance. In addition, when you start giving them experience making small purchases at stores for you or themselves (not covered by allowance), tell them they can keep the change if they put it in the piggy bank, and show them how you empty your pockets each night and put change into a savings jar that you later transfer to a bank savings account. Each week, before giving them allowance, help them count the money in the piggy bank so they can see how it accumulates.

5 • Saving

- **Take a cue from employers** and match all or part of what your child saves and explain that you're not just doing that to be nice but because companies sometimes do that for their employees. If your 401(k) plan does that, show your child the account statements and how your money has grown.

- **Give your children a job** of additional small tasks beyond what they're normally expected to do. Each week, give children a "paycheck" and some bills you make up for services you provide them. "Cash" their paychecks for them with play money so that the amounts will be realistic, and then have them pay you and save the rest. At the end of each pay period, redeem their play money with real money at some conversion rate such as one penny, nickel, or dime for every dollar of play money. Have them pay you what you billed them and save the rest. Give them the opportunity to save more by doing some of the things you do for them so that the bills you give them will decrease. Point out to them that this works when they're adults; the more they do for themselves, the less they have to pay others to do things for them – such as housecleaning, painting, lawn care, hair cuts, and oil changes.

- **When children get a little older**, show them how saved money earns interest – that in a sense, the bank matches part of their savings. Tell them you'll take the place of the bank and pay the interest. Help them set up a "piggy bank account" book in which they can record all the deposits, withdrawals, and interest. Show them that the more they save and the sooner they save it, the bigger the eventual amount because time and compounding work for them.

- **If your children are old enough** to have absorbed most of the credit lessons from Chapter 4, then explain how interest can also work against them if they have debt. Show them how the interest paid on credit-card debt takes away from money available to save, so the longer the debt is held, the less you're able to save. With an inexpensive financial calculator (about $10), you can enter the monthly amounts of interest you've paid in the past few years on your credit card and show how much savings you could have generated from compounding since then if, instead, you'd been able to deposit those amounts each month into savings.

5 • Saving

The piddling two or three percent interest paid by real banks might not excite your children much, so consider using "The Bank of Dave" concept described by Dave Owens in the April, 1998 Atlantic Monthly. Pay them higher interest rates, say 12% (1% per month) so that their money will grow fast enough to keep their interest (on interest!).

- **When children outgrow the piggy-bank stage**, introduce them to the bank or credit-union account in which you've been keeping the larger gifts they've received. Tell them that you'll start putting all the money that they intend to save in the bank account and that they can keep money they want to spend at home in two containers, one holding change and the other holding currency.

- **Explain how putting all non-spending money** in a bank savings account is part of an approach to money which makes it harder to spend than to save. Use the adage, "Out of sight, out of mind" and how that suggests that what you don't see, you don't spend. Show them how you have part of your paycheck put into various savings such as your employer plan, monthly mutual-fund investments, savings bonds, etc. Then you have the rest of it put into the checking account, from which you pay bills. When they get their first jobs, help them set up a similar system of split direct deposit of their paychecks into separate savings and checking accounts.

- **Until they can get a job that provides direct deposit**, serve as your kids' conduit for direct deposit of their earnings from neighborhood chores. And prepare them for that future wage job by getting them involved in volunteer work. As an added bonus, the extra hours spent volunteering will reduce aimless free time to go shopping and spend, thus leaving them more of their chore money and allowance to save. Furthermore, kids who do charitable work are often less materialistic because of direct experience with organizations and people whose needs make some of their wants seem foolish and trivial – again leading to more saving for themselves or for charitable donations.

5 • Saving

- **Volunteer work** is also likely to make kids more aware of how bad habits taken to the extreme, such as smoking, drinking, drug use, and gambling can ruin lives financially and physically. It might facilitate their eliminating bad habits that waste money – such as excessive candy and playing expensive and addictive mall video games. Show them how much money they can accumulate between now and some future time by eliminating a bad habit and saving the money.

- **Don't assume that collecting is a bad habit**, especially if it involves stamps, trading cards, fan-club memorabilia, something related to nature, or any other healthy, possibly educational interest that isn't prohibitively expensive. Collecting has been shown to help kids develop the type of discipline that also contributes to successful saving – and some collectibles do make good investments. Coins are a natural if you're encouraging your kids to save leftover change because when they count what they've got, they can also be checking for the ones they need for their collection.

- **Get your children to collect savings ideas** and reward them for (say) every 25 they find and for each one they find that your family can actually use – including coupons for things your family actually needs. Tell your children that you'll put 10% of what their ideas save into the family savings account and show them monthly how those savings have contributed to the family savings.

Where to Find More Money-Saving Ideas Online

- www.nefe.org/hsfla/secondplaceweb/66ways.html
- www.chicagofed.org/consumerinformation/projectmoneysmart/moneysmartweek.cfm
- www.dollarstretcher.com
- www.allthingsfrugal.com
- www.frugalmoms.com

5 • Saving

- **Teach children that one way to motivate yourself** to find money-saving ideas is by establishing a budget for spending that sets limits on how much can be spent on different expense categories and how much must be put into savings. Show them how money-saving ideas allow the purchase of more of what a family wants in each expense category. For example, if you find a way to save on meat purchases, then more is left over to buy premium meats such as steak, or for indulgences such as ice cream. In other words, once you set a savings goal and stick to it, then you can enjoy yourself when you find ways to cut expenses instead of penalizing yourself by having to put additional money saved into savings. You'll find a helpful, detailed budgeting worksheet at Federal Reserve: www.chicagofed.org/consumerinformation/projectmoneysmart.

- **Once you've gotten children actively participating** in small-scale money-saving, show them how your family achieves big savings through consistent good habits such as usually preparing and eating meals at home, taking bag lunches to work, keeping cars as long as feasible instead of trading for a new one every few years, and setting spending limits in advance for vacations, expeditions to amusement parks, or professional sports events.

- **Set short-term, medium-range, and long-term savings goals** and reward your children proportionately for achieving them; that way saving won't seem like an endless process.

Get children's schools involved in savings education by helping them coordinate with many organizations and financial institutions offering free educational programs online:

- **Kid Teller for a Day** –
  http://detnews.com/2001/schools/0112/04/c05l-357587

- **Banking on Kids Program** – www.bankingonkids.com/index2

- **Teach Kids to Save** – www.aba.com/Consumer+Connection/tcts_bankers

- **Save for America Program** – www.saveforamerica.org

5 • Saving

Save These Links for Even More Saving Tricks

- **Direct Deposit** – www.directdeposit.org/
- **Collectibles** – www.freep.com/money/business/kids28_20020128
- **American Bankers Association Collectible Coins** – www.abacoins.com
- **Savings from Quitting Bad Habits** – www.investoreducation.org/cindex
- **How to Balance a Checkbook** – http://ianrwww.unl.edu/pubs/nebfacts/nf4
- **Books, Software, Other Materials** – www.merrill-lynch.ml.com/family/kids/list
- **Findings of Focus Group on Saving** – www.hec.ohio-state.edu/hanna/kenn.pdf

Savings Vehicles

Getting kids to save is step one, and getting their savings in the right place is step two. Although bank accounts earn interest and increase savings, when children are young, it's better for them to have tangible savings so they feel like the money they've saved is really theirs – at least the money they get from allowance, small gifts, and chores. So before they're in kindergarten, let them use a piggy bank. When they're old enough to understand some simple arithmetic, you can start acting as the bank, still keeping the money where they can see and handle it, but paying interest and other bonuses (as discussed above).

Banks and Credit Unions

Once children are old enough to fully understand that money in the bank is still really one's own money, it's time to have them start putting most of their money into a second companion account to the one you should have already established for their bigger gifts. That first account should have been set up as a Uniform Trust for Minors Account (UTMA) in the child's name, with you or your spouse (or another adult) as custodian. The money that goes in that account is the child's, but the adult has control of it until the child reaches age 18 or 21, depending on the state in which you live. One big UTMA advantage is that grandparents can establish such accounts for grandchildren and name *their* children as trustee for their grandchildren. Each grandparent can then deposit up to $11,000 annually in each grandchild's UTMA account without incurring gift tax.

5 • Saving

Named Accounts Versus UTMA Accounts

In some cases, a "named account" is preferable to a UTMA account. The named account is set up in the name of the child (e.g. "for Lisa Jones") with you as owner, and the interest earned on it is taxed in your name. While that taxation is a disadvantage, one advantage is that you don't have to turn over that money when the child reaches the age of majority. Secondly, if you don't share information about this account, or gifts you've put into it, with your child, then in good conscience, you can take money out for reasons other than for the benefit of that child; for example, you might want to transfer some of the money into a new account you set up upon the birth of a second child.

To give your child the strongest sense that the second account is hers, set it up as a joint account, listing your child's name first. You'll both have the ability to deposit and withdraw funds for your child. However, there might be a requirement for your approval of each of your child's transactions (although she can usually get at the money with an ATM card), depending on the child's age and your state of residence. The interest income will be taxed as your child's, although your child will not have to file a return for amounts under $750 and will owe no tax.

Even if interest income exceeds $750, your child might not have to file a separate return. Sometimes that "unearned" income (interest, dividends, and capital gains) can be reported on the parent's return. If your child is under 14, then amounts above $750 of unearned income will be taxable at the child's rate for amounts ranging from $750 to $1500, and at the parent's rate for amounts over $1500.

Shop carefully for the bank where you'll establish your child's account. Many banks and credit unions offer all kinds of fun incentives for children's accounts, enrolling children in some kind of kids' saving club. Kids can earn prizes for each deposit, for meeting certain savings goals, or by satisfying other conditions. Many send attractive monthly account statements and offer online access to account information and a kids' web site. (Best of all, none give away free toasters – although that might be due to liability issues).

In the long run, though, the most important factor in choosing a bank is what types of interest-earning investments it offers, what interest rates it pays, and what fees it charges to maintain savings accounts, open and use a checking account, and use an ATM or debit card. Involve your children in shopping for the best deal by picking up literature from banks, looking up their web sites, and using web sites such as Bankrate.com to compare banks. Generally,

5 • Saving

credit unions will pay less interest than banks, but also have lower fees. They're often the better choice for kids because they stress education and have a more "user-friendly" atmosphere. For information on local credit unions, check out the Credit Union National Association website (www.cuna.org)

Once you've opened an account, you must decide how to invest the money. Although some banks now offer brokerage units that allow you to invest in stocks and bonds, we'll cover all such accounts separately below and focus here on banks' bread and butter: safe bank investments that earn interest and protect principal. These are your typical choices (descriptions provided verbatim from the Securities and Exchange Commission web site: www.sec.gov).

 ## The Bank's Bread and Butter

- **Savings Accounts.** If you save your money in a savings account, the bank or credit union will pay you interest, and you can easily get your money whenever you want it. At most banks, your savings account will be insured by the Federal Deposit Insurance Corporation (FDIC).

- **Insured Bank Money Market Accounts.** These accounts tend to offer higher interest rates than savings accounts and often give you check-writing privileges. Like savings accounts, many money market accounts will be insured by the FDIC. Note that bank money market accounts are not the same as money market mutual funds, which are not insured by the FDIC.

- **Certificates of Deposit.** You can earn an even higher interest if you put your money in a certificate of deposit, or CD, which is also protected by the FDIC. When you buy a CD, you promise that you're going to keep your money in the bank for a certain amount of time.

All these choices have their place in the conservative part of an overall investment portfolio – especially when your child is younger and might not understand how he lost money that he had "saved." As the SEC puts it (regarding bank accounts, money-markets, and CDs): "Your money tends to be very safe because it's federally insured, and you can easily get to your money if you need it for any reason. But there's a tradeoff for security and ready availability. Your money earns a low interest rate compared with investments. In other words, it gets a low return."

5 • Saving

Savings Bonds

Chances are that your children will receive gifts of savings bonds at birth and in early childhood from relatives, and you might decide to invest in them for your kids through your employer's payroll savings plan. Thus it's reasonable to consider adding to this collection by helping your child use some of her savings to buy additional bonds – if for no other reason than to encourage learning about another form of investment. In addition, they seem valuable to kids because of how they look and are made, and it's easy to explain to kids that a bond will be worth the amount of money shown on it at a specific time – when you'll accompany them to cash it in. These features encourage them to save because they feel they're handling a valuable commodity.

Like bank accounts insured by the FDIC, bonds are fully backed by the U.S. government, so they're a completely safe investment, and have become much more attractive in the last decade as the government took steps to make their returns more competitive. The government also took steps to make bonds easy to understand with an excellent web site that includes the following (almost verbatim) overview.

Savings bonds are issued by the U.S. Treasury Department. They are non-marketable securities. This means you may not sell savings bonds to, or buy them, from anyone except an issuing and redeeming agent authorized by the Treasury Department. Savings bonds are registered securities, meaning that they are owned exclusively by the person or persons named on them.

I Bonds and Series EE Savings Bonds are accrual securities. They earn – accrue – interest monthly at a variable rate and the interest is compounded semiannually. You receive your earnings when you redeem an I Bond or Series EE Savings Bond.

Series HH Savings Bonds are current income securities. You receive your earnings semiannually, and you receive the face value of Series HH Savings Bonds when you redeem them.

5 • Saving

General Features of the I Bond and Series EE Savings Bond

 ### *Overview of Benefits*

- **Attractive Interest Rates.** The I Bond tracks inflation to prevent your earnings from being eroded by a rising cost of living. The Series EE Savings Bond earns market-based rates, keyed to five-year Treasury securities. Both series offer rates that are comparable to the rates of similar savings tools.

- **Tax Advantages.** Savings bond earnings are exempt from all state and local income taxes. You can defer federal income taxes on earnings until the savings bonds either reach final maturity or until you redeem them. If you use savings bonds to pay for qualified higher education expenses, your earnings may be exempt from federal income taxes, too.

- **Safety.** Savings bonds are backed by the full faith and credit of the United States. Your principal and earned interest are safe and cannot be lost because of changes in the market. Savings bonds are registered with the Treasury Department, so if yours are lost, stolen, or destroyed, you may have them replaced at no cost to you.

- **Affordability.** You can buy savings bonds for as little as $25. Participants in the Payroll Savings Plan may buy them in even smaller installments. The Treasury Department never charges fees or service charges when you buy or redeem savings bonds. Because savings bonds come in eight denominations – $50, $75, $100, $200, $500, $1,000, $5,000 and $10,000 – you can tailor your purchases to meet your goals and needs.

- **Accessibility.** After an initial holding period of six months from the issue date, the money you place in savings bonds is available whenever you want it. However, if you redeem a savings bond earlier than five years from the issue date, you pay an early redemption penalty equal to the last three months of earned interest.

- **Convenience.** You can buy savings bonds in several ways. The easiest is through the Payroll Savings Plan with an automatic allotment. If you do not have access to payroll savings, the EasySaver Plan offers similar convenience by allowing automatic purchases with allotments from your checking or savings account. You can also buy savings bonds at 40,000 financial institutions nationwide and online with a credit card at Savings Bonds Direct.

Interest Accrual and Compounding

- **Interest Earned on I Bonds and Series EE Savings Bonds Accrues Monthly.** This means that these savings bonds grow in value each month. The amount of this monthly growth is determined by the current interest rate and total value of a savings bond. Each month's earnings are applied to a savings bond's value on the first day of the next month. For example, interest earned in January is applied on February 1.

- **Interest Accrued by I Bonds and Series EE Savings Bonds Is Compounded Every Six Months** – on a savings bond's semiannual anniversaries. When interest compounds, the savings bond's value on that date is used to calculate monthly interest accruals for the next six months.

- **Savings bond semiannual anniversaries** are simply the months in which a savings bond is issued and six months from that. For example, a savings bond issued in January will have January and July as its semiannual anniversaries.

Tax Exemption, Deferral and Reporting

- **Savings Bond earnings** are exempt from state and local income taxes.

- **You may defer payment of federal income taxes on its accrued earning** until a savings bond reaches final maturity – 30 years from the issue date, or until you redeem it, whichever comes first. The Internal Revenue Service requires that you report savings bond earnings for federal income tax purposes no later than the year in which a savings bond reaches final maturity, even if you do not redeem it.

5 • Saving

- You may also elect to report your savings bonds earnings to the Internal Revenue Service and pay applicable federal income taxes annually.

Restrictions on Redemption

- You may not redeem a savings bond until six months after its issue date. For example, a savings bond with an issue date in January may be redeemed beginning in July. Under extreme conditions, such as a widespread natural disaster, the Treasury Department may waive this holding period to assist people in a crisis.

- After the six-month holding period, you may redeem your savings bonds at any time. However, if you redeem I Bonds or Series EE Savings Bonds earlier than five years from the issue date, you pay an early redemption penalty equal to the last three months of earned interest.

Maturity Periods

- I Bonds earn interest until they reach final maturity at 30 years from the issue date. At that time, they stop earning interest and you should redeem them. You must report your earnings for federal income tax purposes in the year in which your I Bonds reach final maturity.

- Series EE Savings Bonds will double in value to reach face value no later than 17 years from the issue date. This 17-year point is called original maturity. At that time, if the savings bond has not grown to face value, the Treasury Department makes a one-time adjustment to bring it to face value. The Series EE Savings Bond will then continue to earn interest, growing greater than face value – depending on market rates – until it reaches final maturity at 30 years from the issue date. At that time, the savings bond stops earning interest and you may choose one of two ways to proceed. You may redeem your Series EE Savings Bonds and report your earnings for federal income tax purposes in the year in which they reach final maturity. Alternatively, you may exchange your Series EE Savings Bonds for Series HH Savings Bonds and defer federal income tax reporting for up to an additional 20 years.

- You may redeem savings bonds before their final maturity dates, but you'll incur a penalty that in effect yields you a lower interest rate than you would have if held to maturity.

5 • Saving

The Education Tax Exclusion (Education Savings Bond Program)

- **Your earnings from I Bonds and Series EE Savings Bonds** may be excluded from federal income tax if you pay for qualified higher education expenses in the year in which you redeem the savings bonds. Generally, tuition and fees at an educational institution or program that receives federal tuition assistance qualify. Your household income in the year of redemption must meet guidelines for you to use the exclusion. Other restrictions apply.

More About Savings Bonds Online

You can get more detailed online information on rules and restrictions regarding savings bonds purchase, ownership, redemption, and taxation from the web site (www.publicdebt.treas.gov/sav/sav.htm). It includes a downloadable savings-bond calculator that calculates any bond's redeemable value, as well as the current rates that apply to bonds with variable rates. You can also get written information and savings-bond software from the Treasury Department, Federal Reserve banks, or thousands of commercial financial institutions. Reach the savings-bond area of the Treasury Department by calling 304-480-6112, or write to Bureau of the Public Debt, Savings Bond Operations Office, Parkersburg, WV 26106-1328.

Brokerage Accounts

In the roaring and booming 90s, references to kids' financial education were usually synonymous with how to invest in stocks. We read articles about kids' investment clubs that outdid Wall Street experts, kids who started investment newsletters with hundreds of adult subscribers, kids who cut school to stay home and trade online all day, and kids who perpetrated stock scams and made millions. And we saw commercials with a spiky-haired kid showing adults how easy it is to make money investing.

But just as the spikes in hair eventually collapse, the spikes in the stock market aren't permanent either. So although many of us now have deflated portfolios (and egos), the bursting stock-market bubble is a good thing, because kids (and many adults!) have now learned that what goes up, can go down – in fact will, somewhere along the way. That doesn't mean, though, that it's time to stop investing; instead, start viewing investing as just one piece of the overall financial puzzle that kids must learn to solve. In other words, you should teach your kids how to invest and get them started, but leave out the steroids and hysteria.

5 • Saving

Before starting them in actual investing, take advantage of at least a few of the many great books, online courses, and games devoted to investing. You can have your child simulate real investing that's actually tied to current market performance – including the fees they must pay for buying and selling and the taxes on the profits. Some brokerage firms actually allow you to set up an "account" with virtual money so that you completely simulate what happens when you open a real account. The only difference is that you don't actually deposit money, and don't actually gain or lose money – although many online games give real prizes for top performances of simulated portfolios.

Once your child has mastered simulated investing, you can set up the same types of accounts referred to earlier in regard to banks: a joint account in her name with you as co-owner, a UTMA account, or a "named account." You can save some on taxes for realized capital gains if you have a joint account with your child listed first. However, under current financial-aid rules, that benefit could be more than wiped out by reduced financial-aid eligibility.

How Kids' Investments Can Impact College Financial Aid Availability

Currently, most college financial aid formulas use 35% of assets in a child's name annually and only 5.6% of parental assets. However, several elite private universities have recently changed their aid formulas to treat both parent and child assets as "family assets" – using 5.6% of the combined total annually. There's a good chance that formulas used at most schools and for federal aid will soon follow suit. That would make who controls the money and who gets taxed as the main considerations in titling assets – eliminating the need to consider financial aid repercussions.

In Chapter 7, we'll talk more specifically about these games and provide a good primer on investing; so we'll limit this section to the role investing should play in your child's financial education and activities. Most of what your child saves now will be eventually spent before and during college. By starting early, though, she can achieve enough investment growth to offset enough college costs to reduce or eliminate the need to assume educational debt.

Kudos to you and your child if investing his money achieves that objective, but don't limit your ambition. Your child can also get an immense head start on adult financial objectives by starting to invest in a Roth IRA as soon as he has earned income. In 2002, he can invest up to the lesser of his total earnings or $3,000 (going up incrementally to $5,000 over the next several years.)

5 • Saving

 ## *Advantages of a Roth IRA*

- **Earnings in a Roth IRA are tax free forever** if they're held at least until age 59.5. You do not get a current tax deduction for the money put in a Roth, but that hardly matters to a child who can earn up to $4,500 annually without incurring any tax anyway.

- **Once funds have been in a Roth account for at least 5 years**, you can withdraw up to $10,000 tax free towards the purchase of a first home.

- **You can establish a Roth IRA** at virtually every brokerage, so you can minimize fees with a little shopping.

- **You can withdraw principal at any time** without incurring tax – although you normally wouldn't want to because it limits your investment growth. You can also withdraw beyond principal but will incur a tax penalty and have to pay taxes on the portion of the withdrawal that represents earnings. That's good to know because it means your money isn't locked in the account if you have a dire emergency need for it, and withdrawals for some emergencies can be done without tax penalty.

- **Funds in an IRA** are normally not considered as part of a family's assets when colleges determine financial aid eligibility. Furthermore, current formulas treat assets in the child's name much more harshly than assets in the parent's name, so the more the child can shield in an IRA, the better.

- **Funds in an IRA can be invested** in any types of individual stocks, mutual funds, bonds, or interest-earning accounts, and can be shifted within the IRA as often as you like, subject to transfer rules of the investments (mainly mutual funds).

- **Provided you're investing** in a diversified portfolio of moderate-risk equities, time is the single biggest factor in long-run investment growth. The sooner you start, the more years money has to grow. For example, if your child invests $3,000 for each of the next five years and keeps it invested until age 65, it will result in a bigger nest egg than if he waits until age 45 and invests $3,000 in the same investments each year for the next twenty years after that.

- **If you own a business or are self-employed**, you can hire your children to do legitimate work for you and pay them earned income they can use to start a Roth. Thus, you achieve a double family tax benefit: the tax-free Roth earnings for your child and a tax deduction of what you pay your kids from your business income.

- **Roth IRAs are truly an adult investment** that can be made by a child. This isn't "play investing," it's the real thing, so you can engage most children in serious financial education by having them start one.

Section 529 Investment Plans

Because of recent developments, no discussion of kids' finances is complete without covering a new way of saving for college that has exploded on the scene. In typical Uncle Sam fashion, it has the sexy name of Section 529 plan. It allows you to invest more money annually than you probably have (and if we've offended a few of you bluebloods who picked up this book to fan yourselves at the opera, so be it!) in what amounts to an unlimited but somewhat restricted Roth IRA for college. The chief attraction of Section 529 plans is that all earnings are Federal tax-free (and often state-tax free) when withdrawn to pay for college expenses, and many states allow contributions to be deductible against income for state income tax purposes. In addition, unlike the UTMA account, the parent retains control of the money, so the child can't skip college and walk off with it at age 21 and hop on a flight to Tahiti. Furthermore, anyone (usually grandparents with significant assets) can contribute up to $11,000 annually without incurring gift tax; in fact, there's a special rule that allows up to 5 years worth of gift tax exemption to be taken in one fell swoop. Thus, each grandparent can contribute $55,000 this year to each grandchild's Section 529 account without incurring any gift tax – making 529s immensely popular among grandparents over the age of 75.

Section 529 plans might seem too good to be true, but they're not so good that they don't come without some rules, restrictions, and limitations.

5 • Saving

 ## *Limitations and Restrictions on Section 529 Plans*

- **Almost every state has one or more 529 plans** run by various financial institutions who've been awarded administration of particular state plans. You can invest in any state's plan, but state-tax benefits are only applicable if you invest in your own state's plan.

- **Unlike an IRA,** you cannot control your investments. Instead, you pick a particular manager or investment style (e.g. aggressive growth, balanced, etc.) from those offered in a given state's plan. Furthermore, it's very difficult to evaluate the underlying portfolios of various choices. You can switch between options once every 12 months, but you have minimal control over how the money is actually invested.

- **Much like employer 401(k) plans,** each option has annual fees ranging from a fraction of a percent to a few percent associated with it – which can severely cut into your gains. In fact, an increasing number of plans must now be invested in through authorized financial advisors, adding even more fees. Furthermore, it's not easy to determine exactly what the non-advisory fees are, although there's a push by the financial-planning industry to require more upfront disclosure.

- **If the child doesn't go to college,** you can change the beneficiary to anyone else considered family, even cousins. Earnings on any funds not used for education, however, will be taxed at ordinary income rates (ouch) instead of more favorable capital-gains rates, along with a 10% penalty.

- **Plans are evolving** (or deteriorating, depending on how you look at it) rapidly, so the plan you choose now might seem the best but could be surpassed by many others within a few years. You can shift from one state's plan to another, although there might be fees assessed for such transfers.

5 • Saving

- **For financial-aid purposes**, Section 529 balances are counted as assets in the parents' name, and qualified withdrawals are counted as income to the student (although not for taxes). Thus, they can severely limit financial aid eligibility.

- **All these restrictions belie the much-touted benefit of 529 plans** – that unlike other investments that you must constantly manage, you simply pick a plan and the manager does the rest. In fact, choosing the best 529 Plan for your situation requires more upfront homework and continued monitoring than most investments.

Fortunately, there's great help for those flummoxed by trying to choose the best plan. Joe Harley, a CPA who is the most recognized '529 Guy,' has a highly informative web site (www.savingforcollege.com). Either there or through a bookstore you can also order the latest edition of his book, *The Best Way to Save for College*.

Chapter Six

Earning

We're halfway home in learning how to cultivate four basic financial skills in your children. In Chapter 4, we examined when to put an end to the spend. Chapter 5 was about kids craving saving. Now we'll look at ways to foster their yearning for earning before learning how best to invest, in Chapter 7.

Of course, it won't be hard to get kids yearning for things and money. The trick is to get them to look to themselves instead of you or grandparents to satisfy that yearning. Without scaring them, they need to get the message that in life they'll be out of luck if they don't make a buck. While you certainly don't want to go overboard and produce a materialistic little snot, you do want your child to have a healthy desire for and appreciation of money. As one anonymous sage put it, "All I ask is a chance to prove that money can't make me happy."

6 • Earning

Kids' First Sources of Income

In fact, money and happiness do go together, or so it would seem from a child's early experiences. The first few years of birthday parties and visits from grandparents and other relatives are the occasion for endless presents. But when the novelty wears off, the well starts to dry up and the tears start to flow upon the child's discovery of that Rolling Stones truism: "You can't always get what you want."

Allowance

That's a good time to introduce allowance, when kids start wanting things that they're no longer automatically getting. Experts differ widely on how much allowance to give, what kinds of things children should be expected to use it for, to what extent children should have responsibilities connected with receiving that allowance, and whether bad behavior should be cause for suspending allowance. Asking other parents how much allowance they give or relying on allowance surveys doesn't help much, because families widely differ in all these respects. Comparing allowances is like comparing salaries of two people doing the same job working for different companies that have different benefit packages and different overtime policies.

Find Out How Much the Joneses Give Their Kids

If you are interested in surveys, the U.S. Bureau of Labor Statistics 1997 National Longitudinal Survey of Youth (www.bls.gov/nls/nlsy97.htm) contains details on teen finances, including how much they receive in allowance.

But you're not paying the big bucks for this book for its authors to weasel out of decisive recommendations, so here are some guidelines for developing your allowance policy. (Policy? Hey, when we're done, you can call yourself a domestic bureaucrat!).

6 • Earning

 ## *Allowance Guidelines*

- **Family Financial Condition.** There's nothing wrong with telling your kids that just as the adults must live within the family's means, so must the kids. However, don't give kids mixed messages by spending that exceeds what they sense the family can afford.

- **Neighborhood and School Economic Lifestyle.** You shouldn't feel compelled to keep up with the Joneses. However, you chose the neighborhood you're living in, and it's important that you not be excessively stingy if doing so will exclude your kids from most money-requiring activities engaged in by neighborhood kids. Similarly, don't set your kid apart by being overly free with money.

- **Items That Allowance Covers.** It's best to make allowance cover as much as possible, which will help your kids become increasingly responsible. So start by having allowance cover the kinds of things you'd find in a dollar store: candy, inexpensive gadgets and toys, fancy hair clips, etc. As they get older, increase allowance to cover toys they'll want beyond what they'll get at birthdays and holidays, trips to the movies, and similar expenses. As they approach teen years, factor in an amount to cover clothes beyond what you get them for school and family/religious dress-up occasions. Ideally, their allowance should cover everything by the time they're old enough to get wage jobs and supplement their allowance to the extent their wants dictate.

- **Demonstrated Needs.** Don't impose what you think kids' needs are in determining how much allowance they should get. Give them the opportunity to make a list of their needs, price them out, and negotiate with you on what they should get. Rather than undermining your parental authority, you'll be teaching them negotiating skills that will be useful when seeking adult employment, making business deals, setting prices for services they have contractors perform, etc. In fact, you might find they know more about what they really need and how much it costs than you do.

6 • Earning

- **Household Chore Earnings Opportunities.** You might want to treat allowance like the "straight pay" portion of an adult job that includes annual variable pay bonuses based on performance. Thus, you'd determine the maximum amount you'd give your kids for allowance if they did everything around the house you wanted them to, and then determine the value of those things and subtract it from the maximum to determine a "basic allowance" amount. They could then earn the rest by doing what you want them to do. However, don't "pay them" for chores they should do for themselves such as making their beds, keeping their rooms clean, washing their clothes, taking their turn doing dishes, etc. Those are behavior issues for which they should lose privileges if not performed.

- **Outside-Household Earning Opportunities.** You want to be more generous with allowance if your kids have limited opportunity to earn money outside the household, even when they're old enough to do chores. For example, if you live in a condominium development, your kids won't be able to do yard work for the neighbors, and if you live in a neighborhood with few young children, there won't be much opportunity to baby-sit. In such cases, if you can afford it, give your children more opportunity to earn by doing chores for you – perhaps even helping you with clerical aspects of your job.

- **Age and Demonstrated Maturity.** Your goal should be to keep increasing allowance and the life essentials it covers as your children get older, at least until they can get "real" part-time jobs. And you want them to have full discretion as to how to spend it. Therefore, make it clear each time you raise their allowance that you won't rescue them if they squander it and won't automatically raise it the next year if you see they haven't demonstrated the responsibility you'd expect as they get older. That way, they should never get in a position where they absolutely need something but can't buy it because they've used up their allowance. Instead, they'll have to undergo the indignity of depending on you to buy things for them that their friends are able to buy for themselves.

6 • Earning

Regardless of the allowance policy you settle on, make sure it serves its main purpose, as a teaching tool to foster increasing financial responsibility as your kids approach college and adulthood. After all, you are responsible for raising your child, but it's your choice as to how to do that. So you might as well do it in a way that gives your child the most benefit of your parenting. And because good parenting relies on effective communication, it's also essential that your allowance policy is clear to your child and remains consistent, even as amounts and what they cover change over time.

Teen Allowances, An Extreme View

Kathleen Day, a nationally prominent financial advisor in Miami, Florida, counsels her clients to take allowance to the extreme when their children are seniors in high school. Because so many kids mismanage money in college, she has parents turn senior year into a simulated college freshman year by giving their children enough allowance to cover all of their necessary expenses (except possibly three meals a day at home): clothes, toiletries, school supplies, transportation, a reasonable amount for entertainment, etc. Anything else must be covered with earnings from a part-time job, and if they spend half their allowance on CDs and can't afford deodorant or new underwear, tough luck.

And she doesn't stop at allowance, telling clients that to make this realistic, they must give their kids complete freedom with no curfews. That way, they'll be forced to exercise financial and behavior discipline 24/7. Day says kids are better off making mistakes close to home, where parental guidance to aid them in corrective action is still available, instead of possibly sabotaging their higher education by going totally out of control once away from home.

Jobs, Chores, and Entrepreneurial Businesses

One thing that's easy for parents to communicate is what to say when children want too much allowance: "Go out and earn some money." That was easy to do in the flush 90s when newspapers nationwide ran numerous stories about the difficulties fast-food restaurants and other traditional teen employers were having in hiring enough qualified, dependable workers. In those days, minimum wage meant those employers would get a bare minimum of desirable employees, so some employers were paying 15-year-olds $7.50 an hour, and 11-year-old babysitters were demanding as much as $5 an hour, with supplements for multiple kids.

6 • Earning

Although the boom is over, kids still have plenty of earning opportunities. There are always the usual suspects: babysitting, yard work, house-cleaning and car-washing, and caring for dogs and other animals while neighbors are on vacation. However, hectic and changing lifestyles provide several additional opportunities.

 ## *Money Making Opportunities Beyond the Usual*

- **Music-Practice "Enforcer" and Lesson Reinforcer.** Your child might be a good enough musician to be a less expensive alternative to a professional musician giving lessons. But a better bet is to offer services to supervise neighbor children's music practices. After all, many parents don't play the instruments, so can only be of limited help when practice time comes. Your child's relative mastery, though, might be just the ticket to coax and cajole other kids to success.

- **"Recycler" and Shredder.** Even if your neighbors don't work for Enron, the mass of direct mail they receive with private financial information can be overwhelming. It shouldn't just be thrown away because enterprising identity thieves sift through trash. Enter your little "have shredder will travel" entrepreneur. While she's at it, she can also offer to organize recyclable stuff that gets picked up at curbside and cart the rest off, with your "driver's" help, to the local recycling center.

- **Home Organizer.** Your systematic little "neatnick" can take the Recycling/Shredding several steps further and help neighbors organize their homes. Professionals do this for $100 an hour or more. Your child can charge 10 bucks hourly and make huge improvements. Uncluttered kids' minds often can see a way to cut through clutter that we regard as hopeless.

- **Kids' Party Master of Ceremonies.** Have your child and one or two friends give parents an alternative to a roller-skating or bowling birthday party by customizing parties for their kids. Advertise as someone who customizes a party for what the particular child likes and come with games, mini-plays, other forms of entertainment, and props. Your child's enthusiasm and lower prices should provide a big competitive advantage over college students and adults who do clown acts or magic shows. If your child has some food-preparation skills, he can even act as party caterer.

- **Neighborhood Camp.** Taking the party idea one step further, or perhaps in a different direction; your child and some friends can offer a neighborhood summer part-day camp for toddlers and kindergartners. Save nearby parents valuable "soccer mom" time by giving them an alternative to driving back and forth to a commercial camp, or simply provide them a halfway step for their children to get camp "experience" before taking the plunge into a commercial camp. This is also good preparation for your child to become a junior counselor and then full counselor at a commercial camp.

- **Computer and Technology Consultant.** Help families set up web sites, teach them and their kids to use computers in more than basic ways, and to search the Internet like a professional researcher. Install new computers and software for your neighbors and set parameters that will customize screening of viruses, sites that child filters block, and protection against invasion over a cable modem or DSL line. Your young technology whiz can also help install and program family entertainment systems. Computer professionals who do this charge huge hourly amounts, and your kid will be a lot more customer-friendly than most of them.

- **Digital Photographer.** Are families or friends holding special events? Have they just had babies? With some photography skill and computer expertise, your child can use digital photography to take pictures, develop and touch them up electronically, and post them within hours of the event on a web site (and/or create CD mail packages) so that people who attended and distant relatives and friends can get instant access.

- **Athletic Coach.** Parents don't have much time to play catch, shoot hoops, or kick soccer balls around with their kids enrolled in local sports leagues. If your child has some sports skill and experience, she can provide structured practice for neighborhood kids.

- **Freelance Writer.** As you're reading this, are you thinking, my five-year-old can write better than these clowns who call themselves authors? Well, who's to say they can't make some money starting a neighborhood newsletter, or even writing for web sites oriented to kids? Although opportunities are fewer now that unlimited funds are no longer being expended on web publications, there's still money to be made by kids with something worthwhile to say or teach.

6 • Earning

- **Home Office Administrative Assistant.** Most people who work from home would never consider paying $15 an hour for an administrative assistant. Your mature, efficient child can charge half that much and learn about possible careers by helping those in your town who work out of their homes.

One Author's Bona Fides

Why is the senior author on this project now a writer, when an adult on his street used to tell his 10-year-old self he should become an accountant? Because his incredibly long list of kid and grownup jobs gave him the ability to do almost nothing, but know something about almost everything. Having made the point more than once about career flexibility, here's a list of his major kid and professional non-achievements in the work world.

- **Selling** flower and plant seeds and aluminum-siding cleaner door to door.

- **Snow shoveling** and lawn mowing.

- **Soliciting** people on the sidewalks of the main thoroughfare in Cleveland to sign up for prize drawings held in a downtown department store.

- **Checking** people's toes and clothing bags at a municipal swimming pool, and vacuuming the pool bottom in the mornings.

- **Movie Theatre Usher.**

- **McDonald's Staffer** (fired after two weeks...)

- **Running** the popcorn concession at Cleveland's old Municipal Stadium, where vendors came to get the bags and boxes that they sold in the stands. Work was usually done by the third quarter and then watched the rest of the game for free.

- **Caddy** at a posh country club, where first client gave him a dime tip and upon getting home, his father told him he should have given it back and said, "Thanks, but I think you need this more than I do."

- **Hardware Store Clerk** and later traveling to different cities and states to set up product displays in hardware stores.

6 • Earning

- **Babysitting**, camp counseling, and working as a kids' activity assistant at a YMCA.

- **Working** in a concession stand at an amusement park where he used to estimate the cost of huge orders in his head and tell customers that was the price; nobody ever questioned it. (And he did NOT pocket any of their money; it was just fun.)

- **Intramural Sports Referee**. One touch football team got so mad at a call that they ran the next play right at him and knocked him down.

- **Breaking** down trays in the girl's dorm cafeteria for small wages but great sightseeing fringe benefits – especially the smile of thanks when they came back to retrieve keys they so often left on the trays.

- **College Mailroom clerk**.

- **Psychology Research Assistant**.

- **Popsicle Factory Production Line Worker**; it'll be a cold day in you know where before he does that again.

- **Academic Tutoring**: elementary school kids in a summer math remedial program; college kids in Project Upward Bound; later teaching math in middle school and high school, and statistics, computers, and computer software in college.

- Actuarial **Trainee** for a major insurance company.

- **Computer Programmer** for a group of mathematicians and statisticians at one of the laboratories where the atomic bomb was developed, and statistical programming consultant for professors and graduate students in a university computing center.

- **Systems Engineer** for the research arm of the company that invented the telephone, and then later working as a marketing analyst, mathematical consultant, facilities coordinator, technical writer – and finally, preparer of speeches, presentations, and journal papers for an executive.

- **Technical Writing Contractor** for a variety of companies.

- **Help Desk Analyst** for a major computer company.

6 • Earning

Emphasize to your kids how lucky they are to have so many ways to make money, because adults today are so busy that they'll pay for many more services than they did in earlier, more self-sufficient times. If they balk, don't hesitate to inundate them with stories of your pre-professional work experiences. Your experiences will make work more real to them, and they might be amazed at the types of jobs you did. And make sure to emphasize their good fortune at having such opportunities, versus kids in poor, crime-infested neighborhoods whose main opportunities are sometimes limited to dangerous and illegal errands and services.

To avoid making the making of money too grim and glum a subject, be sure to tell them about how you used to walk five miles uphill through blizzards to shovel a foot of snow for $5 a driveway – and then walked five miles uphill back home. If nothing else, you'll drive them crazy enough to drive them out of the house and out into the neighborhood to seek refuge, and work.

Adult Sources of Income

Before children start making money from these neighborhood chores, they're unlikely to have much interest in how your family and adults in general get money – only that they get some from you. But once they've exercised their power to earn, you'll have their attention, so take full advantage.

Salaries and Wages from Jobs

Amongst your peers, your salary is probably treated as classified information to be disclosed only to those with an FBI-approved need to know. If so, here's your notice that your kids have been granted top-secret clearance. Show them your pay stubs, and explain how your company's compensation system works. Compare your salary to others in your profession and explain how it's influenced by the local competition your company faces in hiring, the local and national supply of people who can do your job, and the value of your benefits package.

Don't do your child a disservice by shielding her from the realities of your situation. If she wonders why you didn't aspire to more education, and a better job, or why you don't have a higher salary, explain honestly. "When I took maternity leave for your sister, my skills got rusty and I'm just now catching up," or "When you were born, I realized how important family is, and I'd

6 • Earning

rather make a little less money and have more time to be here with you," or "I just wasn't that motivated when I was younger, but I take pride in what I do; I hope you'll be more motivated, but the most important thing is that you be able to support a family and not disappoint yourself by not working hard enough."

However, if you're a superstar, don't hesitate to extol the merits of hard work that has gotten you ahead of the pack, while also bemoaning the fact that it was necessary to cut into family time in order to hang onto your good standing in today's very competitive market. Make sure you explain things in a way that doesn't make your child feel like she'll be a failure if she doesn't live up to your accomplishments.

Don't focus only on your current job. Exploit your child's interest by explaining how you got to where you are. Explain when and why you decided on your career path, where you went to college and what you studied there, and your job history – including salaries, positions, promotions, and reasons for changing jobs or companies. Especially emphasize the uncertainties you've felt along the way; perhaps you're even now still deciding what you want to be when you grow up. Sharing these feelings will make the whole prospect of adult responsibility less daunting to your child. She'll be less likely to be over-whelmed by college and career selection pressure applied in increasing doses as she progresses through school. By sharing the facts and feelings behind your education and career, you'll be doing far more for her than any high school counselor or college advisor ever will.

Self-Employed and Business Income

Everything just said also applies if you're self-employed or own and operate a business. But there are more and different things to tell your kids about these situations. Start by recounting how you conceived the business, what invest-ment it took to set it up, how much it requires in continuing marketing and operational costs, and what the revenues are. Be sure to address the costs of insurance and complying with regulatory filings and fees, as well as the choice of how you set up your business to avoid driving the family bankrupt if the business should fail or get sued. Mention the old adage about having to spend money to make money in regards to one's own business.

6 • Earning

So how much money do you make? Explain that unlike working for someone else, your income is how much you take out of the business from the difference between revenues and expenses. The rest gets reinvested for further business growth, and that means having to make decisions about how much income is needed versus how much the business must grow if it's to stay viable. Follow up by talking about the differences in taxation between a regular wage job and one's own business, and how you must save for retirement with special tax-advantaged plans that the government approves. Point out that even if you have other savings and assets that will make for a comfortable retirement, using these special retirement plans is almost mandatory because of how punitively small businesses are taxed.

Assuming that you're as "into" your business as most self-employed people are, the enthusiasm you radiate during this discussion should be contagious – more than offsetting the "downer effect" of the tax and liability burdens you've mentioned. Be prepared for lots of questions and to be approached later by your child concerning ideas for her own business. Because of this likely effect, you should talk to your kids about small businesses and self-employment even if you're employed by a company. Explain you're doing it because given the economic shift in job creation from corporations to small companies, chances are better than even that she'll someday work for herself. Encourage her to engage in some of the kids' entrepreneurial money-making ideas discussed elsewhere in this chapter.

Hands-On and Passive Investment Income

While running a business full-time is the ultimate form of hands-on investing, many families do hands-on investing part-time while holding full-time jobs. In addition to the most common, real estate, these investments include antiques, classic automobiles, coins and stamps, art and other collectibles, jewelry and rare metals. Although the 70s and 80s rental boom has somewhat abated due to fewer new duplex and triplex units being built, and old ones being torn down, hundreds of thousands of individuals still actively invest in real estate. Your child will probably be intrigued by your personal experiences involving any of these types of investments.

6 • Earning

Even if you're not such an investor, a friend or relative probably is, so get your child together with that person for a mini-lesson. Explain that real estate is particularly popular, because it provides a regular source of income from monthly rents, while also serving as a long-term investment that you can generally sell for considerably more than the buying price. Or, it can be a source of quick-income for people who buy and fix up property needing repairs, remodeling, and decorating – then selling for more than the sum of what they paid, the cost of improvements, and sales commissions. Explain how credit can be used to leverage such an investment, based on likely revenues from a continuing income stream, and that's why multiple-unit dwellings are more desirable – in case one unit goes vacant. Teaching your child about rental investments provides the added bonus of an early education in the consumer side of renting, leases, security deposits, etc.

In addition to providing diversification, the advantage of such investments is in doing something you enjoy and know something about. In some cases, you can add value by investing some of your "sweat equity;" for example, you can buy and restore old furniture or cars, and sell them for much more than your buying price. Investing where your expertise lies is a more definite path to a profit, and has the further advantage of offering additional profits if you're more knowledgeable about what things are worth than the people you buy from and the people to whom you sell. That's because investments that aren't governed by a central market are part of an "inefficient market" – this means shrewd, knowledgeable investors can buy lower and sell higher than less knowledgeable investors. That's in contrast to the stock market where people generally can buy a stock at any given time within pennies of what the world of investors thinks it's worth at that instant. On the other hand, inefficient markets are also more subject to manipulation and fraud, so investors shouldn't sink a large percentage of their capital into them. Furthermore, it's unethical at the least to pay only a song when buying something you recognize as extremely valuable from an elderly person selling stuff before moving out of a house, for example. So encourage your child to consider "inefficient market" investments, but to do so with some integrity and not rely on them as a primary route to great wealth.

6 • Earning

If It's Too Good to Be True...

Now that the remaining financial virgins amongst us have lost their innocence to Enron, Worldcom, etc., the idea that stocks and bonds are less subject to fraud might bring a pained smile to your lips. Even so, if you have a diversified investment portfolio of stocks and bonds, you're less likely to be victimized than tangible property investors subject to crooked real-estate appraisals, art and jewelry forgeries, and the infamous Hunt family cornering of the silver market. Tell your child about all this; rather than scaring him off, he might find it the most absorbing of the financial lessons you deliver – ending with "if it's too good to be true, it probably is."

Market Investment Income and Gains

We'll devote Chapter 7 to teaching your child about market investments, but before that, you should make your child aware of the part these investments play in your family's finances. Show her the various financial records associated with income from investments: stock certificates; dividend checks and bond-coupon payments, or paperwork showing how they were reinvested; printed or online brokerage and employer 401(k) statements; online accounts for "book form" ownership of stocks; how and where you check prices and net asset values of stocks, bonds, and mutual funds; annual reports you receive from companies and mutual funds; and a copy of a 1040 Schedule D showing how you report sales gains and losses to the IRS. Tell your child about how in the 90s hey-days, the "day trading" profession emerged, and people thought they'd be able to earn their full living making hundreds of real-time, online purchases and sales. For awhile, some did, but in the end most wound up losing their shirts (no visual aids with this lesson, please) and the main profiteers were companies that trained and housed day traders, and institutional investment firms that were just a bit shrewder and outsmarted them. The point is that market investments should be relied on as an important source of income, but only through long-term investing – particularly to provide a nest egg big enough to provide sustenance throughout retirement. Explain that the theory behind investing is that we live in a growing economy and over the long run, good companies will increase in value and those who maintain ownership of stocks will benefit overall, even if some of the stocks lose value.

Other Cash Inflow Sources

Similarly, those who maintain ownership of their rightful place and responsibilities in a family often benefit in the long run as well. In the next ten to twenty years, some economists estimate that baby boomers will inherit more than $50 trillion dollars from their parents, and their children, now young adults themselves, stand to inherit significant amounts as well. Of course, you're going to prepare your kids so well financially that you'll guiltlessly spend your children's inheritance. However, in case your luck runs out before your money does, your children should know that, as the old detective books put it, they might come into some money.

Lawsuit Awards

Or perhaps they'll be lucky enough to get burned by a cup of coffee in a fast-food restaurant and successfully sue for $4 million dollars – which is how one person was made to smile by a popular chain a few years back. Hopefully your kids won't be such opportunists, but they should be aware that litigation is legitimately used to recover real damages that people suffer from physical or financial injuries that are the fault of another person or company. Undoubtedly, you have a friend or family member who has either collected or had to shell out due to a court award, so explain to your child why and how that occurred.

Lawsuit awards often are paid by insurance companies, so use that fact as a jumping-off point to cover insurance payments that protect people when another person or company can't be found at fault: driving your car into a ditch and totaling it, having a tree fall on your house, or compensation for a significant percentage of medical bills. Explain that such insurance is not "making money," but compensating for life's risks when they become realities. Show them your last year's family medical bills, and the insurance payments that were made to partially cover them, and the premiums you paid to have the insurance – emphasizing that medical insurance is very expensive, but absolutely necessary in modern America. Your children might ask why the insurance company doesn't give you your money back if these things don't happen. Respond with an example that shows how some people get back far more than they pay in, and others get back less, and that's why insurance works – as a way for a large group of people to protect everyone from the possibility of being among the few that suffer catastrophic losses.

6 • Earning

Lotteries and Gambling

Unfortunately, too many people are more driven to protect themselves from losing out on huge non-catastrophic luck-based contests and lottery winnings. Hopefully, you won't have personal experiences to relate on this subject. Do share your knowledge of people you know (of) that have won money this way, but also discuss the statistics about the likelihood of winning (another great teaching opportunity), which are usually in microscopic print in an unlikely place on the contest-rules form. Furthermore, tell your child about the enormous taxes that cut into those winnings and the fact that some of them pay off over a number of years – a perfect opportunity for you to explain how inflation erodes the value of money. In addition, point out that the type of people who put their biggest hopes in winning large sums of money are often the least well-equipped to handle sudden wealth. Studies have shown that an inordinate percentage of lottery winners have had miserable life experiences following their "good fortune."

Worse, many people who can ill afford it blow 5 to 10 percent of their income on lotteries, making such lotteries a true form of compulsive gambling. And even more people have had life-ruining experiences chasing good fortune in the dangerous, growing epidemic of illegal sports gambling and legal casino gambling. With the explosion in online gambling, minors no longer have to sneak into casinos to get addicted and lose their money. All this adds up to the absolute necessity of your talking with your children about how gambling is hardly a source of income, but instead a threat to the proper use of income needed for living expenses and investment. Close out your discussion by comparing gambling to the stock market. Gambling is a zero-sum game that's tilted to the gambling establishment (if you lose, they win), while in market investing, everyone can theoretically win from the growth of the economy. And while investing losses can reduce the taxes you owe, gambling wins are taxable, but losses are not deductible, making them very painful indeed.

6 • Earning

Kids and Gambling

When March Madness rolls around in 2003, tens of thousands of pre-teens and teens will have their first gambling experience, an "innocent" participation in a bracket pool. Don't be guilty of allowing it or encouraging it by your own participation. 7% of college students have serious gambling problems, which usually originate in high school, and continue throughout their lives. About 3 million American adults are lifetime pathological gamblers, and another 5 million lifetime problem gamblers, with those numbers rising due to the teenage gambling epidemic. Given these horrifying statistics, the idea of state lotteries supporting education is laughable at best – unless their supporters mean education in how to gamble. Now do you want to know what we authors really think!?

Game Shows

In contrast, trying to earn a big windfall by participating in a game show – especially if it requires skill and knowledge – is a legitimate educational gamble. Encouraging your children to participate in skill-based contests could have big payoffs later if not immediately, by giving them valuable experience they can later put to use in winning college scholarship contests. Just make sure to help them separate scam contests from the legitimate ones.

Odds and Ends

To complete their lessons in family cash inflows, tell kids about other miscellaneous sources: selling cars and other personal property that no longer meet your family's needs, royalties from the sale of an invention or book (hint, hint, help out starving authors by spreading the word), participating in market-research or medical studies that pay a stipend, and getting tax refunds. Now that you've got them dozing, snap them back to attention by telling them how stupid it is to get tax refunds, because refunds from the IRS amount to making an interest-free loan to the United States government, instead of having money withheld at the right rate to just meet your tax obligation. That will allow you to review everything you've told them about cash inflows in terms of whether they're taxable or non-taxable – such as taxable contest winnings and non-taxable proceeds of garage sales and insurance payments that cover expenses you've incurred

MONEY

6 • Earning

Teenage Jobs and Entrepreneurship

As much as non-taxable income seems like a good thing, taxable income is good also, if it comes from your child earning it in her first wage-paying job. Let's look at what the rules are regarding child employment, how to prepare your child to search for and land a job, and what to expect regarding how much and how she'll be paid.

Federal and State Work Regulations

When your child can get a job, the number of hours she can work, the kind of work she can do, and when she can work are all subject to both federal laws and your own state laws. For information on state laws, refer to the chart and accompanying information at this address on the Department of Labor web site: www.dol.gov/dol/esa/public/programs/whd/state/certification.htm.

The Federal Laws, from the U.S. Center for Disease Control

The Child Labor Laws were established to protect the working conditions of adolescents. A summary of the Federal Child Labor Laws follows. Many states have their own Child Labor Laws. If your state's laws are more protective than the federal ones, then those apply. Make sure you know the laws of your state.

> For a complete look at federal child labor laws, visit the CDC's website, **www.cdc.gov/niosh/99-14111.html.**

 ### By Law, Employers Must Provide. . .

- **A safe** and healthful workplace.

- **Safety and health training**, in many situations, including providing information about chemicals that could be harmful to your health.

- **For many jobs**, payment for medical care if an employee gets hurt or sick because of your job. Employees may also be entitled to lost wages.

- **At least the minimum wage of $5.15/hour for most teens**, after their first 90 days on the job. Many states have a higher minimum wage than the federal wage. Lower wages may be allowed when workers receive tips from customers, provided that the tip plus the wage is

6 • Earning

equal to minimum wage. Call your State Department of Labor listed in this guide for information on minimum wage in your state or visit the Department of Labor web site (www.dol.gov/dol/esa/public/minwage/america.htm).

Not all teens may do all types of work. Here is a summary of the federal laws that let you know what the restrictions are depending on the adolescent's age.

No worker under 18 may:

- Operate a **forklift** at any time.

- Operate many types of **powered equipment** such as circular saws, box crushers, meat slicers, or bakery machinery.

- Work in **wrecking**, **demolition**, **excavation**, or **roofing**.

- Work in **mining**, **logging**, or **sawmills**.

- Work in **meat-packing** or **slaughtering**.

- Work where there is **exposure to radiation**.

- Work where **explosives** are manufactured or stored.

- **Recent changes** in the law state that minors under 17 may not drive a motor vehicle; 17-year-olds may drive occasionally, if they meet certain requirements.

- Also, 14- or 15-years-old may not **bake** or **cook** on the job (except at a serving counter).

- Operate **power-driven machinery** (except certain types that pose little hazard such as those used in offices).

- Work on a **ladder** or **scaffold**.

- Work in **warehouses**.

- Work in **construction**, **building**, or **manufacturing**.

- **Load or unload** a truck, railroad car, or conveyor.

- **Federal Child Labor Laws** also have guidelines for the hours that a teenager may work.

MONEY

6 • Earning

For young workers between the ages of 14 and 15, work hours are as follows:

- **Not before** 7 a.m. or after 7 p.m. between Labor Day and June 1 and not after 9 p.m. between June 1 and Labor Day.

- Not during **school hours**.

Maximum hours when school is in session are as follows:

- **8 hours** a week, but not over.

- **3 hours** a day on school days.

- **8 hours** a day Saturday, Sunday, and holidays.

Maximum hours when school is NOT in session are as follows:

- **40 hours** a week.

- **8 hours** a day.

Getting the Job

Despite all the restrictions, kids can find work, provided they've prepared themselves well and go about their search in a thorough and systematic way. When your kids are younger and you're out with them, point out help wanted signs you see in businesses you patronize. If your child expresses any interest, ask for employment applications, even if your child is several years away from eligibility. (You might even tell a white lie in front of your child and tell the store manager that 11-year-old Billy will be 14 next year; how's that for boosting your kid's ego!)

Once you get home with the application, don't drop the ball. Younger children love filling out forms (one good reason we should change child labor laws and hire them to do all the paperwork we adults hate), so encourage them to complete the applications, making up things if necessary to make the exercise realistic. Then you can review the application together and talk about what sorts of things he can do between now and when he's old enough so that when it comes time, he'll be able to fill out the application with real stuff that will impress prospective employers.

6 • Earning

Don't restrict your child to jobs that have advertised for help and have official applications. Just as adults have discovered, many kids get jobs through networking and the best way to get their feet in the door is with a resume. A resume for kids? you ask. Yep, and there are several web sites on which kids can answer a series of questions and a resume will magically appear on the computer screen, which can then be edited and printed.

Online Resume Resources for Kids
- www.teachingkidsbusiness.com
- www.careerkids.com/1152x864/resume.html
- www.myfuture.com/career/objective.html
- www.groovejob.com/job-seekers_resume_builder.php

Once children have worked with these, show them yours and some other adult resumes. They might even improve on the online result by applying their own creative skills, or they can graduate to one of the many resume-building software packages for adults that are available as downloadable shareware or in office-supply stores. Just put the phrases "resume builder" and "resume software" into a search engine and you'll be inundated with possibilities.

Of course, the resume or completed application could be great, but it won't help if your child flunks the interview. That won't happen, though, if you prepare him when he's younger with some realistic interview training at home. On your refrigerator, advertise chores to be done around the house for which you'll pay. If your child expresses interest, tell him he has to interview for the job. Set up a time for the interview and instruct him on acceptable grooming standards for it. Make sure the time is when you'll be able to give your undivided attention and do it somewhere in the house behind closed doors, preferably in a spare room or home office. Obviously, you're going to give your child the job, but you might want to make him go through a second interview if the first one didn't go well, and you can smooth it over by taking him out for ice cream to celebrate getting the job.

6 • Earning

Understanding the Paycheck

Your child's first paycheck might come as quite a shock if she's not prepared for the difference between the gross (hourly rate times hours worked) and the net (what she's actually paid). It's up to you to explain how she's helping take care of you in your old age via Social Security and Medicare taxes (FICA), as compensation for you taking care of her until after college. Show her your paycheck (or a computer printout of your direct deposit) and explain how those deductions are calculated, as well as the federal tax withholding (which teens should usually be able to avoid through filing a W-4 with an appropriate number of exemptions, or getting a tax refund of federal withholding if they make less than $4,500 annually). Then cover the possible state income taxes, including possible separate unemployment insurance and worker's compensation taxes.

Explain that the reason for withholding is so that Uncle Sam and the state get approximately their pro-rated share of what you're going to owe for the year as you make it. If too little is withheld, you'll have to pay a penalty because you've been getting an unwarranted free loan, and if too much is withheld, Uncle Sam will laugh if you ask him to pay a penalty – even though you've been giving him a free loan that you'll get back as a tax refund. Instead, it was up to you to file a W-4 with an appropriate number of exemptions. Then ask your child if she's planning to get married while a teenager. Assuming (hopefully!) that she gives you one of those exquisitely pained rolled-eye looks, say, "Whew, that's good, because it's really complicated to file W-4 forms that avoid having too little or too much tax withheld when both spouses work."

Now that your child has deducted even more points from your sane parent score, it's time to explain the other possible deductions that adults might have on their paychecks.

6 • Earning

 A Long list of Possible Payroll Deductions

- **Employee share** of medical and other insurances.

- **Other cafeteria plan deductions** (flexible medical and dependent care accounts, and 529 educational savings plans).

- **U.S. Savings Bond purchases.**

- **Company Stock Purchase Plan.**

- **401(k)** or other retirement plan contributions.

- **Union Dues.**

- **United Way** or other charity contributions.

- **Direct Deposit** into non-employer investment accounts you've chosen.

- **Involuntary deductions,** including tax levies, child support, creditor garnishments, bankruptcy orders, and student loan collections.

Finally, explain the importance of reviewing paychecks thoroughly, even when they'll be pretty simple in teenage jobs. Although they're almost always prepared by computer, they still can be wrong due to incorrect data entry, such as the wrong wage rate, wrong determination of higher-rate overtime, incorrect tax calculations, etc. Then point out how much more likely errors are in adult paychecks, due to all the other possible deductions. Although you don't want to turn your child into the world's biggest cynic, you can even point out that in the dying days of the Internet boom, a number of small companies were failing to deposit money into 401(k) accounts, instead using it to cover daily operational expenses because they were losing so much money. In other words, when in doubt, question authority – but only after making sure you understand the way things should work (the reason you're teaching him all this stuff).

6 • Earning

Payroll Deductions: A Worst Case Scenario

Paychecks aren't as simple as they once were, and your child might get quite frustrated when he discovers all the different possible deductions. Show him this one first, and then the real one might not seem so bad. (Read down, not across!)

Gross pay: $1222.02	Ma'am Tax: $2.60	Union Dues: $5.85
Income Tax: $244.40	Parking Fee: $5.00	Union Don'ts: $3.77
Outgo Tax: $45.21	No Parking Fee: $10.00	Cash Advances: $0.69
State Tax: $61.10	F.I.C.A: $81.88	Cash Retreats: $121.35
Interstate Tax: $5.89	T.G.I.F: $9.95	Overtime: $1.26
County Tax: $6.11	Life Ins: $5.85	Undertime: $54.83
City Tax: $12.22	Health Ins: $16.23	Eastern Time: $9.00
Rural Tax: $4.44	Disability: $2.50	Central Time: $8.00
Back Tax: $1.11	Ability: $0.25	Mountain Time: $7.00
Front Tax: $1.16	Liability Ins: $3.41	Pacific Time: $6.00
Side Tax: $1.61	Dental Ins: $4.50	GMT: $24.00
Up Tax: $2.22	Mental Ins: $4.33	Bathroom Time: $4.44
Down Tax: $1.11	Reassurance: $0.11	Time Out: $12.21
Tic-Tacs: $1.98	Coffee: $6.85	Oxygen: $10.02
Thumbtacks: $3.93	Coffee Cups: $66.51	Water: $16.54
Carpet Tacks: $0.98	Calendar: $3.06	Electricity: $38.23
Stadium Tax: $0.69	Floor Rental: $16.85	Heat: $51.42
Flat Tax: $8.32	Chair Rental: $4.32	Air Conditioning: $46.83
Surtax: $3.46	Desk Rental: $4.32	Misc: $144.38

Take Home Pay: $0000.02 (This is where the expression "just my 2 cents" came from...)

6 • Earning

The Entrepreneurial Road

Your child doesn't have to question authority, however, if she makes herself the authority through an entrepreneurial venture. The Internet age has meant that a person's age is becoming increasingly irrelevant in the world of business, with teen moguls becoming ten million dollars a dozen. PBS recently broadcast the story of Tom Williams, who started a software company at age 12 that sold computer games he developed. By age 17, he was a school dropout and Director of Creative Development for MultiActive Technologies, a Vancouver firm that develops educational technology. The *Wall Street Journal Sunday Edition* revealed how Jessie Mabry, a 13-year-old Raymore, Missouri girl started a successful business to clean up after the construction crews had finished building new homes. Ellen Matthews, a 16-year old graduating from Mary Baldwin College this year, was offered telecommuting jobs, sight unseen, when at age 11, she detected and solved a number of problems that she reported to software company help desks.

Does Your Child Have Entrepreneurial Qualities?

Entrepreneurs are not necessarily born, but they're not totally made, either. If you're wondering whether your child has what it takes, this section is an overview of entrepreneurial characteristics (based on material taken from the U.S. Small Business Administration web site).

What does it take to be an entrepreneur? Which personality traits make for success?

FICTION: To be an entrepreneur you must be born that way.

FACT: Anyone can learn to operate like an entrepreneur.

Successful entrepreneurs? They have persistence, desire for immediate feed-back, inquisitiveness, strong drive to achieve, high energy level, and goal-oriented behavior. They're "change agents" who are independent, demanding, self-confident, calculated risk-takers, creative, innovative, competitive, highly reliable.

Entrepreneurs also have vision, commitment, problem-solving skills, tolerance for ambiguity, strong integrity, personal initiative, ability to consolidate resources, strong management and organizational skills, tolerance for failure, desire to work hard – and luck!

6 • Earning

Many entrepreneurs also had a role model to influence them early on, or parents who were entrepreneurs.

Two of the traits mentioned that are necessary for successful entrepreneurs are creativity and innovation.

Creativity

Creativity is being able to develop new ideas and ways to solve problems that in turn provide interesting business opportunities. Creative people are bright and adaptable, have high self-esteem, are oriented to ideas and challenges, and are inquisitive and curious.

 ## Can Innate Creativity Be Improved? Yes

- **Gather as much information** as you can (read, talk with experts, etc.) and "brainstorm" over time.

- **Think about the problem** or issue until an idea comes to you. Is the solution reasonable? If so, try it. Did it work? If so, great. If not, begin the process over again.

- **Don't put barriers on your mind.** Put these steps to use. Use your left brain for analytical and rational approaches and your right brain for intuitive and artistic approaches. You need both sides of your brain when being creative because they compliment each other.

Innovation

Innovation can be invention, such as the creation of the CD, or it can be an improvement or variation on an existing idea or product, such as SuperWal-Mart. Innovative ideas come from unsatisfied customers, demographic changes in society, luck, imagination, vision, and problem-solving. To foster it, look for new ideas, keep it simple, start small, and try, try, try again.

6 • Earning

Entrepreneurial Development Resources

Recognizing the startlingly mature money-making abilities that so many kids have, a range of youth-oriented entrepreneurial programs and organizations has evolved to support kids' efforts. Junior Achievement was once a buttoned-down haven for business people who liked to help kids design, develop, and sell cute, but questionably useful, gadgets. Today, it's an information-age organization that reaches four million American kids led by thousands of volunteers – many with high-tech skills. Its web site (www.ja.org) has or directs you to numerous educational resources, including the Entrepreneur Center. (www.bplans.com/miniplan/), a new personal-finance literacy program (www.ja.org/personalfinance), and JA TITAN (www.jatitan.lycos.com/) – an online, "new economy" interactive business simulation competition among teams of JA members countrywide.

More Resources Online to Help and Encourage Young Entrepreneurs

JA is hardly the only game in town for facilitating the development of young entrepreneurs. Check these out:

- **Bankrate.com** features articles on resources for starting a business, and business ventures for kids – www.bankrate.com/brm/news/biz/Green/states/states.asp, and www.bankrate.com/brm/news/sav/20000509.asp

- **Wall Street Journal Classroom Edition** – www.wsjclassroomedition.com

- **YoungBiz Magazine** – www.Kidsway.com

- **YoungBiz Web Site** – www.youngbiz.com

- **National Academy of Finance** – www.naf.org

- **Whiz Teens** – www.whizteens.com

- **U.S. Small Business Administration Discover Business** – www.sba.gov/young

- **Youth Venture** – www.youthventure.org

- **Future Business Leaders of America** – www.fbla-pbl.org

- **Young Entrepreneurs Association** – www.yea1.org

- **Entrepreneurship Education** – www.entre-ed.org

MONEY

6 • Earning

College and Career Planning

Even if your child never becomes an entrepreneur, developing those skills is useful in almost every profession today – as we continually move towards a "free-agent" economy in which it's everyone for themselves. Loyalty is great for boy and girl scouts, but it's no longer carrying much weight in business. Instead, those who are successful have the sales skills to present themselves as the right person at the right time for the job, and have the flexibility to reinvent themselves as circumstances and needs change.

To become such people, kids must treat career and college planning as the first stage in setting up the business of adult financial life. The effort and money they expend in this stage amounts to the start-up capital, and they must budget for the ongoing expense of continuing education. They must also be adept in mergers and acquisitions: finding a marriage partner who has the flexibility and adaptability for such a "business plan" will also be key. Of course, you're not likely to have much say in that, but it will help your child to learn how you and your spouse or other family and friend marital pairs have had to adapt as the nature of employment life has changed during the last 20 years.

Yet, although you should continually stress the importance of, and opportunities for, college and career planning, you shouldn't stress your child about it. Just as the rest of life is a tapestry of colors and shades of gray, so too is the proper place of work and money. Take opportunities to have informal chats with your child about finding a balance between work, family, and involvement in community. Encourage him to think about his choices all during life in terms of this question: Am I living to work, or working to live (and, of course, the answer is not strictly one or the other).

Make it clear to your child that his whole life won't be based on the decisions he makes now. The important thing is to get off to a good start, but not to get it exactly right, because work life is a moving target; people his age are expected to have as many as five different careers during their lifetimes because the world is changing so fast. Thus, continuing education will become an essential part of life, a form of career exercise for career health in the way that physical exercise promotes physical health. Here's a financial fitness plan for getting your kids to work on college and career planning that will lead to the earning power that will fit into their life plans.

6 • Earning

School, Extracurricular, and Social Activities

Schools try, they really do, to make their curriculums relevant to career preparation. Until recently, however, few teachers had significant professional work experience outside the classroom that could help them make the curriculum-career connection in their presentations. That's changing gradually as the teaching profession tries to solve its shortage by reaching out to early retirees and prospective career changers.

You can't afford to wait, though. Help make what your child learns relate to future work by what you do both in school and at homework time. When teachers give assignments that involve aspects of students' own lives, give your child all the relevant input possible concerning your work. When teachers ask students for parent volunteers to come in and talk about their work, make it a point to be there. And if your student doesn't come home with such assignments or requests, talk to the teacher about the importance of doing so, and volunteer yourself to talk to the class, and your time to coordinate such efforts and recruit other parents. Finally, break the standard "What did you do in school today?" – "Nuthin" impasse by engaging in interesting and positive dialogue about how what your child is learning relates to the world of work and adult life in general. For example, when they have to bring in current events, buck the trend of finding something that's easiest to understand. Instead, help your child comprehend an article about how rising health-care costs are changing the medical profession, putting financial pressure on all employers, and in turn affecting employee benefits and job security.

Don't stop there, though. Many middle schools and high schools have clubs with career preparation themes, such as Future Business Leaders of America. See what's offered and who the advisors are, and call those to which you could make a contribution based on your professional training and experience. Other schools have career nights, where you can be one of the parents who give brief talks about careers or staff booths where medical professionals, scientists, computer professionals, and others give demonstrations of what they do, or hand out literature to interested kids. In addition, too many school districts offer reasonably good vocational education for students not planning to enter college, but fall short on professional career-oriented curriculum elements. Attend school board meetings to voice your support for expanding offerings to fill this void.

6 • Earning

Outside of school, encourage your child to get involved with organizations, such as the aforementioned Junior Achievement, that can help your child build financial, business, and career skills – and offer your expertise as an adult leader, coordinator, or advisor as appropriate. The Girl Scouts have all kinds of ways that adults can get involved and emphasizes getting girls more interested in, and prepared for, careers in math, science, and technology. Although careers as a professional athlete are a long shot, kids who participate can become aware of careers in the fields of sports medicine, physical training, nutrition, representation and financial planning for athletes, financial management of organizations, entertainment promotion, and designing improved equipment or more functional athletic apparel (for example, sports bras).

A Career-Success Trifecta

About five years ago, Nancy Barnes, the Sunday Editor of the **Raleigh News & Observer**, was instrumental in helping one of this book's authors get his foot in the door with an opportunity to do freelance personal-finance writing for the paper. In addition, she arranged for him to bring this book's co-author, his daughter Gibora – then a pre-teen – into the press room on a weekend day, where Nancy showed us both how the paper was put together. She also gave Gibora a story rewrite test given to entry level job applicants. This was special personal treatment, but the **News & Observer** regularly gives tours to schools and other groups of kids no younger than nine, and many other businesses provide such opportunities for first-hand observation of the professional world at work. Interestingly, to illustrate an earlier point about career flexibility, Ms. Barnes is scheduled to complete a MBA degree from Duke University's Fuqua School of Business in August, 2002. It prepares her for options such as getting more involved in the business side of journalism.

6 • Earning

Work: Theirs and Yours

If you can't bring work to the school, bring kids to work. It's well worth the day off from school to participate in the new "Take Our Daughters and Sons to Work Day" (www.takeourdaughterstowork.org) premiering on April 24, 2003. If your company doesn't participate in this expansion of the original "Take Our Daughters to Work Day" that has occurred every April since 1993, then it might be one of hundreds of companies that have their own annual "Take Our Children to Work Day." Sponsoring companies such as IBM often have several fun career-related activities supervised by assigned company personnel that let Mom and Dad work most of the day, while also allowing time for children to observe their parents working and meet their colleagues. Of course, many companies also allow this type of work visit on an informal basis.

Unfortunately, many companies so inundate their employees with work that children get to observe more than they care to on nights and weekends at home (so at least the day at the office proves to kids that you really have colleagues and a company, and aren't just trying to avoid them!). So one way or another, you should have ample opportunity to directly expose your kids to the world of adult work.

The next step is getting them involved in experiences that will expose them to possible adult work-avenues that they might choose. For this purpose, volunteer work stands out, with numerous opportunities either advertised or subject only to your child's creativity or initiative. If your child is thinking of medicine, hospitals offer many opportunities beyond the traditional "candy-striper." For animal medicine, look to animal shelters and zoos. For social work, consider nursing homes, hospices, and teen-support hotlines. Your aspiring architect should get involved in Habitat for Humanity. If environmental engineering is a possibility, numerous lake and river cleanup projects are underway nationwide.

MONEY

6 • Earning

Or create an opportunity. If your child is eyeing law, find an attorney or law firm doing pro bono work, and have her do some of the supporting research, or volunteer at a nearby law-school library. If accounting appeals, you should volunteer to do tax returns for seniors and have your child come along to assist you. In fact, depending on your child's age, many such volunteer efforts might be open only indirectly to children through the parent as volunteer.

As your child approaches college age, volunteer work will naturally start giving way to paid work. However, weigh the value of a relevant school activity or volunteer internship versus doing a paid job that will do little to develop your child's career skills. For example, if your child is interested in journalism, he might be better off burning the midnight oil on the school newspaper or yearbook instead of emptying the french-fry oil when the fast-food place closes at midnight. Furthermore, by creating meaningful volunteer internships while in high school, your child will make herself a more desirable candidate for paid internships while in college. The money foregone from character-building (but menial and mindless) labor might easily be made up in a para-professional internship.

6 • Earning

College/Career Research and Visits

All this work exposure – what your child does and what she learns about yours and other adults' work – makes your child a formidable quadruple threat. Her first three weapons are the experience gained from meeting work responsibility, the money earned, and the career preparation. The fourth is the leg up it gives her in doing college planning – making her a more desirable candidate, narrowing the possibilities to those that are most compatible with her career-interests, and becoming a more desirable candidate for admission through work experiences. In fact, having a direction when entering college makes it more likely that your child will graduate on time, or even early – a major money saver and momentum builder toward eventual professional work.

Nevertheless, choosing colleges and careers still amounts to somewhat of a crapshoot. You can tilt the odds more in your child's favor with thorough research, a well-planned campaign for identifying college possibilities and campus visits, solid knowledge of the financial-aid determination process, and aggressive pursuit of outside scholarships. All this can start well before junior year in high school, though, through the summer programs that many colleges offer to students at middle-school level and above. Although your child might initially balk at the idea of spending vacation going to school, these programs have strong social and learning-as-fun elements and compare favorably financially to expensive summer camps.

Enough said about college planning, though, because so many excellent web sites, books, and other information sources are available concerning them and career planning. They contain helpful career information and tools, including aptitude tests, interviews with people in different careers, training you need, lists of colleges that have the best preparation programs, and salaries you can expect.

A Short List of College and Career Planning Resources

- **PBS Teacher Source: Students, Jobs, and Work** –
  www.pbs.org/teachersource/thismonth/jun99/index.shtm#younger

- **Librarians Information Network for Essential Curriculum: Student Resources** –
  www.bcps.org/offices/lis/resources/studentres

- **U.S Bureau of Labor Statistics Career Information for Kids** –
  http://stats.bls.gov/k12/html/edu_over

- **College Board College Search** – http://apps.collegeboard.com/search/

- **College Organizer** – www.collegequest.com

- **Virtual Campus Tours** – www.campustours.com

- **The Career Key** – www.careerkey.org/english

- **New Directions** (Kid Career) – www.bcit.tec.nj.us/KidCareer

- **What Do They Do?** (Career Descriptions) – www.whatdotheydo.com

- **Central Square School District** (Career/Education Link List) –
  www.cssd.org/careerweb/clinks

- **Quintessential Careers** (Teen Section) – www.quintcareers.com/teens

- **Next Step Magazine** (Career Exploration Section for Teens) –
  www.nextstepmagazine.com/Career_Exploration/archive

- **Campbell Interest Inventory** (U.S. News description of this online service) –
  www.usnews.com/usnews/edu/careers/ccciss

- **Job Profiles** (Job Descriptions) – www.jobprofiles.org

- **Family Education** (comprehensive article on teen summer jobs) –
  www.familyeducation.com/article/0,1120,69-15552-1,00

- **Summer/Seasonal Jobs for Teens** – www.quintcareers.com/summer_job_sites

- **My Career Blast** (Summer Jobs/Internships) –
  www.mycareerblast.com/my_summer_job.html

- **Summer Jobs** – www.summerjobs.com

Chapter Seven

Investing

Now comes the easy part. After all, who really wants to control their spending, become obsessive about saving, or have to work for money? But what about once you've earned the money, spent (hopefully, only) part of what you've earned, and saved the difference? Surely, it's more fun to try and do something with it than to just let it sit there – at least for kids, anyway.

So don't be surprised if the problem you have teaching investing to your kids is keeping their attention, rather than getting it in the first place – because they'll be chomping at the bit to get started. Although stocks might no longer seem so sexy to adults after the market's harsh return to reality, kids who are exposed to them quickly catch the bug. It's an incurable bug, but not harmful as long as you keep your kids' high-finance fever down so that they'll become prudent investors and not would-be high rollers.

7 • Investing

Why Invest?

Some of the smartest or most talented high-earners in the world don't invest in stocks, so why should you? For one thing, people who have more money than they know what to do with get that way for a reason. Some do because they save a good percentage of what they earn and take care in spending it once they're no longer earning. If they're not greedy, they do fine by earning modest returns without risking their principal. Their conservative investments in treasury securities and various other interest-paying instruments will ensure they never run out of money, even if prices rise significantly during their lifetimes.

Don't Let Inflation Sap Your Purchasing Power

For the last several years, inflation has been averaging about 2.5% annually, but historically, it's averaged 3.5% and there have been stretches where it averaged between 5 and 10% annually. At a 3.5% annual rate, 20 years from now, your money will have halved in buying power. In other words, if you put $100 under your mattress today and took it out 20 years from now, you'd be able to buy stuff worth only about $50 in today's dollars. It might be better (or bedder) to invest that money in a quality company that manufactures premium mattresses for baby boomers; after all, they're getting worn out faster than ever now that we have Viagra.

Economic Investment Reasons

You and your kids, however, are unlikely to be fortunate enough to have the option of not taking investment risk. You need to earn big enough investment returns to offset the rate at which inflation is eroding your buying power. But even that's not enough, because you have to generate additional funds to ensure that you don't run out of money if you live to a ripe old age.

Furthermore, if you want to raise your standard of living, you need to do it using the system that raises the standard of living for everybody, the growth of our economy. For example, when you hear that we had 5% growth in the Gross National Product last year, that means our economy produced 5% more goods and services (in dollar value) than it did the previous year. Ideally, everyone should be able to share equally in that growth by having their salaries increased to be able to buy more stuff; after all, if the companies we work for grow, shouldn't we be paid more to get our fair share of the growth? However, we know it doesn't always work that way. The next best thing is to own part of our country's economic growth by owning companies that produce that growth – and that means owning stock.

7 • Investing

Thus, we invest first to offset inflation, and it's possible to do that over the long run by using almost 100% safe investments – meaning no risk of losing principal – without investing in stocks. If it works, the result is that even if we don't save a dollar more than we saved now, we'll be able to buy just as much in the future with our savings as we can buy now. But most of us want to do more than beat inflation, so we need investments that will grow so that we can buy more with our total savings than we can now – even if we didn't save another dime. For example, if inflation is 2.5% and our investments grow by 7.5%, then we've achieved roughly 5% real growth – meaning we should be able to buy 5% more with our money then, versus now.

Adult Investment Reasons

Once you've taught your children the overall concept of investing, achieving personal financial growth in line with global economic growth, it's time to cover the reasons why they should hone their investing skills now to meet lifelong needs.

- **College, Continuing Education, and Career Changes.** When babies born today go to college 18 years from now, the average cost of a private or out-of-state public school for students receiving no aid is expected to exceed $200,000. And the cost of state public schools is starting to catch up as states feel the enormous pressure of the end of the 90s boom and much less help from Uncle Sam, while the schools themselves suffer through scaled-back alumni donations and declines in their endowment investments. Investment is essential to keep up with college-cost inflation that generally exceeds overall inflation by several per cent annually, and the better prepared you and your child are to pay for college, the less debt she'll carry into adulthood. Furthermore, once your child graduates from college, she should save and invest towards the cost of continuing education to keep up earning power and to cover time off that might be needed in the course of making career changes. Although it used to be said that a house is the biggest purchase most people will make in a lifetime, it could well be that the total cost of education, plus career-related expenses, could surpass your child's home purchase costs.

7 • Investing

- **Their Weddings and Their Children's.** The average wedding today costs more than $20,000 and many cost as much as $50,000. While we think it's ridiculous to spend that much, you might feel you owe your child that, and your child might feel he owes his children that. It will take a lot of mutual fund to pay for those occasions of mutual fun.

- **Home, Furnishings, and Improvements.** The national-average price of a new home now exceeds $200,000. Those seeking a cheaper resale starter home find that few meeting their needs for space and proximity to work are available. Like college costs, home prices are rising faster than the rate of inflation – except in a few areas hit especially hard by the tech-sector slump. And many young adults neglect to consider the high costs of minimally decorating and furnishing a home. Combining an adequate 20% down payment with extra funds needed for furniture, furnishings, and initial repairs – it takes many young adults at least $50,000 to realistically enter the home-ownership club.

- **Kids.** Refer to Chapter 2. Enough said.

- **Cars.** By the time children born today are ready to buy cars, new models might run on hybrid engines to dramatically reduce fuel consumption and pollution. That will raise the cost of a car several thousand of today's dollars, and adding in inflation, an entry-level car could easily cost $25,000 by then.

- **Hobbies, Charitable Contributions, and Vacations.** This strange grouping exists because young adults interested in social change and social entrepreneurship sometimes combine all three. For example, someone who likes to backpack and camp and is passionate about the environment might arrange vacations in other countries that combine backpacking with an environmental cleanup. The costs add up when people start pouring their passions and pocketbook contents into causes, so it might be necessary to invest money financially now in order to invest money socially later.

- **Life Reverses and Emergencies.** What if your grandchild becomes anorexic? An increasing number of severe cases are bankrupting families whose insurance has little or no coverage for treatment in specialized facilities that can cost thousands a week. Investing towards amassing an adequate emergency fund for the unexpected is more essential than ever.

- **Starting a Business:** With loyalty between employer and employee becoming as irrelevant as the British royalty, smart young adults today are soaking in all that they can from each of their employment experiences. When the time is right and the non-compete clause is no longer operative, starting a business might prove the only viable way to long-term stability for those who seek it. But as Mark Twain said, "A banker is someone who will lend you his umbrella when the sun is shining, but demand it back at the first drop of rain." In other words, raising start-up capital is about as painless a process as posting-up Shaquille O'Neal, with a similar likelihood of success. The obvious answer: they must raise it themselves during their "employee apprenticeship stage" through savings and investments.

- **Retirement.** If she reads the first chapter of *Alpha Teach Retirement Planning in 24 Hours* by this book's senior co-author, your child will either immediately jump off a bridge or jump on the investing bandwagon. If the latter, then the answer to "how high should she jump" is "the sky's the limit."

MONEY

7 • Investing

Your Child's Investment Reasons

While you should teach children the critical investing concepts, chances are they'll be overly abstract for many children younger than high-school age. So reach them by making the need for investment clear to them in the types of childhood goals they have.

For example, take a 7-year-old child who wants to accumulate enough money to buy a serious bicycle by age 12. She's eyeing a 10-speed made by one of the best bike manufacturers. The model she wants is a deluxe model selling for $500, but the manufacturer also sells a basic model for $425. So far, through gifts and allowance, you've helped her manage to save $300 – a little short of either goal.

For simplicity's sake, let's make a few assumptions that aren't realistic but will make it easier to illustrate how investment growth works. First, assume there's no inflation, and that the same bikes at the same prices will be available five years from now. Also assume that there are no taxes on investment gain, no fees to buy or sell the investments, and your daughter won't get any additional money between now and then from work or gifts. Her challenge is to come up with either $125 or $200 more dollars, depending on whether she wants the basic or deluxe model, by making what she has grow through investment. If she puts the $300 in a 5-year CD paying 4.5% annually, she'll have $375 in 5 years, not nearly enough for either bicycle. If instead she invests in something that requires taking a risk but it earns 7% a year, she'll have enough for the basic bike, but if she earns a little over 10% annually for the next five years, she will have right around $500.

Compound that Interest!

In referring to annual returns, we're referring to compounded returns. In other words, if you start with $100 and earn 10% annually, then you'll have $110 after one year, $121 after 2 years, $133.10 after 3 years, etc. Thus a 10% annual return over 3 years grows your original amount to more than the $130 versus from an uncompounded 10% per year (3 times 10% or 30% more than the original amount).

7 • Investing

Reasonable Investment Returns and Risk

Although it didn't seem that way a few years ago, 10% annually is a pretty high return. Your daughter might have to invest in stock that has a lot of potential – perhaps some great new medical technology that unclogs arteries in a 30-minute outpatient procedure. But even though the technology works, the company will have to succeed in bringing it to market on a timely basis and producing it at a price that will attract a lot of customers and still yield a decent profit for each unit sold. You're "betting" the company will succeed and investors will push up the value of its shares an average of at least 10% a year. However, you're also betting against the company failing, which will almost certainly push its shares down by 20% or more. Once upon a time, Microsoft was such a stock, and wound up growing much more than 10% a year for some time. But alongside it were some other promising young companies that no longer exist – their investors losing some or all of their money depending on when they sold out. Generally, the higher the return you seek from stocks, the more risk that you'll lose a large percentage of your money if things don't go well.

Do you really want your daughter betting on just one stock? If not, there's another way to invest in promising but risky companies and have a better chance of not losing all your money, while still having a chance at a good but not stupendous return. Your daughter could buy a mutual fund consisting of many such companies; the fund might be called "moderate growth" if the companies had already started earning some money, but seemed to have the potential to earn quite a bit more, or an "aggressive growth" fund in which the companies were all potential Microsofts or Macrobusts! In either case, if things go well, a few of the stocks in the fund will hit it big over the next five years, others will hit it smaller, some will do nothing, quite a few will perform poorly, and a few will even go out of business. You're hoping that the combined performance of all the stocks in the fund will yield your target return – even if some are total duds.

If your daughter chooses the moderate fund, she's probably not going to achieve the 10% return unless she's lucky, because the successful stocks aren't likely to be so successful that they'll approach Microsoft's dramatic growth. In the aggressive fund, more stocks are likely to do poorly and fewer hit it big, but a big hitter could be a new Microsoft. Here, your daughter could very well earn as much as 15% annually, but have a much higher risk of losing more

7 • Investing

than 25% of her money. With the moderate fund, the downside risk is significant but not as high, perhaps more like 10 to 20% loss. So if your daughter really wants that deluxe bike and is willing to take a big gamble (thought not as big as a trip to Las Vegas), then the aggressive growth fund is the way to go. If she's willing to take moderate risk and have a slim chance at the deluxe bike and a good chance at the basic one, then she should go for the moderate fund.

Taking this one step further, what if you your 7-year-old daughter wanted to skip the kid stuff and instead invest towards a car she'll buy at age 17. She'll now have 10 years to invest. Suppose she starts with $2,000 (cobbled together from cash gifts on all her birthdays) and has her eye on a 5-year-old sub-compact economy car that currently sells for $4,400. If she earns just under 8% annually, she'll have enough to buy the car, again assuming no inflation and no additional savings. 8% annually is perhaps a little more than you can hope for from a moderate risk fund, but your daughter now has one additional advantage on her side, an extra 5 years. Those extra years make it more likely that by the time she's cashed out of the fund, she'll have earned close to its expected return, and will be less likely to have suffered a sizable loss; that's the same principle that says you'll get closer and closer to having 50% heads and 50% tails the more times you toss a coin.

Investing Principles

Given this analysis, your daughter shouldn't even consider the aggressive fund, but put her faith in the moderate fund earning about its expected return over the 10-year period. However, this solution is not the main point of this long example. Instead, the example is meant to highlight some of the following key principles of investing that you should teach your child.

Eight Simple Investment Rules

- **Objective/Goal.** When undertaking an investment, know what you're trying to achieve because it might affect the degree of risk you're willing to take. In fact, it definitely should curb your risk-taking if it's clear that the objective is crucial and can be achieved with little risk.

- **Time Horizon.** The longer you have to invest towards a goal, the more likely the investment will perform about as well as similar investments have done historically. Trying to achieve the expected annual return over a short time horizon increases the risk that your investment will have achieved a much lower return and increases the chance it will have achieved a much higher return. When looking at the market as a whole, the longer the time horizon, the more likely the market averages will have risen over time at about the rate of growth of the economy – smoothing out the bumps of spectacular rises and cataclysmic drops.

- **Risk/Return Principle.** The higher the possible return from an investment, the more risk that you'll lose all or a substantial portion of your investment. Think in terms of the lottery. Your $1 ticket could return multiple millions but almost always returns nothing, occasionally returns amounts of $10 or less, and rarely returns $5,000, $1,000, $500, or $100. Compare that to betting on a horse race by placing $2 each on the three most highly favored horses to place (finish 3rd or higher). You have a very high chance that one or more will do it, but you won't win very much money. You take only a small risk that you'll lose all of your total $6 bet, and a slightly higher risk that you'll lose part of your bet.

From reading Chapter 6 on Earning, you know your authors do not advocate gambling because it's usually a bad investment and is seriously addictive. However, gambling examples were chosen because we're betting that these examples will clarify the notion of risk. (And if we're wrong, then we'll wager 10 bucks right now (check the hidden pocket containing our bet on page 1157) that your kid will understand the example even if you don't...Just Kidding.)

- **Diversification:** The more you spread your investment into many stocks of different sized companies with different levels of risk, and from different industries, the more likely that you'll get a return close to the overall market. Compared to buying shares of just one or a few companies, diversification shields you more from catastrophic investment loss, but also limits your upside. That principle is taken to the extreme with the Wilshire index fund of the 5000 largest public companies (by the time you get to 5000, companies aren't so large). Mutual funds offer diversification without requiring you to go out and buy all those stocks separately.

7 • Investing

Taking diversification one step further, financial advisers working with substantial client portfolios employ a technique called portfolio allocation to determine the mix of investments appropriate to current economic circumstances and the client's specific circumstances: family situation, age, risk tolerance, etc. The idea is that a certain amount of your portfolio should be held in cash or cash-equivalent securities, some in real estate, some in precious metals, and most in equities (stocks or mutual funds). Further allocation is done within each category – particularly stocks: international companies, small companies (small cap), medium-sized companies (mid cap), and large-sized companies (large cap). Consequently, they might have some clients invested in four or five different mutual funds.

What's in a NAV?

The price movement of mutual funds is indicated by the Net Asset Value (NAV). Think of the NAV as the value of one share (portion, not a stock share) of the total value of all the securities the fund owns. When you buy into a mutual fund, you buy a number of shares determined by dividing your total investment by the NAV at the time you buy. Thus, you're buying 40 shares of the mutual fund if you invest $1,000 when the NAV is $25 (1,000 divided by 25 = 40). If the NAV goes up to $30 and you sell your 40 shares, you've made $5 per share times 40 or $200, not subtracting fees or taxes.

- **Timing Loses and Quality Wins.** The saying goes that all you have to do is buy low and sell high to be an investment winner. But even top experts don't know how to time the stock markets' ups and downs – even those who've correctly predicted 11 out of the last three recessions. Studies show that those who pull their money in and out of investments in attempts to succeed at picking the lows and highs actually do – except that they buy high and sell low more often than the opposite. Therefore, you want to pick investments for their long-range quality and hang onto them through their ups and downs.

- **Dollar Averaging Helps Prevent Under-Average Performance.** One form of timing does win, investing repeatedly on a regular schedule over time in a mutual fund or each of a portfolio of individual stocks. Typically, adults do this by having the same amount (say $100) of their monthly paychecks sent to a mutual fund to continually increase their total investment in it. When the fund is in a slump, each $100 buys more shares, and when the fund rallies, each $100 buys fewer shares. Say you do this for 10 years, investing a total of $6,000 versus having invested $6,000 at the beginning of five years. Studies show that over a 10-year or longer period, the monthly-investment portfolio does better than the lump-sum portfolio. Furthermore, few people have a large lump sum to invest all at once, so doing it monthly lets you get your money starting to work for you instead of waiting to accumulate the amount you plan to invest.

- **Bulls Win and Bears Win, But Hogs Lose.** This philosophy says that those who are upbeat all the time about the economy will win in the long run by picking stocks that should benefit from a good economy, as long as they hang onto them. Similarly, those who are always pessimistic might pick stocks of companies that do well when the overall economy doesn't do well – so called defensive stocks (and that doesn't mean companies who will build Star Wars missile defense systems). But if they hang onto them over the long haul, they'll also do well. Those who base their investment on guessing about the economy, however, are trying to get the best of both worlds. They're the Hogs who often end up holding stocks that are wrong at the time they have them and right after they sell them.

- **Fees Matter.** Frequent buying and selling racks up brokerage commissions that must be paid, cutting into profits (or adding to losses). But even mutual funds that are held for a long time can rack up fees. Load funds charge either an upfront percentage (usually 2% or 3%) to buy or a similar back-end percentage to sell – and sometimes both. Increasingly common, though, are so-called no-load funds that don't charge upfront or backend fees but sometimes charge excessive "hidden fees" of which naïve investors are unaware. These are 12(b)-1 and other fees that mutual funds charge as annual percentages for marketing and other operational expenses. They can sometimes exceed 2% annually – putting a major dent into profits if the fund goes up less than 10%.

- **Taxes Matter.** Buying and selling frequently also racks up bigger tax bills because profits on any security sold within a year of its purchase are treated as "ordinary income" (the same as job wages) instead of capital gains. The tax rate on ordinary income is generally higher. Again, naïve investors are also hit by hidden taxes when they own mutual funds that frequently change their holdings. Every year, mutual funds report their internal capital gains, which is the difference between all profits and all losses on the transactions they made that year, and that amount is taxable, even if the fund recorded a net loss in the overall value of its shares. (See sidebar on the NAV.)

Trade Less, Earn More

In recent years, financial experts have paid more attention to how much frequent trading can hurt investors, so they've increasingly recommended funds that have a policy of keeping their portfolios more stable, only occasionally switching holdings from certain stocks to others. The ultimate use of this strategy is to buy an Index Fund, which consists of stocks that comprise commonly reported stock indices such as the Standard & Poor 500. These Index funds require very little trading to keep the proper balance of all the stocks in the indices they represent, so annual capital gains are minimized.

Investment Vehicles

Adults who apply these investment principles appropriately generally assemble a portfolio of many types of investment vehicles and many specific investments within each type. To do that intelligently, they need detailed information on these investment types and even more detailed information on the specific investments they're considering. Such information is available in numerous books, magazines, newspapers, and web sites – so there's no point repeating it here. Instead, let's examine these investment vehicles with regards to how you should get your children started learning about them and using them, and how you should be using them for your children.

7 • Investing

Savings Accounts, Money Markets, and CDs

Interest-earning accounts are not investments per se, but primarily a resting place for money that either needs to be invested, will be needed soon enough that investment risk shouldn't be taken, or provides a cushion for emergency cash needs. Establish them when your child is born and put baby-gift cash in them until you determine an investment strategy. Continue using them as interim storage for gift cash as your child matures, but start making the transition to allowing your child to choose the investments to be made with that money. Also teach your child to use these when an investment she makes achieves its objective before she's ready to spend the money. Have her then cash in the investment (say stock earmarked for a bicycle) and park the proceeds in a money-market account until it's time to use it.

Savings Bonds and Other Government Securities

Somebody's going to give your child savings bonds (covered thoroughly in Chapter 6). Like bank accounts and CDs, they're interest-earning vehicles, rather than growth investments. However, it makes sense to give those gift bonds company by having your child buy a few more when he's old enough to understand them, for educational purposes if nothing else, because they provide a good lesson in tracking the value of an investment. Furthermore, families with modest incomes can redeem their bonds totally tax free if they're used to pay for college, so check the tax laws to see if this might apply to your family.

Like savings bonds, most other U.S. government securities aren't growth investments either – although some negotiable (transferable) treasury bonds go up or down in value on the open market based on current interest rates. Generally, though, they're purchased because they pay interest comparable to bank CDs of the same duration and can actually earn a better net return because of the no state/local tax break. Explain to your kids that government bonds are a way for the United States to raise money relatively inexpensively. So they're one possible way to fill the cash portion of an investment portfolio while being patriotic by investing in America – as a means to lessen U.S. dependence on foreign capital.

7 • Investing

In addition, you can have your child use government securities as a way to learn "laddering" – an investment technique employed by sophisticated investors who purchase many corporate bonds. The purpose of laddering is to avoid a situation where you lock money in for a number of years at a low interest rate and then miss out on the chance to earn higher rates if they suddenly go up. Although treasury bonds are negotiable, you're effectively locked in when rates rise because the open-market value of your bonds decreases. After all, who would want to buy your lower-yielding bond when they can buy newly-issued bonds with higher rates.

To implement laddering, you must understand the different securities available. The most common are 91-day and 182-day treasury bills, 2-year and 5-year treasury notes, and 10-year treasury bonds. Assuming you have enough money ($1,000 minimum investment per security), you can start out buying an equal amount of each. As the various securities mature, you reinvest the money in the newest issues of the same securities (although sophisticated laddering is more complex). This strategy is similar to the dollar-cost averaging mentioned earlier related to mutual-fund investing because over the long run, it smoothes out the highs and lows in the movement of interest rates, yielding a better overall return than trying to guess at what durations to choose and how to split up your investment between them. For detailed information on the way interest is paid, other features, rates, and how to buy these securities directly from the U.S. government, visit the Treasury Direct web site: (www.publicdebt.treas.gov/sec/sectrdir.htm)

Climbing the Ladder Online

- **Building a Bond Ladder** (Motley Fool) –
  www.fool.com/retirement/retireeport/2000/retireeport000724.htm

- **Laddering Your Bonds** (Smart Money) –
  www.smartmoney.com/retirement/investing/index.cfm?story=investing6

- **Interest Rate Proof Your Bond Portfolio** (CNBC/MoneyCentral) –
  moneycentral.msn.com/articles/invest/CNBC/8338.asp

7 • Investing

In addition to savings bonds and treasury securities, many government agencies and affiliated entities also sell securities, including GNMA (Ginnie Mae), FNMA (Fannie Mae), FMAC (Freddie Mac), TVA (Tennessee Valley Authority), SBA (Small Business Administration), and SLMA (Student Loan Marketing Association). These are virtually safe investments for guaranteeing your principal and interest payments, but are not guaranteed with "the full faith and credit" of the U.S. government. They're too sophisticated to get your child involved in, but you should make her aware of their existence.

Corporate and State/Municipal Bonds, and Bond Funds

Unlike interest-bearing accounts, CDs, and U.S. government securities, most other bonds are much more of an investment – starting with the fact that you generally can only buy them through brokers. More significantly, however, they carry significant risk that you could lose your principal if the company or government entity goes into default or bankruptcy. And most significantly, they're now again regarded as a serious part of an investment portfolio, whereas most investors scoffed at "wasting their money" on them during the booming 90s.

Bonds are back for several reasons. First, they provide a hedge against weak growth in the economy by offering an alternate, relatively assured attractive return for a significant percentage of your funds. This is increasingly attractive to retirees the older they get, because they want to assure an increasing percentage of their capital (moving it from stocks to cash-oriented investments gradually over the years) and replace a portion of the income they no longer get from work with a steady stream that supplements Social Security and pensions (if they have them!).

Bonds also seem attractive in an inflationary economy because those who offer them must offer higher rates to attract investors seeking a return that exceeds inflation. They're also targeted by more speculative investors who look for even higher rates in "junk bonds" issued by companies or government entities that have questionable credit and must offer a "return premium" to attract investors. Investors who feel that rates for quality bonds are near their peak buy them both for the high return and the increase in their principal (market) value if rates drop – which happens because they then offer coveted higher returns that people are willing to pay a premium to get.

173

7 • Investing

All of these factors make these types of bonds very tricky investments. Investors must check out the credit-worthiness of the companies and government entities that issue them by consulting information provided by AM Best, Standard & Poor, or similar rating companies. However, high ratings (A++) are no guarantee because we've seen recently how these agencies have sometimes failed to detect serious accounting irregularities that made companies much riskier than their ratings suggested. To dampen this risk, most average investors shun individual bonds – leaving those to wealthier investors. Instead, they purchase shares in bond mutual funds, which are intended to lessen risk through diversification. However, these funds have their own tricky aspects and should be studied carefully before funds are committed.

So if you're looking for a way to get your child's interest, bond with them by teaching them about bonds (see www.investinginbonds.com). Just make sure they fully understand the risks – that they shouldn't assume they'll be reaping a bon(d)anza.

Real Estate

So far we've looked at investments that are at least as much income-oriented as growth-oriented. Rental real estate is the next step towards growth, while still offering income through a combination of rental receipts and tax deductions that lower the taxes owed on the rental income. One theory behind real estate investing goes back to what Will Rogers said: "Buy land, they're not making any more of it." Of course, income-oriented real estate consists of both land and the structure on it – but the same idea applies: there's only a limited amount of room for desirable – particularly residential – rental property. Thus, in buying rental real estate, you're hoping for an income stream that exceeds the monthly loan payments and other monthly expenses you incur, plus appreciation of the property due to increased demand tied to scarcity.

The problem with real estate is that it requires the investment of significant capital and time, plus an established credit record. That rules it out for most kids, but that doesn't mean you shouldn't teach them about it. In fact, because it's not the type of thing people do because everybody else is doing it, your willingness to teach them real estate investment basics might be the difference between whether they seriously consider it as an adult or not – and most adults should because of the diversification it offers.

7 • Investing

Also make your kids aware of indirect ways of investing in real estate as another way of diversifying an investment portfolio. Indirect investments emphasize commercial real estate: Real Estate Investment Trusts (REITs), mutual funds with real estate holdings, and Real Estate Limited Partnerships (RELLPs). Sophisticated investors can do quite well with these, but they are quite complex – particularly REITs and RELLPs, which also offer a combination of income and growth of capital, but on an irregular and unpredictable basis. Naïve investors who pay for "premium crops" can wind up getting the bitter outside skin of the fruit while the insiders get the sweet inside nectar.

Stocks and Equity Mutual Funds

Just shy of the extreme end of the income-growth investment spectrum you'll find stocks. True, they pay dividends, which at one time represented the company's return of its income to its shareholders. That was particularly true of utility stocks, which were coveted by retirees and conservative investors because of the generous dividends they paid. But utility stocks aren't what they used to be, many beset by financial problems from nuclear power plant construction and deregulation that has made the price and supply of energy unpredictable – helped along by the market manipulations of companies such as Enron. Today investing in a utility for its safety and dividends is at best an exercise in financial futility, and at worst, an exposure to business brutality.

Widows and Orphans Brave the Street

AT&T was once known as the "widows and orphans" stock because it was considered such a safe way to invest for growth while also getting a good dividend. It typically paid annual dividends of 5% or more, and was counted on to rise slowly over the years, with very little downside risk. Today, AT&T is one of the riskiest large-cap stocks on the market, paying very low dividends (when not suspended outright). It bears little resemblance to the company it was 50 years ago, having divested its local telephone operations to regional telecommunications companies including Bell Atlantic and Ameritech, and having spun off a number of its businesses into separate companies such as AT&T Wireless and AT&T Broadband. There's a good lesson here for your kids in showing just how drastically the business landscape has changed from the time you were a kid until now – AT&T's changes alone substantially affected millions of shareowners and hundreds of thousands of employees. This author should know; in a previous life, he worked for AT&T and owned a significant chunk of its stock.

7 • Investing

In today's economy, most companies give little more than lip service to dividends – their executives know that much of their compensation is tied to the performance of their stocks and that their executive boards expect increases in shareholder value. Therefore, dividends are mostly sacrificed to provide more growth capital from the company's reinvested earnings. Your child will be eager to plunge into stocks as part of trying to grow up as fast as these companies. So you must draw this realistic picture of what investing in stocks is about today, and how hard it is to get it right by emphasizing individual stocks. And that's all the more reason to emphasize mutual funds over stocks, despite the fact that your child will view it as having to settle for kissing a sibling on the cheek instead of necking with the school siren or stud.

Collectibles, Precious Metals, and Other Non-Dividend Investments

Your child won't be turned off for long, though, if you allow her a little indulgence in small-scale R(isk)-rated investing in collectibles. Kids collect all kinds of things from their natural curiosity, but turning collections of things they naturally enjoy into possibly profitable financial ventures broadens investment skills. The old standbys are great – including autographs and sports memorabilia, coins, currency, stamps, and antiques – and it's easy to find price information about them. These are just a sampling of other collectibles that are becoming common and have investment potential: figurines, miniature cars, match covers, toy soldiers, dolls and dollhouse furnishings, comic books, postcards, greeting cards, shells, and bumper stickers.

True, collectibles pay no scheduled monetary interest or dividends, but they do pay off in holding your child's interest and providing the dividend of their passionate enjoyment of something fun and educational.

 ### *Collecting: More Than Its Own Reward*

- **Relatively inexpensive** but rewarding 'together time' with your child going to garage sales and flea markets (provided you make online auctions out of bounds – a good idea considering exploitation and fraud to which your child will be more susceptible).

7 • Investing

- **Assessment and negotiating skills** from determining what things are worth and then getting them at sales for prices no higher than you can afford.

- **Networking skills** from the various contacts made in pursuing collections.

- **Research skills** from finding all different types of information about collecting in general and the particular types of collections.

- **Practice in making carefully considered financial choices.** With limited funds, collectors must ration their funds in getting their most desired items.

- **Incentive to earn money**, save it for collecting, and not waste it on frivolous things.

- **Career preparation possibilities:** one Lego collector never built anything based on the directions but collected enough different types to build his own model city, and grew up to become an urban planner.

- **Kids who you don't have to nag** to clean their rooms because they have, by necessity, developed respect for order, cleanliness, and space.

Good collectors are systematic and organized, so it makes sense to start prepared, instead of haphazardly. These books might help:

- **101 Great Collectibles for Kids**, Diane L. Oswald, Brent Roderick (Illustrator)

- **Complete Idiot's Guide to Making Money with Your Hobby**, Barbara Arena, Phillip L. Reed

Once your child has learned the fundamentals of investing in collectibles, introduce her to the world of investments in paintings, fine art, vintage cars, and other "real assets" that pay no interest or dividends. Like land, these investments get their value from their finite availability (relative scarcity) as much as their aesthetic appeal. They provide a further means of diversification because they don't move in lockstep with the stock market, although they do tend to suffer when the economy is weak, limiting the number of flush investors who have interest in them.

7 • Investing

However, real assets have several drawbacks for potential investors. They lack liquidity (the ability to liquidate quickly for full value), because their value depends much more on finding the right buyer. If a quick sale is necessary, the seller is likely to get much less than nearly maximum value. This also necessitates a skilled broker or auctioneer, whose commission further reduces profits. Finally, there's the increasing potential for fraud; these are not investments for those unwilling to do their homework, or find and pay expert – and trusted – appraisers and buying agents. Nevertheless, rewards can be quite substantial, so these investments are worth considering despite the obstacles – especially if your kids take up collectibles now as a prelude to entering this arena as adults.

Precious Metals

A final type of real property deserves consideration by all investors, whether they've had experience with collectibles and other real property or not. Gold, silver, other precious metals, and gems were once commonly used as currency throughout the world and are still used that way in some places. Although substantial amounts remain to be mined, we know that like fossil fuels, there is a finite supply that we can estimate. Therefore, markets for them are fairly well defined – provided they're in standard raw or processed condition (e.g. gold bars, ingots, etc.) Although speculators once dominated the market, prudent investors are increasingly using them as a hedge against severe inflation and other economic calamities that can seriously weaken currency value.

It's not essential to own precious metals and gems in their physical form, which can literally be back-breaking in the case of gold if you own enough – not to mention the security issues. Generally, people buy gold certificates, but they can also invest in individual gold or other precious metal stocks or mutual funds as an indirect approach to diversification. Be careful of investment pitches for gold-related investments, however, because frauds abound: with respect to gold brokers, all that glitters isn't (always) gold.

Investment Scams and Fraud

Gold is only one of hundreds of investments that are offered in fraudulent forms by scam artists. Even if you teach your child to invest only in U.S. Savings Bonds, he'll be ahead of the game by simply avoiding the tens of thousands of scam-laced investment schemes he'll be pitched by mail, email, Internet pop-up ads, cold calls, infomercials, and other means during his lifetime. In fact, chances are that you, your spouse, or someone close to you has been taken in by such a scheme already. After all, nobody's immune – including numerous celebrities such as sports legend, Steffi Graf, who lost more than one-half million dollars in a non-tennis racket (not to mention President George W. Bush's mother-in-law, who lost almost $8,000 in the Enron debacle, a mere 20% of the typical Enron employee's loss).

Enron appears to be the biggest pump-and-dump scheme ever perpetrated – although the media has routinely been incorrect in referring to it as a Ponzi scheme. Oh, so you're not sure what either one means. Well, here's a list describing some of the most common investment scams and frauds for which you and your kids should be on the lookout.

 ## Common Scams and Frauds

- **Pump and Dump Schemes.** These are numerous ways in which people, looking to make artificial stock profits, buy large quantities of a stock and then spread false positive information through numerous channels, such as cold calls, Internet chat-rooms, bribed brokers, and phony press releases. People start buying the stock, its price rises, more people buy, and the price gets pumped up to extremely artificial levels – at which point the perpetrators start dumping the stock gradually (to avoid panic) at huge profits on its way back down to its realistic price level. Enron was a pump and dump extraordinaire because top executives with large holdings (including stock options) were telling employees to buy more of it when they knew the company was facing serious financial problems. They got out with huge profits while employees were left holding the empty bag.

MONEY

7 • Investing

Enron: A Cautionary Tale

Enron employees who lost almost all of their retirement savings should have known better because they violated a fundamental investing principle by putting all their (later to be proved) rotten eggs in one basket. Apparently, they didn't take the lesson about diversification seriously, were never taught it, or were just plain greedy. Furthermore, it should be noted that the losses Enron employees suffered weren't totally real, in that the shares they held weren't really worth the price they were selling at, and if they'd all tried to get out at once, the stock would have fallen harder and faster than a cable-less elevator – netting most of them much lower sales proceeds than their shares' market value before the plunge.

- **Ponzi Schemes.** These typically involve unrealistically high guaranteed returns on (guaranteed principal) investments, such as 20% per month. The perpetrators actually pay these returns to the first batch of investors they attract, using the very principal of the duped investors to pay their dividends or interest. This goes on until they've attracted enough investors that they don't continue paying the return, close down shop, and take the money and run. Such schemes multiply like rabbits during periods of low interest rates because greedy investors want to believe that such returns are possible with no risk.

The SEC web site (http://www.sec.gov/answers/ponzi.htm) reveals the history of Ponzi schemes:

Ponzi schemes are named for Charles Ponzi, who duped thousands of New England residents into investing in a postage stamp speculation scheme back in the 1920s. Ponzi told investors he could take advantage of differences between U.S. and foreign currencies used to buy and sell international mail coupons. He promised investors that he could provide a 40% return in just 90 days, compared with 5% for bank savings accounts. Ponzi was deluged with funds from investors, taking in $1 million during one three-hour period – and this was 1921! Though a few early investors were paid off to make the scheme look legitimate, an investigation found that Ponzi had only purchased about $30 worth of the international mail coupons.

Decades later, the Ponzi scheme continues to work on the "rob-Peter-to-pay-Paul" principle, as money from new investors is used to pay off previous investors until the whole scheme collapses.

7 • Investing

- **Boiler-Room Schemes.** Depicted in scarily realistic fashion in the movie *Boiler Room*, these are schemes using a combination of pump-and-dump and Ponzi. They get their name from the fact that they're typically run from cheap rented space that the perpetrators furnish with telephones and desks – from which they aggressively telemarket nationwide. The people called are enticed to buy fraudulent over-the-counter securities, lured by the potential of spectacular returns that are "promised" – but not guaranteed. They initially invest small amounts and are elated when they see the price skyrocketing. If they decide to cash in, the money generated from the "investments" made by other investors is used to redeem their shares. Most investors don't sell, however, and they're then pitched for larger investments. After a time, the price falls some from its peak, at which point they're further pitched to grab this buying opportunity to get even more at a never-to-be-seen-again low price. Once those additional funds come in, the fraud artists close up shop and abscond with the loot – only to open up shop somewhere else with a new offering in sparsely-furnished low-rent "boiler rooms" in other states.

- **Fool-Me-Twice Fraud Compensation Schemes.** Some of the most vulnerable targets of scams are those who've already been victimized. The perpetrators of the original scams sell lists of their successful targets to other criminals who then pose as law-enforcement officials or private detectives trying to track down the people who ripped off the investors. They concoct schemes that require the once-duped investors to put up some money for a sting operation that will bring down the scamsters. Instead, they've just been stung for a second contribution to the Criminals' Retirement in Paradise fund.

These are just the tip of an iceberg jam of hundreds of successful investment frauds. Below are some web pages containing listings of excellent government publications on the cold hard facts concerning investment fraud, describing numerous schemes in detail.

7 • Investing

More About Investment Scams Online

- **Investment and Consumer Scams –**
  www.pueblo.gsa.gov/scamsdesc.htm

- **SEC Investor's Toolkit –**
  www.sec.gov/investor/pubs/toolkit.htm

- **SEC Investment Questions to Ask –**
  www.sec.gov/investor/pubs/askquestions.htm

- **FTC Fraud Information –**
  www.ftc.gov/reports/Fraud/toc.htm

- **SEC Online Investing Fraud Information –**
  www.sec.gov/investor/online.shtml

- **FirstGov for Consumers –**
  www.consumer.gov/yourmoney.htm **and,**
  www.consumer.gov/yourmoney2.htm

- **Phony Treasury Securities Offerings –**
  www.publicdebt.treas.gov/cc/ccphony.htm

- **Surprise Site** (Worth the Trip) –
  www.mcwhortle.com/

Starting to Invest

You've got the prerequisite information you need, or know how to get it, so learn it yourself and teach your child. Then you're ready to get your child involved hands-on – starting with investment-simulation software and moving on to kids' investment clubs and individual investment accounts. After he gains his own experience, take the next step by including your child in the family's investment planning so that he'll have a start at doing his own family's investing as an adult.

Here's how to get started.

7 • Investing

Your Wall Street Whiz Kid

Why let the movers and shakers have all the fun messing around in the market with their millions? Your child can do the same thing, and it won't cost more than your monthly Internet fee. Investment games abound on the Web, some designed by kids themselves, educators, or non-profit organizations promoting financial literacy. Others come courtesy of Wall Street itself, its major financial institutions pulling out all the stops to entice your child with the excitement of investing and hoping it carries over into using real money. Here are just a few, with more available on web sites listed in the Resource Appendix.

Online Investing with Play Money

- **The Stock Market Game™** –
  (Stock Market Simulation and Market Mysteries web site) –
  www.smgww.org

- **InvestSmart Fund Challenge** (a mutual-fund investing simulation) –
  http://stocksquest.thinkquest.org/10326/market_simulation/mutual.html

- **Virtual Stock Exchange** –
  www.virtualstockexchange.com

- **Edustock Stock Market Simulation** –
  http://library.thinkquest.org/3088

Although children can use many of these simulations on their own, the best approach is to use them under the direction of a teacher for a school project, or with your involvement in explaining how realistic the game is. For example, in order to "win" some simulations, you might have to "go for broke" rather than develop the kind of sensible, diversified portfolio that is needed in real life. There's nothing wrong with that if you explain that while some participants will win or do really well using such a strategy, many will lose all their money. Therefore, such strategies might be okay in a few select real-life situations, such as using a small portion of total investment funds as "mad money" in a way that gives you a better chance to get rich than playing the lottery or going to a gambling casino.

7 • Investing

Limited-Budget Investing Vehicles

Once your child has used these games, he might not be an expert investor, but he'll have a good overall understanding of basic stock market dynamics and some methods for evaluating individual stocks. The next step is to put his head together with other members of your family or equally enthusiastic peers in one of the hundreds of nationwide family or kids' investment clubs. Think of an investment club as a private micro mutual fund in which each participant's share is based on the proportional investment that he's made. Rules usually require a certain minimum monthly investment by each member, and all the money is then pooled to make investments that the club as a whole decides upon. These clubs can be ideal for allowing participants to each feel they're developing a realistic portfolio that they'd be unable to do otherwise due to limited funds.

The best place to start looking for kids' investment clubs is the non-profit National Association of Investment Clubs (NAIC) at www.better-investing.org. In addition, Buy and Hold (www.buyandhold.com/bh/en/education/oak/qa/qa 10.html) and other financial institutions also sponsor them. While it's true that kids can't run such a club totally on their own, thousands of such clubs enable kids to make all the investment decisions, with the securities held in the club name, with a parent as custodian. These clubs also provide excellent career training, in the sense that they require kids to work together the way adults must do on work projects. Kids make group decisions about most aspects of the particular club they establish, including its bylaws and specific investments.

Kid's Investment Clubs: Where to Start

- **National Association of Investment Clubs (NAIC) –**
  www.better-investing.org

- **Buy and Hold –**
  www.buyandhold.com/bh/en/education/oak/qa/qa10

7 • Investing

Dividend Reinvestment Plans (DRIPs) are another approach that allows kids to assemble portfolios of several stocks with limited amounts of money. Their magic comes from the partial shares that kids can buy of any stock offering a DRIP once they've bought at least one whole share, which allows them to enroll in the DRIP. The rules allow them to send in amounts of money at specified intervals to be used for purchasing additional whole and fractional shares. In addition to allowing kids to invest with small amounts of money, the beauty of DRIPs is that they don't require a broker and the DRIP companies charge very small service fees per transaction, versus larger broker commissions.

For more information about DRIPs, refer to these online sources:

- **The Moneypaper, Inc. –** www.moneypaper.com

- **DRIP Advisor –** www.DRIPAdvisor.com

Another way to buy fractional shares and pay less than normal brokerage commissions is offered by Folio(fn) and Buy and Hold. Buy and Hold works much like DRIPs, with the amount of money you choose to invest buying an amount of shares based on the current market price, fractional and whole. But the investor doesn't have to join the DRIP and has more flexibility than DRIPs provide. Folio(fn) is like a miniature mutual fund that offers you ways to buy fractional portions of groups of stocks that it packages in "folios." Although both these approaches cost more than you'd pay in DRIP fees, they enable you to save considerably compared to brokerage fees or mutual fund internal loads and internal fees.

7 • Investing

Investing with the Big Boys/Girls

When children outgrow clubs and start to regard partial-share investing as a DRIP in the bucket, it's time to let them set up their own brokerage accounts, with you as custodian. Your most important consideration in choosing a broker will probably be the extent it caters to custodial accounts involving a minor, the minimum balances it requires, and its pricing for a low frequency of limited-share transactions. Otherwise, the choice should be based on the same set of factors you should have already considered: frequency of trading and suitable selection of individual trade and trade-package pricing plans, desire for state-of-the-art online trading tools, need for and availability of unbiased investment education and research materials, quality of records and reports detailing trading activity, and responsiveness to customer problems.

It's important that you closely monitor your child's trading when the account is first established, because it's mighty tempting to trade frequently, and studies show frequent traders almost always register worse performance. Agree in advance with your child to a phase-out approach to your monitoring and having a say in her transactions. However, if you've given your child a real voice in family investments, then it's likely she'll continue seeking your opinions even after you've given her investment freedom.

Your Junior Family Financial Team Member

Want an investment opinion you can trust? Now that you've unleashed your child into her own investment world, chances are that she'll soon be as knowledgeable as you, if not more so. Why not now let her have a go (at least on paper) at the family's investments – a logical extension of activities described in earlier chapters that enlisted your child's help with the family budget, consumer research and shopping, and money-saving campaign.

7 • Investing

Family Financial Assessment

Your child's involvement in family investing needn't be an all-or-nothing proposition. Start by introducing her to the current family investment portfolio. Explain the rationale behind it (if there is one!), and your current ongoing strategy. This discussion should include the various family financial goals and how you've translated them into investment objectives. Also cover any tax considerations (see Chapter 8) in your choice of investments and the timing of their purchase and sale.

When you make investment decisions, tell your child about them to keep her updated. If you have some kind of monitoring system you use on paper or on the computer, encourage your child to learn how to do it and start keeping it for you, and let her set one up for you if you don't have one. After awhile, start inviting her input during future discussions of family financial objectives and the strategies that will best achieve them. Ultimately, once she's proven herself with the "entry-level" investing experiences just discussed earlier, you want her input on the family's investment decisions. Some of what she says will probably be off target, but some or a lot could be useful and you should act on it, perhaps in modified form, to show that you're taking her role seriously. Most importantly, give her feedback on all of it, whether good or bad.

Specific Investment Decisions

To involve your children in your investment decisions, you must first have a thorough understanding of all of them yourself, and if you're like most of your peers, you can use a little remedial review. So as that old fogy (either Dean or Witter, before they paired up with Morgan and Stanley – and Livingston, we presume) in the fake film clip brokerage commercial might suggest, let's take a look at them, one investment type at a time.

7 • Investing

IRA Investments

Although funds in these can be taken out in certain circumstances before retirement, think of these as an important source of your retirement funds – a place to invest for the long-term at moderate-plus risk. That's because earnings in an IRA grow tax-deferred and you get no tax deduction for losses; higher-risk investing should be done outside this and other tax-sheltered accounts so that you can deduct losses. Your IRA is a self-managed plan. You can open one with virtually any financial institution and can invest in any stocks, bonds, and mutual funds (and even some other investments, but stick to these).

Your investment strategy shouldn't be any different regardless of which of the three types of IRAs you have, although the type might affect how you eventually withdraw funds. They all allow each spouse to contribute up to $3,000 annually in 2002 – even if only one spouse has earned income – going up to $5,000 by 2008. Parents can also set up a custodial IRA for a child with earned income for up to the lesser of the child's income or the current limit.

 ### A Quick Explanation of IRA Types

- **Traditional IRAs give you a current tax deduction** on amounts you contribute, and your funds grow tax-deferred. Therefore, all money you withdraw after age 59.5 is treated as income and taxed at "ordinary income" (not more favorable capital gains) rates. Many couples aren't eligible for this type, though, because if they participate in an employer retirement plan, their joint annual incomes must not exceed $62,000. And even if they were eligible, if they're in the 15% tax bracket, they'd be better off using the Roth IRA.

- **Roth IRAs don't give you a current tax deduction** on amounts you contribute, but the payoff is that your money grows tax-free, forever – and unlike the traditional IRA, you have total flexibility on your schedule of withdrawals once you reach age 59.5. Eligibility stretches to couples making a maximum of $150,000 joint annual income. Set up your kids' IRA as a Roth.

- **Non-Deductible IRAs are for couples** who don't qualify for the other two types. Their contributions don't get tax deductions, but their money grows tax-deferred and only the earnings are taxed (as a prorated part of any withdrawal) upon withdrawal.

7 • Investing

Employee-Contribution Employer-Sponsored Retirement Plans

Even if you work for one of the dying breed of employers that still offers a pension plan to which it solely contributes, you have no say in the investments – only in the amount for which you might be eligible based on service length and salary. So let's turn our attention to employee-contribution 401(k) or 403(b) plans – or the SEP, SIMPLE, and Keogh if you work for a small employer or are self-employed, or own a business.

401(k) Plans

Your 401(k) plan allows you to contribute up to $11,000 annually (rising incrementally to $15,000 by 2006) depending on your company's rules. In addition, your company can match all or part of the portion of that $11,000 that doesn't exceed 6% of income. (A typical match for someone making $40,000 might be one-half up to 6%; 6% of $40,000 is $2,400 and half is a match of $1,200.) Therefore, it's almost a no-brainer to effectively increase your investment return by contributing at least the maximum that your employer will partially or fully match.

Like traditional IRAs, the amount you contribute in a given year is a current tax deduction. Both your and your employer's contributions grow tax-deferred, and you pay ordinary income tax on distributions you take from the account starting at age 59.5 (or later). Chances are that you'll have to rely on your 401(k) as the major source of your retirement income, so you should try to contribute the maximum (not just the maximum that gets matched) every year.

Sounds great, but the value of a 401(k) plan is considerably dependent on how good your employer's plan is, and many – as your kid might say – suck! Unlike IRAs, you can't invest in individual stocks and bonds – except for

7 • Investing

employer stock (Enron, need we say more) – and are usually limited to a choice of mutual funds. That's okay if your employer offers a wide range of choices, but to save on expenses, some use 401(k) administrative companies that offer only a handful of choices. Worse, those choices are sometimes funds that have high annual expense ratios – which (here's that word again) suck a substantial amount away from your annual returns. Furthermore, many have rules that restrict your ability to move fund balances into different funds more than once a year.

Thus, you must weigh how much your employer's plan might adversely be affecting the growth of funds that you contribute, versus the tax benefits and matching contributions it provides. In some cases, it actually makes sense to contribute only the amount your employer matches and invest the rest in investments that aren't in a plan. In any event, you should use the same strategies for investing in 401(k) plans as in IRA plans – relying on the tax-deferred feature. Thus, you needn't concern yourself with avoiding funds that frequently change their holdings, because you won't be paying any capital gains tax the way you would if you held those funds outside a tax-deferred plan. However, you should be leery of any fund that trades too excessively.

For more information on problems with 401(k) plans, visit **www.timyounkin.com**

403(b) Plans

If you work for a college or university, school system, not-for-profit hospital, or other non-profit organization, you probably don't have the opportunity to invest in a 401(k) plan, but might have a 403(b) plan. Although these two plans are intended to serve the same purpose, they could hardly be more different.

 ### 401(k)s versus 403(b)s

- **Both provide tax deductions for contributions and tax-deferred growth of the contributions and earnings.** However, rules for making withdrawals from 403(b) plans are less flexible.

- **Most employers** don't match any 403(b) employee contributions.

7 • Investing

- **Plan administrators rather than employers** have fiduciary responsibility for a 403(b) plan, and the plan administrators needn't be as concerned about employee education, provision of good choices, etc. In fact, some employers providing 403(b) plans allow insurance agents from the company providing the plan to meet with the employee in "financial counseling" sessions.

- **403(b) investment choices focus on annuities,** which are big profit-makers for insurance companies and REALLY can suck a lot of internal fees out of the employee's investment. When annuities are appropriate investments, it's usually for retirees looking to get a guaranteed monthly payment for the rest of their lives through a low-fee fixed annuity or for wealthy individuals looking for additional avenues to make tax-deferred investments through a variable annuity.

- **Maximum 403(b) contributions are based on different rules.** You're usually not able to contribute as much as in a 401(k), so they're often not concerned about employee education, provision of good choices, etc.

- **Employees with 403(b) plans make less money on average** due to the nature of their employers versus the private and corporate sector. The tax advantages of making contributions are therefore not as significant because of the employee's lower tax bracket.

If you get the impression that these are "403(b)ad" plans, in many cases you'd be on the money – or out of some of your money if you participate in the worst ones. Teachers in particular are becoming militant in some districts around the country for reforms that will make these plans worthwhile – particularly in campaigning for good mutual-fund choices to be included. Depending on your salary and particular plan, however, 403(b) investing might be appropriate, but make sure you understand all the details of your plan, and monitor its performance carefully.

For more information on problems with 403(b) plans, visit **www.403bwise.com**

7 • Investing

Educated investors should certainly have knowledge of annuities, and annuity providers are reacting to bad press by making their products more attractive. However, it's highly unlikely that readers of this book (and certainly not their children) should be considering annuities now, so they're not covered any further.

Business Owner and Self-Employed Plans

If you work for a small employer, you might not have a 401(k) or 403(b) plan available to you. Instead, your employer might offer a type of employment-related IRA that you control, called a Simplified Employee Pension (SEP) or Savings Incentive Match Plan for Employees (SIMPLE). (On rare occasions, your employer might also offer something called a money-purchase Keogh.) The plans are like 401(k)s in that you make tax-deductible contributions and employers provide a match, but under their more complex matching rules, most employers provide less match for a given amount than the average 401(k) employer. Because you totally control your SEP or SIMPLE contributions and your employer's matches once they're made, you should participate to the maximum amount you're allowed. Use the same investment strategies as you do for your other IRA (although these employer-related accounts shouldn't be co-mingled with personal IRAs).

The news is better if you're self-employed or own a business, because you can set up these plans for yourself, and can arrange to contribute more to your own than you're generally able to do as an employee. Furthermore, the tax hit on the self-employed is so great (due to paying almost double an employee's social security tax) that you should pick the plan that will let you contribute the maximum and then contribute that much in order to minimize taxes. If you have employees, however, the rules require that what you do for them is tied to what you do for yourself, so you might not be able to afford such generous contributions. Finally, if you don't have employees and have a very successful enterprise, you should consider a "defined-benefit Keogh" – which might allow you to sock away more than 50% of your earnings tax deferred. These plans are too complex to go into further detail here, so consult the following IRS publications for full details.

7 • Investing

Not So Simple: More Details on Self-Employed Plans Online

- **Tax Guide for Small Businesses –**
  www.irs.gov/formspubs/display/0,,i1%3D50%26genericId%3D11457,00.html

- **Individual Retirement Arrangements (IRAs)
  including SEP IRAs and SIMPLE IRAs –**
  www.irs.gov/formspubs/display/0,,i1%3D50%26genericId%3D12598,00.html

Tax-Advantaged Section 529 and Education IRA College Savings Plans

Yet another type of IRA allows you to save for your child's private-school and college education by making an annual contribution of up to $2,000 to an Education IRA for each of your children. They work somewhat like a Roth IRA; contributions are not tax deductible, but all funds grow tax-free and can be withdrawn without taxation if used for eligible education expenses. And like other IRAs, you have control of your investments. But unlike other IRAs, you're dealing with a shorter time frame of about 20 years until your child is in the middle of college instead of 30+ years until you're well into retirement. Therefore, you must take a slightly more conservative approach in your investment strategy – particularly when you get within five years of your child entering college.

Take advantage of (Coverdell) Education IRA plans – even if you're not sure your child is going to college – because you control the account and, at worst, the earnings will be taxed normally if not used for college. Furthermore, the tax-free earnings from these accounts, if set up when your child is born, should more than outweigh the negatives of these funds reducing eligibility for financial aid.

Of course, 529 plans are the massive education-savings playground bullies you've heard so much about. They're covered in Chapter 5, but revisited here to focus on investment strategies associated with them. Unfortunately, your use of strategy is far more limited than with IRAs and somewhat more limited than with 401(k)s. That's because many state plans don't even allow you to pick a specific fund in which to invest. Instead, you pick a state you think offers the best overall plan and choice of sub-plans. You then pick one or more sub-plans in which to put your contributions, based on the stated investment strategies of your sub-plan choices. Your control is now gone until a year later, when you can switch between sub-plans, because most states' investment managers for your chosen sub-plan(s) make the actual investment allocations and handle continued management of those sub-plans.

7 • Investing

While information is available on how each sub-plan currently allocates to investments within it, those allocations can change. For example, the manager can dump 5 funds and add 8 others, making your choice a very different animal than it was when you chose it. Of course, you can always vote with your money by pulling it out of a state's plan and putting it in another state's, but restrictions might delay your switch and penalties can apply if you switch sooner than when you're able to do so without penalty. Because of the way these plans work, it can be difficult to gauge the effect of investment fees within each of the mutual funds they hold, which we've already mentioned is an important consideration in investment decisions. All these drawbacks don't mean you shouldn't invest in a 529 plan. However, be painstakingly exhaustive in making your initial choices between state plans and between a state's sub-plans. Follow that up with obsessive vigilance concerning your investments' performance and how your plan continues to compare to other states' evolving plans.

Your Non-Plan Investment Plan

A man, a plan, a canal, Panama. If you're exhausted from seemingly covering everything about investments backward and forward, invest a few seconds to read that anagram backwards (the way General Noriega did things). Then you'll be ready to pass through the canal that begins at the employer and other tax-advantaged investment plans that we've covered, and ends at the unfettered taxable remainder of your investment portfolio.

The View from the Free Choice Taxable Investment Side

- **Taxable investments are made to reach a variety of goals** that occur at different times, requiring you to divide up your funds into "strategic portions" that go into various investments tailored to differing time frames – such as a car you plan to buy in five years, a major home improvement project you plan in ten years, a vacation home you hope to purchase in fifteen years, and your child's wedding in about 25 years.

7 • Investing

- **Your portfolio of investments that isn't shielded** by a tax-deferred plan should include some percentage of full or partially tax-free investments, such as municipal bonds and government securities. These types of investments should never be held in tax-deferred accounts because they generally have lower returns than taxable investments. Why shield an investment from tax when it's already shielded from tax?

- **The timing and amount of tax exposure** should be considered. For example, excess capital gains in a given year might be taxed at the higher Alternative Minimum Tax rate. If you're in a high ordinary-income-tax bracket, there's a strong incentive to hold securities long enough to qualify for long-term capital gains treatment. And because only $3,000 of the excess of capital losses over gains in a given year can be deducted from income that isn't capital gains, timing the sale of gainers and losers can be critical.

- **Titling of investments outside of a tax-deferred plan** comes into play because children over 14 are usually in a much lower tax bracket than parents. Thus, making gifts of stock that has already achieved considerable appreciation transfers the gain to the child at a lower tax bracket. Counterbalancing that, however, are the current financial-aid determination rules, which consider much more of a child's assets as being available to pay for college than parental assets. (However, this might change soon so that all assets are treated the same as family assets.)

- **Index funds** are much more attractive for taxable investments because they have low transaction costs, thus minimizing annual capital gains while you continue holding them.

- **Riskier investments** should be made in your taxable portfolio, where losses are deductible.

7 • Investing

- **You might have more money that can be used for taxable invest-ments** versus tax-deferred plan investments, because of the limitations on contributions to the latter. The larger the portfolio, the more it makes sense to invest in a broad selection of individual stocks. Limited funds within a plan might preclude that kind of investing because you'd be unable to achieve enough diversification.

- **You can raid funds** that aren't invested in tax-deferred plans at any time, and only have to pay normal income tax, while premature use of funds in tax-advantaged plans also carries a stiff tax penalty.

- **Some types of investments aren't allowed** in tax-deferred plans – including most precious metals, collectibles, and some types of real estate. Outside of plans you're limited only to avoiding illegal invest-ments. (There goes that 25% money-laundering monthly return.)

The results of investing are uncertain, but one thing that is certain is how you'll fall behind inflation if you don't grow your money enough through investment. Although the wag who first uttered "If you don't use it, you'll lose it," had a different kind of inflation in mind, it is equally applicable to money: if you don't use it for investing, you'll lose its buying power.

Chapter Eight

Family Financial Planning and Management

We're confident that what we've covered so far will help you be financially better prepared to have kids. And once you have them, you should be able to get some control of your family's spending, take steps to keep up or increase your earning power, act on the need for saving, and more effectively invest what you save. Furthermore, you should be able to enlist your kids to help accomplish those objectives and to develop those skills for themselves.

But how do you know whether what you're doing is good enough and will lead to enough financial success to maintain a viable, happy family unit? Will everyone in your family be able to pursue their life dreams, with a realistic shot of attaining one or more of them?

8 • Financial Planning

To determine that, you must be able to view and coordinate all your family financial activities in an integrated fashion. That's called financial planning, a task big and challenging enough to send millions of Americans to professionals who help them do it. Financial planners take a magnifying glass to all the tiny pieces of your spending, earning, saving, and investing puzzle, and help you put them together into a complete picture that looks like your desired family future.

You don't have to hire a financial planner, though, to assemble your own puzzle – or at least solve most of it. But you do have to know how to start putting the spending, saving, earning, and investing pieces together. This chapter will show you how.

Manage Your Finances to the Max

Fine-Tune and Integrate Spending, Saving, Earning, and Investing

The road from being a winning financial management family to becoming the consummate successful financial management family is much like the progression of a young baseball pitching phenom. Although you and your spouse might not be baseball fans, we'll trust you know enough about it to find this analogy useful.

A Fast (Ball) Lesson in Becoming a Complete Pitcher

Our phenom starts as a raw "thrower" and becomes a "complete pitcher." That's the kid in little league who only looked like he was lying about his age and struck out the entire opposing lineup as effortlessly as Danny Almonte (you remember, the little leaguer from 2001's Little League World Series who lied about his age). Knowing he could always fall back on his un-hittable "heater," our phenom starts fooling around with breaking pitches and change-ups, which allows him to maintain success in pick-up games with older kids who can only occasionally get their bats on his fastball. When he gets into high school and college, he still has the "nastiest stuff" around, but after awhile he's been scouted enough so that the better hitters learn to lay off his pitches just out of the strike zone. So his walks occasionally get him bases-loaded jams that he manages to escape with a little extra mustard he's saved for such occasions.

8 • Financial Planning

But in the minor leagues, he runs into more sophisticated scouting, and opposing teams learn his pitching-pattern tendencies and note that in certain situations his fastball doesn't have a lot of movement. They learn to "guess" at their best-chance pitches, and soon the outfield walls are being scuffed by wicked line drives. Fortunately, though, this player is almost as fast mentally as his arm is strong and decides that two can play the same game. He starts reading scouting reports on the opposing batters, learns to outguess them in some situations, and prevails against dangerous hitters with a series of foul-ball two-strike pitches that wear them down. And he also learns when to pitch around some of them by issuing walks that can be erased by striking out the next batter or two.

Don't Rush Your Phenom's Growth

Dr. Mike Marshall, one of the few relief pitchers to ever win the Cy Young award, has strong opinions on the damage done to pre-teens and teens who are rushed into becoming pitching prodigies. Using his doctoral training in kinesiology, his research has shown that many pitchers are dominant as teenagers only because their growth plates have developed faster than their peers' have. More importantly, he's found that stress on still-developing growth plates, caused by too much pitching practice or pitching in little league or scholastic competition, often permanently injures youthful pitching arms. As an alternative, he offers a Florida-based 40-week training program for high-school graduates that teaches them to pitch properly at a time their growth plates have fully developed. Many prospects have deferred college and learned from "Dr. Mike" – some moving on to successful college and professional careers that haven't been derailed by serious injuries. Check out www.drmikemarshall.com for more.

But he's not quite all the way there. Now that he's regained his dominance, teams realize they must make maximal use of the precious few base runners they get. They start their fastest lineups against him and resolve to get on base any way possible through walks, bunts, and beating out deep infield ground balls. Once they're on, they drive him nuts by stealing bases or bluffing, using hit-and-run plays, or hitting behind the runner to advance him. When they get a runner to third with less than two outs, they bring him home with squeeze bunts or sacrifice flies. But our hero has one last weapon. He becomes an adept fielder who charges off the mound to throw out the lead runner on bunts and develops a nasty pick-off move that occasionally nabs base runners

8 • Financial Planning

outright, or inhibits their leadoffs enough that they're less successful on steals or advancing an extra base. And against speed demons, he selectively employs pitchouts to make them sitting ducks that the standing catcher can easily throw out.

Finally, our fellow on the mound gets a bit long in the tooth and a bit short of overpowering. He learns to make even more use of his change-up and develops a sinker to get more ground ball outs instead of relying on strikeouts. Perhaps he experiments with a knuckler or screwball, as well – but one way or another, he replaces the power lost in his arm with more powerful thinking.

Our flaming-torch thrower has evolved into a polished (possibly Hall of Fame) pitcher, much like a fellow named Tom Seaver once did. Think of the qualities he cultivated: investing in perfection of a diversified pitching repertoire and in strategic preparation towards the long-term goal of winning rather than the short-term goal of dominating, earning a reputation for creativity and unpredictability, spending less unnecessary physical energy, saving his "out" pitches for the most critical situations, and earning the chance to prolong his career by using his arm in new ways and making more use of his legs and brain.

A Pitch for Becoming the Complete Family Financial Manager

Even if you've never played baseball, and think a hit and run is strictly a police matter, your development into a hall-of-fame family financial manager isn't unlike our pitcher's evolution. Your fastball is your earning power. Like most of your peers, you were encouraged to develop it to the maximum extent through higher education and hard work. At first, though, you spent most of what you earned, confident that you could stay ahead with your increasingly overpowering earning potential. But as you matured, you realized that the boom might not last forever, so you had to learn to spend carefully and save most of what you didn't spend in order to ensure your ultimate victory. Finally, you became the complete family financial manager by realizing that even the tightest spending and maximum saving won't work forever when your earning power plateaus and perhaps even shrinks a bit (in real dollars – due to inflation). So you learned the financial curve ball, investing, which will get you back the long-term edge in a roundabout way. (As we've seen, markets don't just keep going straight up!)

8 • Financial Planning

Of course, that's a simplified synopsis of how mastery of earning, spending, saving, and investing make you a financial winner – and perhaps your pitching repertoire is a bit different. Somehow, though, you've learned that you need all of them. If you're not there yet, it might help to visualize your family as a financial engine that needs all those parts working together smoothly, just as a pitcher needs to harness all his resources to become an efficient pitching engine.

Of course, the engine is started with earning, which comes from multiple sources of work-generated income, business income, investment income and gains, tax savings from certain deductible expenditures, insurance payments that cover some health and other expenses, and gifts and inheritance. Earnings then flow into either the immediate spending chamber or the saving chamber. Saving drives three different pistons: investing for income or gain (short, medium, and long-term), investment in a business, and interim saving for planned future spending.

The spending chamber of the engine feeds expenditures that aren't tax-deductible, those that are, those that directly pay taxes, those that generate debt because they're made with credit, those that pay down debt, and those that pay interest on the debt. The expenditures that are tax-deductible then generate tax reductions that flow back into earnings. In the savings chamber, gains either flow back into earnings or directly back into savings.

By understanding how this engine works, we can see how to make it more powerful. Its total power at any given time can be measured by "turning it off" and waiting for inputs to flow through the spending and savings paths. Its "net power" (net worth) is the difference between the combined amount in the three chambers coming out of the savings tank and the debt chamber. As the driver, you're trying to increase that net power by integrating a combination of increased earning; reduced, intelligent spending that generates maximum tax deductions; and increased saving and investment earnings. The more success you have, the more it will benefit your family, and by extension, your children – both in providing more for them and showing them how to drive in the process. But this is no ordinary drive; it requires the thorough preparation necessary for a multi-day road rally. So just as you'd map out a road-rally trip, you must map out your financial journey, in the form of a financial plan.

8 • Financial Planning

Prepare to Plan

Before plotting a road-rally trip though, you must know where you're going, what car you're going to use to get there, and what resources you have to make the trip – and then gather the information and materials you need to figure it all out. The same is true before you plan your financial journey.

Determine Your Goals and Objectives

Put the world's best sharpshooter on a cliff overlooking a valley full of farms, armed with the world's most powerful and precise rifle, and she won't even be able to hit the side of a barn with the world's most powerful and precise rifle if a fog rolls in. Similarly, if you're not clear on your family's life goals and objectives, you won't know at what financial targets to aim.

Take your child's career objectives, for example. If she wants to be a high-powered corporate attorney, an Ivy League school might well be the right goal to earn the pedigree and the connections that go with Hah-vud. Yet, how can you swing it if you're one of those in-between families who can't really afford it, but won't qualify for enough financial aid to avoid a crushing debt burden? If your child burns Harvard crimson, however, perhaps you should make an agreement her on splitting the debt burden. After all, you know she'll be able to pay off her part quickly with a high-salary job in which she'll have no time to spend money anyway while working 100 hours a week to make partner.

But if she wants to find the cure for AIDS, she doesn't necessarily have to get her undergraduate education at Johns Hopkins or other universities with the absolute-best scientific research facilities. By getting admitted to the honors program of one of your state universities – or on full scholarship to a good but not quite elite private university – she can gain a solid grounding in all the sciences by taking the toughest courses, serving as a research assistant to a respected faculty member, and graduating with highest honors. She'll have bought a ticket to most of the top-ranked graduate programs in whatever scientific specialty she chooses – probably with a full fellowship. Why go into debt to end up in the same place – especially since she'll be spending many of her career Saturday nights with lab rats and mice, rather than the stuffed-shirt rodents that sometimes populate high-society cocktail parties?

8 • Financial Planning

Imagine the possible difference for you. Your daughter now has a good chance of sharing her future triumphs with a single phone call to you and your spouse, instead of having to call you separately because you're no longer together after the financial stresses of paying for the gold-plated education that ruined your marriage. Consider the ripple effects of making this decision. Now you can afford to take a once-in-a-lifetime family vacation the last time you're all likely to be together as a family before she goes off to school. In addition, you'll possibly have more family time while she grows up, instead of feeling the need to hustle her off to every "enrichment program" offered in your area.

This isn't an attack on elitism, but an appeal to examine goals and objectives carefully so that you can look at the financial alternatives that can achieve them. Far too many parents buy into the conventional wisdom that they're not good parents if they don't give their child the very best. What constitutes "very best" is unique to each family and child and is more likely to be discovered if you don't automatically assume that "very best" equates to "very expensive."

Determine Your Cash Flow and Net Worth

Once you know your goals and objectives, you can quantify them in terms of alternative financial targets. For example, if your goal is to provide your child an undergraduate education, then one alternative is to commute to a nearby college, requiring a quality vehicle. Then you might want to go in with him on an inexpensive new car during high school, which he can then use throughout college. But if the goal is to send him to a good-quality small college because he'll thrive better in a smaller atmosphere with smaller classes, then it probably means going where he gets a good enough financial deal. Now, if he needs his own car during high school, it means a much less expensive used one in decent running condition.

After enumerating all significant goals and the likeliest alternatives to achieve each, you're ready to determine how to get from here to there. That requires knowing what your current net worth is and how much it is increasing or shrinking due to your cash flow (the difference between what's coming in and what's going out).

MONEY

8 • Financial Planning

Online Cash Flow Calculators

- **Kiplinger's Cash Flow Format –**
  www.kiplinger.com/tools/cashflow

- **Kiplinger Net Worth Format –**
  www.kiplinger.com/tools/networth

- **E-Analytics Net Worth and Cash Flow Worksheets –**
  www.e-analytics.com/fp2

Organize Your Finances and Financial Records

In order to do financial planning yourself, or by consulting with a professional advisor, you'll need to compile detailed financial records to have at your fingertips.

Financial Records to Collect and Keep

- Auto, home, life, health, and other **insurance** policies.

- **Statements from bank** and brokerage accounts, stock certificates, etc.

- **Mortgage** and real estate documents.

- **Tax returns** dating back the last few years.

- **List of personal property** that has significant value, bank and brokerage statements, mortgage and other real-estate documents, etc.

For a More Detailed List of Records to Keep...

This article on Kiplinger's excellent web site provides a detailed list of what you'll need, while also providing other information to help you prepare for financial planning.

- **Prepare to Meet Your Financial Planner –**
  www.kiplinger.com/basics/projects/wp_planner

8 • Financial Planning

Plan Financially for Prosperity

You might be pleasantly surprised to discover that you've already gotten a good head start on composing your financial plan. Let's look at the process that leads to a complete financial plan, what a plan contains, and the specific tasks required to complete it.

Embrace the Financial Planning Process

When the profession that has grown up to do formal family financial planning was in its infancy in the 1970s, a financial plan was the equivalent of a financial blueprint. It was meticulously constructed and often "published" in a hundred-page-plus bound document that was given to the client after a number of planning meetings culminating in a final one to go over the plan. But just as today's blueprints can be created with special high-resolution-graphics computers, and easily modified if necessary during the construction or remodeling process, today's financial plans are no longer the immutable financial bibles they once were. Instead, financial planning is regarded as an ongoing process to be comprehensively revisited every year or so – and today's computer tools make that possible. Here's an overview of the planning process taught to Certified Financial Planner® practitioners. The explanations under each numbered step represent our interpretation of what that step of the process should mean to you.

8 • Financial Planning

The Financial Planning Process the Pros Use

1) **Establish and Define the Client-Planner Relationship.** If you're doing the planning yourself, this obviously doesn't apply. But if you're a planning client, you have the right to know what to expect from the planner in the way of written and consultative work products, whether you'll be able to access updated account information on the planner's web site, how much and how you'll be charged, what information you're expected to provide, and the frequency, duration, and accessibility of communication to expect from in-person meetings, phone calls, and e-mail. It's especially important that the planner clearly disclose how she's compensated: hourly, flat fee, annual percentage fee assessed on assets managed, commissions on insurance and investment products that you purchase through her, or some combination of these. That way, you're in the best position to assess whether you feel there's any conflict of interest regarding recommendations the planner might make.

2) **Gather Client Data, Including Goals.** We've already discussed determining your objectives and goals, and the financial records you've gathered will provide the data needed for various calculations involved in assembling a plan. A good planner should also be able to develop the kind of rapport with you that will allow exploration of sensitive issues – such as the nature of your relationships with family members and how that might affect your estate planning, and the solidity of your marital relationship and how that might affect relying on largely joint planning versus planning that caters more to the possibility that the relationship could dissolve under severe financial pressure.

3) **Analyze and Evaluate Your Financial Status.** The Cash Flow and Net Worth statements already discussed form the major basis for determining where you are now financially and the trick is to bridge the gap between #3 and #2.

4) **Develop and Present Financial Planning Recommendations and/or Alternatives.** There's no one right financial plan that results from good planning. Several significant plan variations should be developed that are each the result of changing certain key assumptions such as overall economic variables, how much risk you're willing to take, what kinds of returns you might achieve, different types of colleges your kids might attend, etc. A good planner should be able to make changes quickly to the proposed plans based on clients' reactions to them. In other words, the planner must take into account the validity his proposals have for the client.

5) **Implement the Financial Planning Recommendations.** Financial plans aren't worth the paper on which they're printed if you don't act on them. Many people make the mistake of letting themselves get overwhelmed by all the recommendations in a comprehensive plan, and let it gather dust. Instead, the plan should put priorities on its various recommendations so that you do one or a few at a time, starting with the highest priorities. For example, your planner will probably recommend relatively inexpensive umbrella liability of one or two million dollars in case you have sizable assets that could be grabbed if you're found liable in an auto-collision lawsuit. That might be medium priority, but making sure your child has health insurance if he takes time off from college and is no longer a full-time student would be a top priority; most health-insurance plans don't cover kids over 19 in that situation. Similarly, if you have a mortgage with many years left that's a few points above current rates, then refinancing is a medium priority. But what if you're a middle-income family with a child a few years away from college, are carrying significant debt, and have investment holdings with substantial built-in gains? It's a high priority to liquidate a sizable portion of that stock and pay off your credit-card bills. You'll not only eliminate high-interest debt on which payments are not tax deductible, but will also make yourself far more eligible for financial aid by reducing your savings. (Most colleges don't consider debt that isn't for a house in determining your financial need.)

8 • Financial Planning

6) **Monitor the Financial Planning Recommendations.** Finally, families using financial plans should think of themselves as diligent parole officers, frequently checking up on whether they're complying with the (plan's) "rules," and weighing the "cons" and "pros" of its performance. If you've hired a financial planner and he's not frequently following up and monitoring your plan, send him to jail without his passing Go and collecting (a) $2000 (fee).

If your plan is doing well, add on time for good behavior (for it to operate in its current form). But if it's not doing so well, or circumstances have significantly changed, then give its current version the minimum sentence and start a new trial of a significantly revised plan.

Build a Solid Financial Pyramid

No matter what your specific financial plan, your assets should always be divided into tiers of the "financial pyramid" shown below.

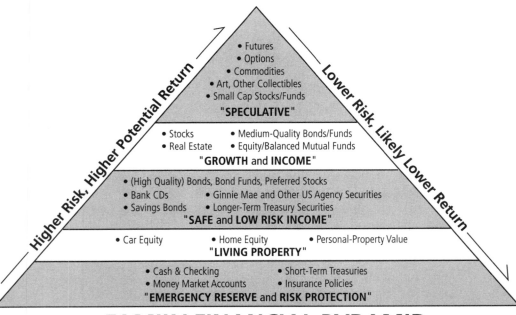

FAMILY FINANCIAL PYRAMID

8 • Financial Planning

The concept is that you build your portfolio from a solid base at the bottom that consists of adequate funds kept in risk-free, liquid investments to take care of immediate needs, a reserve for unexpected emergency expenses, and a further reserve that replaces income should you lose your job – allowing you to continue paying your mortgage and other normal expenses for a period of three to six months. These funds should be kept in "cash or cash equivalent" investments such as checking accounts, money-market funds, and 91-day or 182-day treasury securities. In addition, it includes funds to keep insurance policies in force that will cover catastrophic expenses (health, homeowner's, auto, and umbrella liability policies) or replace lost income (life and disability insurance).

The second-widest tier, "living property," consists of the equity in your house, your automobiles, and the market value of other significant property that you own as part of your lifestyle – rather than as an investment. While it's true that your house is an investment, your decision to purchase it should have been based primarily on how it serves your family's lifestyle needs, and only secondarily on its investment potential. Note that this tier is not at the bottom, even though its value might exceed the bottom, because making sure you've adequately funded the bottom tier comes before buying a home and other significant property.

The middle tier consists of high-safety income-generating investments that might offer some growth, and is actually the most conservative part of your actual investment portfolio. It consists of bank CDs, savings bonds, treasury securities with maturities exceeding one year, government-agency securities such as Ginnie Mae certificates, high-quality municipal and corporate individual bonds and bond funds, and high-quality preferred stock. These are the types of investments that might be held in large amounts by someone in their 80s, families planning to buy a new car in five years, or families with children a few years away from college.

The tier just below the top is the growth-and-income part of your portfolio. These are the moderate-to-medium risk individual stocks or mutual funds that you're holding for long-term growth to pay for college for a current toddler, buy a larger home in 10 years, or retire in 20 years. But it also might include a "balanced" mutual fund that you're holding for both growth and some income from its fixed-income securities and higher-dividend stocks. In addition, this category includes rental real estate or moderate-risk forms of real-estate investments such as certain Real Estate Investment Trusts. Your 401(k), IRA, and other tax-advantaged investments should mostly consist of these.

The top tier is your "mad money" for speculative and "hedge" investments such as "emerging growth" mutual funds or high-risk small-cap individual stocks, precious metals, limited partnerships, more aggressive REITs, art and other collectibles, commodities, stock-market options and futures, and high risk/return "junk" bonds.

Decide Whether You Need a Financial Professional's Help

Unless they have high income and substantial assets, families who have or can develop financial know-how (which you can if you've followed this book this far) probably can't afford to fully engage a financial planner on a continuing basis at a cost of several thousand dollars a year. But they might want to retain one on a limited (hourly or commission) basis to get a second opinion or to help tweak the financial plans they've developed on their own.

We suggest you start with one of the popular personal-finance software packages such as *Microsoft Money* or *Quicken* that enable you to set up and track budgets, manage your credit, invest toward goals, allocate your investments, and monitor your changing net worth. By learning all the features and reading some good sources of personal-finance information regularly, you should be able to do almost as well as a good financial planner could do for you, net of her expenses. And you'll also avoid the too-large chance that you might not get such a good planner.

8 • Financial Planning

A Few Good Sources of Personal-Finance Education and News

- **CBS MarketWatch –**
  http://cbs.marketwatch.com

- **MoneyCentral/CNBC –**
  http://moneycentral.msn.com/home.asp

- **CNNMoney –**
  http://money.cnn.com

- **Kiplinger –**
  www.kiplinger.com

- **Washington Post Personal Finance –**
  www.washingtonpost.com/wp-dyn/business/personalfinance

- **New York Times Your Money Section –**
  www.nytimes.com/business/yourmoney

- **Financial Planner Errold Moody's Web Site –**
  www.efmoody.com

- **iVillage Finance –**
  www.ivillage.com/money

- **Smart Money –**
  www.smartmoney.com

- **Bloomberg –**
  www.bloomberg.com

If and when you eventually reach a critical mass of healthy income and substantial assets, it will be time to engage a financial planner regularly. But whether you use one on a limited basis or regularly, it's essential that you understand the different types of financial planners (e.g. CFP CPA/PFS) and the different types of financial institutions for which they might work (e.g. brokerages, insurance companies), and that you screen candidates thoroughly. Find out about the training they've had, formal certifications they hold, their history and experience in the business,

8 • Financial Planning

how they get compensated, and whether they've had any disciplinary action taken against them by either a professional organization (e.g. CFP Board), industry regulatory organization (e.g. NASD), national regulatory organization (e.g. SEC) or state regulatory organizations.

More on Finding Good Planner Candidates

- **10 Rules to Pick Financial Planner** –
  http://moneycentral.msn.com/articles/retire/basics/5266.asp

- **Questions to Ask** –
  www.cfp-board.org/cons_10qs

- **How to Choose** –
  www.financialfinesse.com/financial_planners/choosing.php

- **Selecting a Financial Planner** –
  www.chr.ucla.edu/chr/ben/selectfp

- **The Right Way to Hire Financial Help** –
  (Charles Jaffe, 2nd Edition, MIT Press, February, 2001)

Assemble and Activate Your Financial Plan

Whether you do it yourself or engage a professional financial planner, your plan should cover all the major financial areas.

Areas Your Plan Should Cover

- **Insurance Protection and Employee Benefit Utilization.** Even if you earn tons of money, save most of it, and invest better than the pros, all your efforts will go to naught if you don't protect yourself from catastrophic financial loss. Arranging to have the proper home, auto, health, and other insurance in place is a small price to pay to protect your nest egg. Sometimes, your employee-benefit plan will offer what you need, but in many cases, you'll have to meet at least part of your insurance needs by directly purchasing policies from agents or insurance companies.

8 • Financial Planning

- **Budgeting and Cash Management.** Your budget is your blueprint for a solid family financial structure – ensuring that all needs, including regular saving, are met first before discretionary spending occurs. But your budget is worthless unless you "manage" it by ensuring the timing of your cash inflow and outgo so that you're never in a position to fall prey to "quick loot" types of predatory lenders.

- **Credit and Debt Management.** Sometimes you do have to borrow in order to meet your cash flow needs. The question is knowing when you need the credit versus when it's simply a convenience that costs more than you should be willing to pay. And you must find the best deals available with straight shooting credit providers that don't trap you with fine-print "gotcha" clauses for cards or loans.

- **Investment Policy.** The way you invest is unique to your (family's) needs and attitudes about risk. Your investment policy is reflected by those factors and should continually guide your overall strategy and specific portfolio selection, subject to changes in your (family's) circumstances and fortunes.

- **Tax Management.** Suppose you clone two families that start out with identical assets and earnings, and then see how differently they end up, say, 10 years in the future. Your evaluation will surely show big differences in how they managed their taxes through choice of investments and timing of buying and selling, spending that generates tax deductions, etc. Good tax management isn't a matter of trickery, but rather using the tax code to your best advantage while pursuing your financial objectives (i.e. never use a financial strategy primarily for tax reasons).

- **Self-Employment and Business Ownership.** Even if you and your spouse both work for employers and could never imagine self-employment in your wildest dreams, chances are good that one or both of you will bring home the bacon that way, someday. That form of income requires a totally new look at tax strategy, family cash flow, and other aspects of your financial plan.

8 • Financial Planning

- **College Funding.** It's not just a matter of setting a savings/investment target based on what you think it will cost your child, and then developing a strategy to get there. For one thing, most families could never hope to pay full price at any college their kids might choose to attend. It's important to understand the detailed rules that govern how college financial aid works, and use your knowledge of them to plan a strategy for your overall finances. Furthermore, making sure you are regularly saving towards your own retirement must come first. You can always get a college loan, but it's not so easy to get a "retirement loan."

- **Retirement Planning.** Most young parents with young children cannot realistically envision a retirement that awaits them 35 or more years ahead. You also can't see the peak of the Himalayas when you start out to climb them from the bottom, yet if you have any hope of getting there alive, you'll have begun preparations for your trip years in advance – relying on what you can learn about the equipment you'll need, the weather conditions you might encounter, and a host of other mental, physical, and fiscal preparations. So you must start your retirement climb now.

- **Special-Needs Trusts, Other Trusts, and Estate Planning.** It probably won't be hard to convince you to write a will if you are going to climb the Himalayas, but even if the riskiest thing you plan to do is commute back and forth to work, you should still develop an estate plan now. All you need ask yourself is how bad things can be for your survivors if you don't. Furthermore, if your child has any special problems that would be unmanageable if you were to die, then you should set up a special-needs trust to ensure the proper care is provided.

8 • Financial Planning

Even More on Financial Planning
(Including What a Good Plan Looks Like)

- **Financial Planning Case Study for the Samples** –
  www.managedcapital.com/financial-planning

- **Middle-Income Financial Planning** –
  www.bankrate.com/brm/news/pf/20010314b.asp

- **MetLife "Map Out a Financial Strategy"** –
  www.metliferesources.com/PDF_Directory/19-022601Map_Out_Fly.pdf

- **My Financial Planning Guide** –
  http://instant.pair.com/financialplanning/finplanprocess

- **Sound Money Planning At Life Stages** –
  www.soundmindinvesting.com/vsection/v_newsletter/0201/feature

- **Get a Financial Life: Personal Finance in Your Twenties and Thirties** –
  (Kobliner, Simon & Schuster, June 2000)

Planning for Your Children and Unique Family Circumstances

Okay, so you weren't planning on this financial planning diversion from this book's focus on kids and money, but it was both necessary and germane. Think about the flight-attendant's little safety lesson prior to takeoff, in which he instructs you about what to do if there's a loss of cabin pressure: "First put on your own oxygen mask and then put on your kids' masks." In other words, if you don't have the proper flow of oxygen (money) for yourself, then you might lose consciousness (financial control) and be unable to properly help your child breathe freely (not struggle to have their basic financial needs met). Put another way, without a sound financial plan, your best-laid plans for raising kids may never come to fruition.

MONEY

8 • Financial Planning

But now it's time to resume our focus on your children. In this final section of the book's final chapter, we'll look at some specific financial-planning issues involving kids moving toward independence and kids in families that don't have the stereotypical happily-ever-after first marriage and 2.3 kids. However, it will be some time until most readers are dealing with kids on the verge of independence, and the issues that involve them and "non-standard" families are quite complex. So rather than covering them inadequately, we'll present the issues and provide some resources you can use to learn more if they're applicable to your situation.

Financial Relationships Between Parents and Late-Teen/Adult Children

Children who've reached their pre-teens are in the decided minority if they're not striving for increasing independence every minute. That's as it should be, but they might not be so eager to assume financial independence in the form of having to live on annual clothing allowances you establish for them, or not being able to go to all the concerts they'd like to or buy every new CD. Don't let your natural desire to slow their move to independence make you soft on the financial issues in (perhaps) a subconscious attempt to keep them closer to you for a longer time. Here's a look at issues involving their transition to full independence.

When Children Start Driving

Teens want to have their own cars, and if you do the right thing and don't automatically just give them one, many will be willing to raise the money by working many more hours weekly than what a good high school student can manage and still maintain health. And some teens will place a much higher priority on the independence the car gives them over their academic performance – even to the extent of going from being a good student to one failing several classes.

8 • Financial Planning

Depending on your child's academic capabilities and goals, it's important that you help your child look at the big picture of college admissions, whether it's really wise to be so single-minded about car ownership and independence, instead of working fewer hours and having time to apply for outside tax-free scholarships, etc. Try to work out an arrangement that allows her to earn a considerable amount towards buying a used car and paying for some of the insurance, but leaving sufficient time for academics, even if it means going a little further in helping out towards the car than you might have wanted to do.

Help for Parents Who Want to Help Their Children Buy Cars

- **Parent's Primer: When Your Teen Works: Is Your Teen Safe on The Job** – www.nclnet.org/kidprime

- **Teens Try to Juggle Worlds of High School and Work** – http://cjonline.com/stories/032701/tee_workingteens

When Children Enter College or Full-Time Employment

All your scrimping, saving, and careful financial planning can go down the drain if your child goes off to college and handles finances disastrously by running up enormous credit-card charges. In addition, many kids who are given substantial financial-aid grants don't realize that they come with academic-performance standards. If they don't meet them, then that lost several thousand free dollars will now have to be made up with additional loans. The answer is that college shouldn't be a quantum leap in independence from high school. By giving your child increasing independence, you'll be able to observe how well he handles it and possibly help him be better prepared for total independence in college.

8 • Financial Planning

Help for Parents Who Want to Help Their Children Make the Leap

- **Transition to College: Separation and Change for Parents and Students** – www.aboutourkids.org/articles/transition

- **Easing the Transition from High School to College** – www.imdiversity.com/villages/african/Article_Detail.asp?Article_ID=5817

- **Bringing Home The Laundry: Effective Parenting for College and Beyond** (Janis Brody)

When Children Graduate From College (Or Don't Go)

During the 90s, college graduates couldn't establish themselves independently soon enough after getting a degree that led to multiple lucrative job offers. Now, however, that space under their parents' roof is far more attractive, given that the free rent will leave them some spending money from their fast-food-heaven paychecks. Times might be tougher, but parents can't afford to be overly soft should their children return to the nest after graduation. Some amount of rent should be assessed, and kids should have to pitch in fiscally to pay the food bill, and physically to keep up the house.

 ## Tips for Parents with Adult Children in the Nest

- **Have a frank discussion with your child about his plan** for staying at home. Does he have specific objectives, such as waiting for particular opportunities to become available and not wanting to move until they do, or trying to save money? Does he have a time frame in mind? Use this discussion to determine if staying at home is part of a well-conceived strategy leading towards independence. Be wary if not, because once he's back in, it's hard to get him out.

- **Set the ground rules in advance**, rather than making them up as you go along. Your child is now an adult "loved tenant" who should not be subject to curfews, etc. – provided that he doesn't disrupt the household. Make sure you're okay with this and with the effect it will have on you, your spouse, and other children to have him back home.

8 • Financial Planning

- **Treat your child's return as a business arrangement** and formalize it in writing. Determine rent and responsibilities based on analyzing how your child's presence will affect grocery and utility bills, insurance, etc. There's nothing wrong with subsidizing him a bit with "below-market" rent, but make sure he's paying enough to feel it. Make sure the agreement has specific consequences should your child fail to live up to its terms – such as a late fee for rent.

- **Offer help in getting your child moving toward his goals** (e.g. suggestions on polishing the resume, and helping in the job hunt by reading online job classifieds), but don't let that help enable him to slack off on his responsibilities. Of course, your child might remain at home because she chose not go to college, chose to attend college or other career-training education locally, or chose to work locally. The way you should handle these cases is less clear-cut, because your child will be in that "tween" stage just shy of adulthood. If you were going to help pay for your child to go away to college, then you shouldn't penalize her for staying at home. Rather than charge rent, you might want your child to pay for any excessive bills due to remaining at home – such as high phone bills, or party food and beverages. Once your child reaches the age at which she'd normally graduate from college, you can then switch to some version of the rules, rent, etc. discussed above for a child returning home after college.

When Children Move Out of The House

If you've taught your children well, their transition into adult life on their own should be minimally painful. They'll know how to budget and choose lodging that will comfortably fit their finances. They'll know about how to buy a car and finance it intelligently. And they'll be faced with mostly student-loan debt, having avoided the kind of college credit-card debt that now burdens so many young adults. Nevertheless, you still can help your adult children in a number of ways (without cramping their style – or yours).

MONEY

8 • Financial Planning

Even Well-Adjusted Young Adults Need Help

- **Evaluating and Comparing Job Offers.** You can help your child go beyond the salaries offered and accurately value the outright benefits such as insurance coverage and the relocation package, as well as the potential benefits of 401(k) matching, flexible spending accounts, etc. As part of this, make sure that he leaves no gaps in crucial coverage such as health insurance. For example, if he plans to move before his job starts, he might not be covered by your family policy in the interim and will have to buy a short-term "stop-gap" policy.

- **Arranging the Move.** Hiring a moving company that offers good value and good service is challenging enough for adults who've done it two or three times. And some kids balk at the cost and put themselves in possible peril by renting pull-along storage to attach to their cars. Help them determine what makes the most sense. For example, an accident while towing belongings can increase insurance rates for the next few years far more than the cost of paying a moving company. If need be, you might consider making a small loan to help with moving expenses and perhaps an apartment deposit.

- **Establishing a Financial Infrastructure.** Your guidance could be useful in helping your child determine where to bank or how to go about finding an insurance broker. You can also help him learn to screen all the unwanted attention he'll be getting from financial salespeople. In addition, offer to assist in establishing a record-keeping system for all financial matters that will serve him well throughout his life.

- **Repaying Student Loans.** Your child faces a dizzying array of options such as consolidation of different loans, various payback schedules, and interest-only (deferred principal) payments. He might welcome your efforts to help make sense of them.

- **Filing Taxes.** Do whatever possible to convince your child that he shouldn't hire help to do his tax returns. Whether he uses a computer program or does it by hand, if your assistance ensures that he files it himself, you'll have gone a long way in helping him develop an attitude of involvement with his finances.

8 • Financial Planning

Should You Help Adult Children Financially?

Once your child has established himself as an independent adult, it might seem that your role in providing financial support and education is over for good, and if you're from the "old-school" mindset, it is. But many parents see no reason why their kids should have to wait as long to afford such family "essentials" as a new minivan or SUV, or a house – particularly if parents can comfortably afford to help their children. However, just as it's a mistake to give younger children everything they want as soon as they want it, it's often harmful to consistently help adult children financially.

 Guidelines for Helping Adult Children Financially

- **What.** If it's not for something major, sensible, important and lasting, forget it. Don't finance your kids' cruises or other vacations, purchase of a new car when they're single and a used one will do as well, or lavish honeymoon. But if you can help with the down payment on a house, then you might want to structure an incentive deal that will match part of what they save for a down payment, closing costs, and planned repairs and maintenance.

- **How.** In most cases, you're better off loaning money rather than just giving it. You can always decide later to forgive part of the loan outright as a gift, or to forgive part of it as an incentive for expedited repayment. Don't worry that your attitude might lead your kids to go elsewhere for the money – such as rolling up credit card debt for groceries. If that happens, then your help would have just made things worse. Alternatively, your child's pride might cause them to look for more expensive commercial personal loans than you would provide, and it might concern you that they're paying more interest than necessary. So be it, the extra they pay is investment in a valuable lesson of self-sufficiency and restraint.

8 • Financial Planning

- **Special Circumstances.** Sometimes your child might get into financial trouble through no fault of her own – perhaps incurring major uninsured health expenses, or getting "screwed" in a divorce settlement, or losing a job in a tough employment market. If your child has been truly responsible and you're able to help her avoid bankruptcy or foreclosure in such a situation, it's worth doing because bankruptcy has such long-range, negative effects. However, don't bail your child out of bankruptcy if clear foolishness or financial excess caused it. As painful as it will be to watch, bankruptcy is a lesson in humility that irresponsible adult children need.

Special Family Situations

Believing that bankruptcy is undesirable, we don't wish to have readers find this book bankrupt of advice for families that don't consist of middle (including upper and lower) class couples who've remained married and (plan to) have two or more "blood children." Families who don't fit that mold are actually in the majority today, so let's take a look at how you might adapt some of what we've covered if yours is such an "atypical" family.

Splintered Families

Families with unmarried-together, unmarried-apart, separated, divorced, or remarried parents all fall into this category. Because of the circumstances surrounding such families, parents might feel that they can't be as open about the family financial situation; they might fear doing so necessitates discussion of child support, alimony, welfare, and similar emotionally charged money matters. Yet consider the alternatives: children's inevitable exposure to arguments, tensions, and problems such as failure to send support checks, or parents trying to outdo each other with excessive gifts to win kids' favor.

Obviously, you don't want blunt, unpleasant information about financial realities to further overwhelm children who are already emotionally burdened. But you're also doing yourself and them a disservice if you try to shield them from realities. Instead, carefully feed them information about your financial circumstances over time, based on their age, maturity, need to know, and likelihood they'll find out anyway. In the end, kids who've made it through such adversity with your loving support and their eyes wide open might be better prepared than their traditional-family peers to deal with the financial vicissitudes of life.

8 • Financial Planning

What to Tell the Kids

- **Single Parent.** If thriving in this status requires some governmental assistance, such as food stamps, don't hide it from your child as though it's shameful. Point out that we're lucky enough to have such government programs – unlike earlier times (before antibiotics) when parent mortality was high and single parents were dependent on the generosity of neighbors and religious institutions. In fact, you can use this as an educational experience by teaching your child about "hidden" government benefits such as the Earned Income Tax Credit that is so valuable to single parents.

- **Divorced Parents.** Do you want to give your child a dual physics/fiscal lesson? Then explain how splitting the atom might create energy gain, but splitting the nuclear family definitely causes economic loss. The joint economic resources of two parents simply can't stretch as well to cover two separate rents or mortgages and the associated upkeep. If you and your spouse kept that in mind in coming to an equitable settlement that put the kids' interests first, don't hesitate to point that out. It can go a long way to easing the pain of some deprivation caused by the divorce, and is a fascinating financial lesson to boot.

- **Blended Families.** It's particularly important for parents in these situations to give their children the straight scoop. You'll not only be setting them straight about the financial circumstances of your own divorce and remarriage, but also counteracting all the false or incomplete information they'll inevitably get from step-family members about the financial circumstances surrounding your ex-spouse.

8 • Financial Planning

Families with "Special" Children

Families with children who have special care needs, life-threatening or chronic illnesses, or physical, mental, or emotional disabilities fall into this category. It also includes adopted children, many of whom have special needs. Such families almost always incur unusually high medical, caretaker, or administrative expenses beyond what's covered in insurance plans, adoption-assistance programs, or adoption tax breaks. These financial burdens not only inevitably weigh on the family's other children, whose comfortable phase of life often come to an abrupt halt, but they often cause the family itself to collapse.

Resources for Families with Special Needs Children

- **How to Make Adoption an Affordable Option**
  (76-page online booklet by NEFE) –
  www.nefe.org/adoption/

- **Families with Special Needs Children:**
  A Financial Guide for the Perplexed –
  www.leimberg.com

- **Article on Estate Planning for Special-Needs Children** –
  www.bankrate.com

- **Article on Financial Planning for Special-Needs Families** –
  www.insurance.com

- **Ordinary Families, Special Children:**
  A Systems Approach to Childhood Disability
  (M. Seligman & R. Darling, New York: Guilford Press, 1997).

8 • Financial Planning

Families That March to Different Drummers

This final category encompasses families whose demographic, socio-economic or political characteristics, or unusual parental backgrounds, gives them outside-the-mainstream perspectives on money. They might be "graduates" (or survivors) of a "hippie" commune, social activists who believe it's better to help others than indulge beyond meeting basic needs, people who enjoy the basic pleasures of life and would rather live simply than pursue the rat race, or traditionalists who feel a mother's place is in the home and only boys should be educated and prepared to work outside the home as adults. Or maybe they're unusually wealthy or have overcome severe discrimination or the hardships of immigration to become financially successful.

If you have any of these family types, your background and beliefs are likely to strongly affect the way you teach children about money. You obviously have the right to raise children (within reasonable limits) as you see fit. However, you should consider whether your philosophies are guiding what you teach them in a way that might make it difficult for them to adapt if they should choose to live their lives differently.

 ### *A Few Considerations for Different Drummers*

- **If you swim strongly** against the consumerist tide, you might not do enough to prepare your child to make intelligent decisions should they later buy the things you never purchased.

- **If you live modestly** because you're so charitably inclined, you might fail to teach your child enough about saving and investing so that they'll do it well enough to be able to give away lots more money by becoming wealthier.

- **Girls raised to believe they'll be homemakers** might be deprived of acquiring necessary earning power should their husbands die, become disabled, or disappear.

8 • Financial Planning

- **If you and your spouse each worked two or more jobs** to provide opportunities for your children, you might exert undue pressure on children to become professionally and financially successful. The same might be true if you've become wealthy from untiring entrepreneurial efforts. Your example alone should be a strong positive influence, so consider easing up just a bit on your expectations of them.

- **If you're affluent**, it'll be hard for your children's views about money to not be affected by your lifestyle. You can turn this into a positive by teaching your children that wealth not only confers privilege but demands responsibility to use money well and for good.

A Few Resources for Different Drummer Families (or for Those Looking to Join Their Ranks)

- **An Odyssey into Frugality: How I Became a Miserly Mom** – www.thelaboroflove.com/forum/miserlymoms/1

- **Better Living Through Austerity** – www.business2.com/articles/mag/0,1640,7129,00

- **Unspoiled Little Rich Kids** – www.kiplinger.com/magazine/archives/2000/December/managing/RICHKIDS1

Of course, in some ways, we all march to different drummers, while joining together as parents in the same parade towards our children's future happiness, health, and success. We hope this book has been the parade band's music in your ears in helping your child march financially forward.

Appendices

Baby Budget

How much does the first year cost?

Use this worksheet to help you determine how much your baby will cost in the first year. If you prefer, you can use it online at www.teenageparent.org/english/costofbaby2B.html.

Enter how many of each item you think you will need, then total it up. Can you think of other items that you will need in the baby's first year? Doctor visits, toys, etc.? If so, add these to your total. And if you're having twins (or more!) don't forget to multiply your figures accordingly, especially for Nursery Items, Health/Safety Items, Diapers, Food and Clothing, and even Additional Items such as Toys.

Note: All figures used for calculating the costs of raising a baby for a year are based on average prices from three discount chain stores. You may find prices near you to be slightly higher or lower.

Before Baby Arrives

1. Monthly check-ups with the doctor for pre-natal care($1,500.00): ....$_____

2. Prenatal vitamins! ($15.00 for one month's supply.): $15.00 x _____ (months) = $_____

3. Hospital ($5,000.00): ....$_____

4. Infant car seat to take the baby home from the hospital.
(You can't leave without one!) ($45.00): ....$_____

Sub Total: $_____

Appendix A

Nursery Items

5. Crib ($100.00 each): ....$_____
6. Crib mattress ($45.00 each): ....$_____
7. Crib sheets ($10.00 set): ....$_____
8. Crib blankets ($10.00 each): ....$_____
9. Crib mattress pad ($7.76 each): ....$_____
10. Receiving blanket ($2.98 each): ....$_____
11. Crib mobile ($14.95 each): ....$_____
12. Crib activity center ($12.57 each): ....$_____
13. Changing table ($89.00 each): ....$_____
14. Changing table pad ($8.00 each): ....$_____
15. Cradle or bassinette ($80.00 each): ....$_____

Sub Total: $_____

Health /Safety Items

(Remember, you are buying these for an entire year!)

16. Hairbrush and comb for the baby ($6.87 each): ....$6.87 x 2 = $_____
17. Digital thermometer ($10.27 each): ....$_____
18. Various items for babys feeling under the weather:
    Humidifier/vaporizer ($35.42 each): ....$_____
    Nasal aspirator ($2.01 each): ....$_____
    Medicine dropper ($1.97 each): ....$_____
19. Toothbrush. ($ .89 each): ....$_____
20. Baby monitor, so you can hear when the baby is crying ($25.00 each): ....$_____
21. Do you have stairs in your house? If so, you'll need stairway
    gate(s) to protect the baby from falling down the stairs
    ($9.96 each): ....$9.96 x _____ (stairways) = $_____
22. Drawer latches ($ .13 each): ....$.13 x _____ (latches) = $_____
    and outlet plug covers ($ .09 each): ....$.09 x _____ (outlets) = $_____
23. Baby bathtub ($14.39 each): ....$_____
24. Baby washcloths ($ .79 each) (Don't forget to get enough for when
    you haven't had time to do the laundry!): ....$.79 x _____ (washcloths) = $_____
25. Bathtub ring ($8.96 each): ....$_____
    and faucet protector(s) ($2.00 each): ....$_____

26. Hooded towel(s) to keep the baby warm
after the bath ($6.00 each): ....$6.00 x _____ (hooded towells) = $_____

27. Additional items for good hygene:
Baby soap ($2.77 each): ....$_____
Baby lotion ($2.81 each): ....$_____
Baby powder ($2.00 each): ....$_____
Baby oil ($2.80 each): ....$_____
Diaper rash ointment ($3.50 each): ....$_____

28. Multiple boxes of laundry detergent
for baby clothes! (Hint - About 2 a month!)
($4.89 each): ....$4.89 x _____ (boxes of detergent) = $_____

Sub Total: $_____

Diapers

(Remember, you are buying for a year!)

29. Disposable diapers.
(Hint - you will use about 75 diapers a
week and about 320 diapers a month)
($ .30 each): ....$.30 x _____ (diapers) = $_____

30. Even if you are using disposables, cloth
diapers come in handy as burp/spit towels!
Buy a few dozen to keep on hand.
($12.00 per dozen): ....$12.00 x _____ (dozens of cloth diapers) = $_____

31. Baby wipes (Hint - you will
use about 2 boxes a month.) ($2.97 each): ....$2.97 x _____ (boxes) = $_____

32. Diaper bag ($15.00 each): ....$_____

33. Cloth diapers
(if you choose to use them instead of disposables).
(Hint - You should have at least 3 dozen clean diapers on hand).
($12.00 per dozen): ....$12.00 x _____ (dozens of diapers) = $_____

34. Diaper pail ($17.95 each): ....$_____

35. Diaper cover(s) ($1.59 each): ....$1.59 x _____ (diaper covers) = $_____

Sub Total: $_____

Appendix A

Feeding Baby

(Remember, you are buying for a year!)

If you plan on breast-feeding –

36. Breast pump (if you plan on nursing
    while you are in school or working). ($24.98 each): .... $_____

37. Nursing pad(s)
    (Hint - about 3-4 a day.) ($ .58 each): ....$.58 x _____ (pads) = $_____

38. Nursing bra(s). (Hint – you will need extras
    because of how quickly they need to be laundered!)
    ($14.00 each): ....$14.00 x _____ (bras) = $_____

39. Pacifier(s). (Better buy a few extra -
    for the ones that end up getting misplaced.)
    ($1.34 each): ....$1.34 x _____ (pacifiers) = $_____

40. Pacifier holder ($1.76 each): ....$_____

If you plan on using formula –

41. Cans of formula. (Hint – you will use 7-8 a week and
    about 32 a month.) ($3.65 each): ....$3.65 x _____ (cans of formula) = $_____

42. Wipes (Hint - about two
    packages per month.) ($2.97 per package): ....$2.97 x _____ (packages) = $_____

43. 4 oz. bottles. (Don't forget to get enough to allow
    for breakage and spares.) ($ .99 each): ....$.99 x _____ (bottles) = $_____

44. 8 oz bottles. (Don't forget to get enough to
    allow for breakage and spares.) ($1.65 each): ....$1.65 x _____ (bottles) = $_____

45. Bottle brush to clean glass bottles ($2.00 each): ....$_____

46. Plastic bottle inserts (if you plan on using them instead of glass).
    (Hint – about four boxes per month.)
    ($3.43 per box): ....$3.43 x _____ (boxes of inserts) = $_____

47. Nipple(s) for the bottles. These are in addition
    to your bottles! ($ .30 each): ....$.30 x _____ (nipples) = $_____

                                                    Sub Total: $_____

Congratulations!

The good news is your baby is getting bigger and more independent. The bad news is there are more expenses involved!

48. Toddler car seat ($55.00): ....$_____

49. Baby food. (Hint - Babies begin on solid foods at
about 6 months.) ($ .47 each):.....................$.47 x _____ (jars of baby food) = $_____

50. High chair ($47.00 each): ....$_____

51. Childproof plates and bowls
($3.96 each): ....$3.96 x _____ (plates and bowls) = $_____

52. Infant spoons ($ .94 each): ....$.94 x _____ (spoons) = $_____

53. Cloth bibs ($2.75 each): ....$2.75 x _____ (cloth bibs) = $_____

54. Plastic bibs ($1.96 each): ....$1.96 x _____ (plastic bibs) = $_____

55. No-spill cups ($1.73 each): ....$1.73 x _____ (cups) = $_____

Sub Total: $_____

Clothing

(Remember, you are buying for a year!)

56. Sleepers ($4.95 each): ....$4.95 x _____ (sleepers) = $_____

57. Hats ($2.78 each): ....$2.78 x _____ (hats) = $_____

58. Booties ($2.39 pair): ....$2.39 x _____ (pairs of booties) = $_____

59. Gowns ($6.00 each): ....$6.00 x _____ (gowns) = $_____

60. Outfit ($12.00 each): ....$12.00 x _____ (outfits) = $_____

61. Socks ($2.48 pair): ....$2.48 x _____ (pairs of socks) = $_____

62. Coats ($24.00 each): ....$24.00 x _____ (coats) = $_____

63. Warm suits ($18.00 each): ....$18.00 x _____ (warm suits) = $_____

64. Shirts ($6.45 each): ....$6.45 x _____ (shirts) = $_____

65. Pants ($9.18 each): ....$9.18 x _____ (pairs of pants) = $_____

Sub Total: $_____

Appendix A

Additional Items

Not necessary items, but they sure make life easier!

66. Carrier ($40.00 each): ....$_____

67. Stroller ($48.00 each): ....$_____

68. Play yard ($60.00): ....$_____

69. Extra diaper bag ($15.00 each): ....$_____

70. Swing ($80.00 each): ....$_____

71. Doorway jumper ($20.00 each): ....$_____

72. Small toys ($8.00 each): ....$8.00 x _____ (toys) = $_____

73. Books ($3.00 each): ....$3.00 x _____ (books) = $_____

74. Baby pictures ($30.00 each): ....$30.00 x _____ (sets of pictures) = $_____

75. Yard toys ($48.00 each): ....$_____

Sub Total: $_____

Add up all the Sub Totals from each category above:

Grand Total: $_____

This is a brief insight into the costs of having a baby. You might not need all of the items listed, but this is the "recommended" shopping list for new parents. There are also additional costs not listed, like going to the doctor, etc.

How much money would you need to earn a hour, a week, a month to be able to afford a child?

(The worksheet is provided courtesy of Idaho Public Television and The Idaho Department of Health and Welfare, from a program entitled "Life in the Fast Lane," which deals with teen-pregnancy issues.)

Appendix A

Talk about Money Worksheet

(This worksheet is provided courtesy of Iowa State Extension Service.)

Directions: Family members should answer these questions separately, then compare answers. Use the similarities and differences to guide discussion of family money attitudes and practices.

1. If you received $5,000 tax free, what would you do with it?

$ _____ for _____

$ _____ for _____

$ _____ for _____

$ _____ for _____

$ _____ for _____

$ _____ for _____

2. Rank the following activities, using **1** to indicate what you would enjoy doing most and **6** to indicate what you would enjoy least.

_____ an evening at home with the family _____ a night on the town

_____ a few extra hours on the job _____ involvement in physical activity

_____ spending time with friends _____ some quiet time to myself

3. If you had to make a major cut in your current spending, what area would you cut first?

_____

4. Do you agree (A) or disagree (D) with the following statements? (Circle one).

A – D I'm basically too tight with money.

A – D My spouse is basically too tight with money.

A – D Equality in family decision making is important to me.

A – D I feel good about the way financial decisions are made in my family.

A – D Sometimes I buy things I don't need just because they're on sale.

A – D I believe in enjoying today and letting tomorrow worry about itself.

5. I'd like to see us spend less money on:

_____

and see more dollars go for:

_____

6. What money problem is the most frequent cause of argument?

_____

7. What was the most sensible thing you've done with money since marriage?

_____

The most foolish?

_____

8. Do you know the dollar figures that go in the following blanks?
Family take-home income $ _____
Rent or mortgage payment $ _____
Money spent on food each month $ _____
Monthly car payment $ _____

9. Buying on credit is:

_____

Government Resources

U.S. Treasury
www.treas.gov/kids
Your kids might not treasure every game the U.S. government Treasury department offers them. But they can also learn about our money history and acquire some money trivia.

IRS
www.irs.gov/individuals/display/
0,,i1=1&genericId=15548,00
Amazingly, the Internal Revenue Service won't tax you or your patience here. But it will help your kids learn and understand taxes. They can find out how much they will actually get if they have a job and how much gets paid in taxes, what the taxes pay for, and how taxes work when you start your own business.

U.S. Mint
www.usmint.gov/kids/index.cfm?Filecontents=/
kids/games
Jump into the colorful and splashy graphics and find a number of games and activities about money that aren't as interesting as they look, but are still worth trying out with your young kids.

Illinois Treasury
http://state.il.us/treas/Education/BASplans
This is a lesson plan of financial basics for meant for schools starting with "What is Money?" and continuing through saving, work, credit, and loans. The lesson plan includes activities and homework.

U.S. Securities and Exchange Commission (SEC)
www.sec.gov/investor/students/tips
Parents or teachers who want their kids to know about saving and investing will find explanations and examples of how interest, stocks, and accounts work. Also see the sections on credit management and how to achieve financial security. In addition, this area (www.sec.gov/investor/tools/quiz) contains a ten-question quiz about investments. Whether you get an answer right or wrong, you get a clear and understandable explanation after you answer.

Federal Consumer Information Center
www.pueblo.gsa.gov/cic_text/children/
kcpy/kcpy.txt)
Many parents want to make sure they are teaching their kids the right lessons about money, but they're not sure about it themselves. If you fit this description, read the information on this site. It explains what you should teach your kids about money and how you should act in front of your kids in order to set a good example for them.

U.S. Federal Trade Commission (FTC)
www.ftc.gov/bcp/conline/pubs/young/realdeal
"The Real Deal" is an activity book for kids. It includes games and other activities meant to teach kids about being a good consumer. The site has more information and tells how to order.

Social Security Administration
www.ssa.gov/kids
Ok, your kids might have green hair, but certainly not gray hair (yet!). Nevertheless, they're soon going to be paying for it, so they should learn about Social Security. For kids, this site uses animals to teach about what social security does. For teens, there's more information and games for learning. Parents and teachers can also find information to educate themselves and their kids.

Federal Reserve (Kansas City) "FED 101"
www.kc.frb.org/fed101
If they absorb everything they'll find here, your kids will soon know more about what Alan Greenspan does than middle-age stock-ticker addicts who watch CNBC all day.

Appendix B

Federal Reserve (Boston)
"Peanuts and Crackerjacks"
www.bos.frb.org/peanuts/leadpgs/intro
Sports-loving kids can learn the concepts of money in relation to sports with a "Sports Page." After reading it, they can play a baseball game with nine "innings," each starting after they've finished the previous one by answering questions about money.

U.S. Treasury Savings Bonds
www.savingsbond.gov/sav/savkids
These words are their (savings) bonds – literally. With word scramble and word search games, your kids can learn about the most popular way to loan Uncle Sam money, and eventually get double back.

Non-Profit/Non-Commercial Organizations, Educational Institutions

Kids' Money
www.kidsmoney.org
Just like you can find valuable old things in the attic, you can find valuable "old" articles and other educational materials on this web site that doesn't appear to have been updated for the last few years. Your eyes will tire before you get through all the great ideas about allowance, earning money, and other financial matters relating to your kids. There's also a store where you can buy games, videos, and workbooks to help teach your kids about money – but make sure it's still in operation before committing your cash.

Junior Achievement Entrepreneurship and Personal Finance
www.ja.org
JA is the long-time most successful program for getting kids involved hands-on in learning about business and entrepreneurship, and applying what they learn. Start by checking out the programs for various age groups (www.ja.org/programs/programs). Then explore Junior Achievement's new personal-finance program (www.japersonalfinance.com/gsjapf/welcome) where your child can find out how much she already knows about money, use the financial calculators, and do the activities for understanding credit, budgeting, saving, and more.

National Endowment for Financial Education
www.nefe.org/pages/collaborativeyouth
NEFE sponsors a great, free High School Financial Planning Program (HSFPP) that currently serves 500,000 students in about 6,000 schools nationwide. This portion of the NEFE web site has online brochures and booklets published jointly with many non-profit organizations, such as Boy Scouts and Girl Scouts, to teach kids about money. They include lessons and activities for learning fundamentals of money – some geared to particular age ranges. You can also find information on how to order some booklets directly from organizations, including some from the Scouts that enable kids to earn merit badges and other awards. Don't stop here, though; make sure to check out all that NEFE has to offer, including the possibility that your creative, financially literate high-schooler might be a candidate for the High School Financial Literacy Awards Program (www.nefe.org/hsfla) sponsored by NEFE. This annual contest allows students to create a project based on a theme having to do with responsible financial decisions. Contestants have a chance of winning up to $5,000.

National Institute for Consumer Education (NICE)
www.nice.emich.edu/child1
How nice that University of Michigan provides this mini-lesson that includes detailed information on what each child age group should be learning about money and how you should be teaching it. Then check out other areas of the web site to find a variety of inexpensive educational materials you can order.

Appendix B

University of Missouri (St. Louis) Wise Pockets World

www.umsl.edu/~wpockets

If your kids have a pocket full of "why's this?" and "why's that?" about money, then let the "Wise Pockets" characters regale them with stories about earning, borrowing, and lending. Wise parents will also take advantage of financial lessons and activities that they can work on with their kids.

EconEdLink

www.econedlink.org

This non-profit National Council of Economics Education site provides ready-made online lessons and a place to make your own lessons. It also has a list of links to other web sites with lessons and activities, and has a section for learning about current economic events.

Jump Start Coalition

www.jumpstartcoalition.org

You'll jump for joy at all the materials here that help kids and teens to become financially literate. You'll find a list of 12 principles about money everyone should know, in a calendar format, and an extensive collection of downloads including budget sheets, worksheets, and surveys. This worksheet/calculator (www.jumpstart.org/madmoney/pgv_money_rc_form) enables kids who think they're ready to live on their own to fill in the types of things they spend money on and the calculator tells how much money they must make to live like that. Your kids might be shocked at how much it is.

Money Management International

www.moneymanagement.org

This great adult learning tool starts with pretests and questionnaires and goes step-by-step through money management (www.moneymanagement.org/Members/Workbooks/MoneyAndCredit.pdf). It includes worksheets and lessons to learn about credit and savings and finishes with a post-lesson test. Continue with these great lesson plans (www.moneymanagement.org/Education/Resources) for teachers of kids from 3-6 years old, which parents can print and use too. They feature characters from favorite book series such as the Berenstein Bears and American Girls. Each month brings a new lesson, with many already in the hopper to choose from.

National Council On Economic Education's "It All Adds Up"

www.italladdsup.org

This is a great site for your kids if they're getting ready to go to college. It has sections on college, investing, credit, and budgeting. They can learn a lot from the interesting games.

National Council of Economics Education's "The Mint"

www.themint.org

Are you looking for money-related games and quizzes for kids, plus lessons about making budgets and investing? Find them here, along with information on government spending and how kids will end up making more money by going to college.

University of Arkansas

This self-study course will teach you money management so you can teach it to your kids (www.arfamilies.org/money/children&money/dollars_and_cents_for_youth). Topics include allowance, child spending, and countering persuasive advertising. In addition, your kids can learn directly using this lesson (www.kidsarus.org/money) on how and where to get money, saving, spending, and sharing.

Appendix B

Future Business Leaders of America
www.fbla-pbl.org
Encourage your middle or high school kids to become part of the FBLA-Phi Beta Lambda at school. They'll learn about leadership and participate in conferences and competitions.

National Academy of Finance
www.naf.org/curriculum/description/cd_aof
If your child is interested in a business career, find out if your school district has, or is willing to adopt, the National Academy of Finance curriculum. The courses are described here, and also consult the National Academy Foundation site map (www.naf.org/sitemap) for related information.

Entrepreneurship Education Consortium
www.entre-ed.org/criteria
If you have an independent-minded child who always seems to be coming up with ideas for making money, encourage it; share this information with her on what it takes to become a successful entrepreneur, and check out the entire web site (www.entre-ed.org) for entrepreneurship resources.

Zillions
www.zillions.org
If your kids want zillions of things, then here are zillions of things they can learn about being smarter and less needy consumers. Click on the apple icon to go to an education section with a bunch of additional resources, including lesson plans to be used in conjunction with **Consumer Reports** magazine.

Consumer Jungle
www.consumerjungle.org
It might not turn your child into the king of the financial jungle, but this is a good place for kids to start thinking about money in their future. There are sections on credit, living on your own, phones, cars, and the internet. For each section there are downloads, activities, and tests to see how much you know.

Institute of Consumer Financial Education
www.financial-education-icfe.org/children_and_money
Trying to think of an easy way to lay down the simple rules of finance for your kids? Show them the "10 Commandments of Personal Finance For Young People in 2002" (www.financial-education-icfe.org/children_and_money/10_commandments_of_personal_finance). Then check out the other articles for kids, parents, and Grandparents about credit, allowances, spending, and more.

Financial Literacy Guide for Students
www.unr.edu/sb204/fls
This portion of the University of Nevada, Reno site has tutorials about credit ("Credit is Due"), buying a car ("Wheel Deals"), and saving money ("Saving Grace")

National Council on Economic Education's Financial Fitness for Life
http://fffl.ncee.net
This program, for kids from Kindergarten to 12th grade, is meant to teach them everything they need to know about money in a fun way. This site has an overview for each grade level and the program can be purchased online.

Foundation for Teaching Economics
www.fte.org
The FTE offers programs for rising high school seniors to learn about economics. Sample schedules and teacher lesson plans are available online.

Financial Literacy 2010
www.fl2010.org
This project promotes financial literacy by teaching teachers so students can learn in school. Its quarterly newsletter, also published on the site, includes articles about current financial literacy in high schools across the nation and about the negative consequences of financial illiteracy.

Aid Association for Lutherans "Rock The Cause"
www.aal.org/LifeResources/Youth_Resources/Rock_The_Cause
This is a great game. Kids get a credit balance and put on concerts to raise money for charity. Depending on the decisions they make, they can get into debt or they can manage money wisely and give to charities and still have savings left over. Kids learn about managing savings and credit, as well as supporting charities.

Thinkquest ("Parent" Site)
www.thinkquest.org
If your quest is to find a place where your kids can learn about almost anything in a fun way by playing sophisticated games, quest no more! First explore the wide variety of "sub-sites" you can find from this vast site. Then have them try the financial sub-sites described below.

Thinkquest "Econopolis"
http://tqjunior.thinkquest.org/3901
Designed a little like Monopoly with different characters to guide you around, each section on the board teaches different things about money and each has a quiz at the end. This is an interesting way for kids to learn about economics and will hold their interest longer than just reading in a book.

Thinkquest "Econostocks"
http://library.thinkquest.org/16500
Whether you want to learn the history, the terms, or the math involved in economics, EconoStocks is the perfect site. The site has tutorials that cover all of these subjects, and also features articles on some of the different topics of economics such as stocks and businesses.

Thinkquest "Investing for Kids"
http://library.thinkquest.org/3096
Is it time for your kids to get started taking an interest in investing? Here, kids can learn about concepts and types of investments then take a financial quiz and find out what level they're on. After that, they can play games at their level that help them learn about investment.

Thinkquest "Market Simulation"
http://stocksquest.thinkquest.org/10326/market_simulation
Widely cited as a terrific teaching tool, this is a great game for kids who want to learn about the stock market. Your child can invest individually, as part of a group, and teachers can even have whole classrooms invest together.

Thinkquest "My Stocks"
http://stocksquest.thinkquest.org/C001759/stocksquest/mystocks.htm?tqskip=1
Here's yet another stock-market game; this one created by a teenager.

Appendix B

Financial Institution Resources

Visa Practical Money Skills
www.practicalmoneyskills.com/english/parents
Talk about striking it rich. You can find practically anything kids should know about money here, with lessons for kids of all different age groups and activities that correspond to the lessons. In addition, teachers can tap into lesson plans that go through college level. Try the budgeting and saving calculators, and the "banking tutor" guide to banking concepts and terminology, bank statements, and ATM cards. Then try Ed's bank (www.practicalmoneyskills.com/english/pop/games/p_ed_bank) and a myriad of other games. At Ed's, players collect money, put it in a piggy bank to save, and later go to the store and buy what they can afford. It teaches a good lesson about saving money in order to afford to buy things, but be careful because it does not teach how to get the money in the first place; don't let your child think that this game is like real life. If you like what you see here, you can go to www.practicalmoneyskills.com/english/consumers/index.php?cat=parents and order two good programs that families should use. "Practical Money Skills for Life CD-ROM" is a fun way for teens to learn. "How to Raise a Money Smart Child" is a booklet with topics and activities for all age groups.

Strong Funds "Strong Kids"
www.strongkids.com
If you don't want to be your family's weak link financially then bulk up with the Strong Funds "Toolbox" – which includes a "ladder," "tape measure," and "hard hat" to teach kids hard lessons about saving and investing, and ensure they know it by passing a quiz. Also check out the "library" of terms and planning calculators for college and other goals. After they have learned the information on this site, www.strong.com provides further knowledge of money matters.

Republic Bank "Cool Bank"
www.coolbank.com
Kids of all ages through high school can cool their heels while learning about money. For the younger kids, there is a "backyard" with animals that kids click on and learn the meaning of different money terms through stories involving money. For the older kids, there are more formal lessons and fun activities for learning.

Fleet Kids
www.fleetkids.com
If your kids want to make money and move to the front of the pack, "Frontyard Fortunes" will help them by taking them step by step through a variety of jobs they might want to try, showing them what they can earn and how much materials will cost. They can also earn "Kindness Coupons" to be used instead of money for jobs such as yardwork and doing the dishes. And don't overlook the games for younger kids and the learning materials and ideas on how to teach kids about money for parents and teachers.

NASDR Basics of Saving and Investing
www.nasdr.com/basics_savings
This section of the National Association of Security Dealers site has a good online financial course meant for classroom use. It includes five units (Financial Decisions, How Financial Markets Work, Investment Choices, Investment Information, and Investment Fraud) that each have lessons and worksheets; a few also have overheads.

CIBC Smart Start
http://www2.cibc.com/smartstart
It's sponsored by a major Canadian bank, but contains many financial games and activities from which U.S. kids can learn as well.

Merrill-Lynch SaveLab
www.plan.ml.com/family/kids/sheet
Four different worksheets get kids thinking about saving. They include studying your own money and savings habits, and developing new plans and interviewing family members about the way they save. These activities will make your child more conscious about what they do with money and hopefully your interview will inspire them to save.

A.G. Edwards Big Money Adventure
www.agedwards.com/public/bma/frontpage
Young kids can choose from among guides who have names such as "Gold Bullion" and "Sell-Hi" – who'll let them choose from games and other activities that teach about money. There is also an interesting story about money that let's the reader determine the outcome by choosing different paths on the way, and a stock picking game which awards prizes to winners.

Sovereign Bank "Kids Bank"
www.kidsbank.com
This is a good site for smaller children because of the characters, pictures, and easy to follow language. The characters teach your kids about money, interest, saving, and checks. It also includes a question board for kids to post questions about money and receive a real person's answers.

Citigroup
www.mpt.org/senseanddollars
So you have teenagers who think they know all they need to know about money? Send them here for great educational games that will help them learn about budgets, earning, saving, and spending. For example, this (www.mpt.org/senseanddollars/games/checkitout) is a great game to have children play if they think they're ready to go off and live on their own. It lets you choose whether you're a high school or college graduate, and then you get the corresponding monthly paycheck and bills. If you spend more than you have, you lose the game. This will show your child that living on your own isn't going to be as fun and easy as he or she imagines.

Sallie Mae
(Student Loan Marketing Association)
www.salliemae.com
From the leading source nationally of college loans, here's everything you needed to know about going into debt, intelligently, to finance college. You and your child can apply for loans – and later repay and track them online. But it's not just about debt, you'll also find information about the free portion of financial aid, scholarships and other ways to help finance your child's education. And the "Wired Scholar" area (www.salliemae.com/ws_frame.html?) goes beyond the money issues and provides tips on college selection and applications, as well as providing an online resume-posting service and job search.

Kid Stock
www.kidstock.com
Kids and their parents can learn about the economy, investing, money, and how to make money. This is a good place to find quick and understandable answers to your children's questions.

ING
www.ing-usa.com/plan/family
Are you thinking about starting a family. If you're not sure if you're prepared, check here first. There's more than a r(ING) of truth to the information on how to start off well financially, deal with taxes, and understand and choose benefits – as well as articles on whether you're ready to start a family and how much it's really going to cost you.

Appendix B

Banking On Our Future
www.bankingonourfuture.com/hope

This site has sections for kids, young teens, and high school students and adults. The kids section has an animated creature making it more interesting to learn about budgeting, credit, savings, checks, and banking. The other sections cover the same concepts, but more in depth as the level increases.

MetLife Life Advice
www.metlife.com

This section of the site (www.metlife.com/Lifeadvice/Money/Docs/kid2) gives good ideas for teaching kids about allowance, savings, and goals. It also has sample budgets for you to help your kids fill in to understand the concept of saving.

Salomon Smith Barney
www.salomonsmithbarney.com/yin/te_classroom

Have you been trying to teach your kids about investments but are not having much success? Don't give up! Show this site to your kids and it will be the last time you have to explain the meaning of terms such as stocks, bonds, and funds.

Ernst & Young Moneyopolis
www.moneyopolis.com

Here's a treasure trove for teachers, parents, and kids. For example, teens in the US save only 21% of what they earn. This lesson plan (www.moneyopolis.com/teachers/answers/teachers_lpsc) compares saving in the US versus other countries and then proceeds to have the kids analyze the differences and then hopefully learn to be better shoppers. Kids should check out the multitude of resources (www.moneyopolis.com/library/library_resources) for learning about money, to either learn themselves, or with teachers and parents. Best of all, though, is a great game for kids who can do calculations, but are still master-

ing them (www.moneyopolis.com/game/login/index). It teaches about gross and net income, fixed and variable costs and much more in easy to understand descriptions. Players answer questions, often involving math, to get to the next level. (They might need calculators.)

American Century Tips for Kids
www.tipsforkids.com/educators

For teachers who are looking for a lesson plan for their students to teach about money, this is a 10 week program whose lessons include the history of money, how money works, credit, debt, and investing.

American Banker's Association
www.aba.com/Consumer+Connection/In_Charge_Resources

You can bank on not finding any thrills and chills here, but you will find useful credit tips, stories for consumers that illustrate good and bad financial practices, and a section of activities to show your kids about money. Another section (www.aba.com/Consumer+Connection/CNC_bankers_prods) offers many videos, booklets, and kits you can order to help kids better understand money management and credit in terms they can understand. These products include videos, booklets, and kits.

Books and Online Newspapers/Magazines

Money Magazine Money Lessons
http://money.cnn.com/pf/101/lessons/12

Don't have enough time to read long articles with your busy life? Don't worry, here are the ten top things to know about kids and money. Then try the other money lessons geared to the whole family.

Kiplinger Magazine "Money Smart Kids"
www.kiplinger.com/managing/kids
This endless supply of articles by Janet Bodnar, author of Dollars and Sense for Kids, covers topics ranging from jobs and taxes to budgeting and investing. Also try the calculator to determine how much it costs to raise a child, and submit questions to Janet about kids and money.

Parenting Magazine "Family Finance"
www.parenting.com/parenting/family_finance
In addition to a wealth of articles, you'll find interesting quizzes and polls. But the real treat is the collection of calculators for determining how much money you have, if you can afford a child, and if you can afford to stay home with your child rather then return to work.

Wall Street Journal Classroom Edition (College)
www.wsjclassroomedition.com/tc_coctr
For your college kids or (even better) your almost college kids, it's time to start thinking about what college costs. This site has good information about college fees, loans, debts, and investing.

Young Money
www.youngmoney.com
Even without the subscription that gives young adults full access, they can read articles on subjects such as credit and investing, and stories about young entrepreneurs.

How to Raise Kids Without Going Broke : The Complete Financial Guide for Parents (A Smart Money Book)
by Peter Finch and Delia Marshall
As the title advertises, this book will explain how you can be a parent without spending excessive amounts of money. Some of the topics include common financial mistakes that parents make, how to choose the right bank, and how to choose the right credit cards.

Growing Money: A Complete Investing Guide for Kids
by Debbie Honig, Stephen Lewis, Gail Garlitz
This is a great book for kids who are interested in learning how to use money to make more money. It explains all about investing, and has quizzes and real-life-experience stories. It also gives kids a chance to do their own "investing".

Allowance Kit, Junior! : A Money System for Little Kids
and
World of Money Allowance Kit!: A Hands-On Money Management System Exclusively for Kids!
both by Michael J. Searls
If you are ready to start your kids on an allowance, these books are fun and helpful ways to teach your children how allowance works, and about saving and spending.

Kids and Money : A Hands-On Parent's Guide to Teach Children About Money Management and Business Basics
by Michael J. Searls, Todd Clary (Illustrator)
Searls returns with another good book, this for kids who've long since mastered allowance management.

Dr. Tightwad's Money-Smart Kids
by Janet Bodnar
Dr. Tightwad didn't get that name for nothing. She'll tell you how to get through your child-raising years without going bankrupt. This book covers money issues for all ages of children and will teach you how to forever banish the phrase "I want it now."

Appendix B

The Kid's Guide to Money: Earning It, Saving It, Spending It, Growing It, Sharing It
by Steve Otfinoski

Looking for a book your child can read himself and understand without your explanations? This book is meant for children in grades 4-8 and covers earning, saving, spending, growing, and sharing money in terms that kids will understand, and won't be bored by.

Kids and Money : Giving Them Savvy to Succeed Financially
by Jayne A. Pearl

Not only does this book cover the basics including allowances and credit cards, but also covers how to teach against harmful money values propagated in the media, how to deal with broken families, and how to deal with money-related problems such as gambling and shoplifting. Find out more at www.kidsandmoney.com – which lists the table of contents and a basic list of what you can find in the book. The site also has an allowance calculator where you can figure out how much the money you got for allowance is worth today.

The Kids' Allowance Book
by Amy Nathan, Debbie Palen (Illustrator)

If you're ready to start your kids on allowance but aren't sure exactly how to go about it, this book should give you some ideas. The book includes information from 166 students ages 9-14. They will tell you their ideas about allowance and how it works in their families. From this, you can figure out what is best for your children.

Kiplinger's Money-Smart Kids
by Janet Bodnar

It's Dr. Tightwad again and from preschool to young adult she's got advice and ideas about teaching kids about saving, spending, budgeting, and investing. She also discusses insurance, wills, and college.

Debt-Proof Your Kids: An Interesting Thing Happened on the Way to Getting a Financially Confident Life ... My Kids Got One Too
by Mary Hunt

So you're tired of hearing the whines for more money all the time. In this book, Mary Hunt will teach you how to set a salary for your kids that they have to stick to. This will prepare them for the future when they don't have you to fall back on for more money. If they learn it early, there's a great chance that they'll be debt-free for the rest of their lives.

Money Sense for Kids!
by Hollis Page Harman

This book will be entertaining and informative to you and your child. It has puzzles and games and also includes information about where money comes from, investing, and bank accounts.

Totally Awesome Money Book for Kids
by Adrienne Berg and Arthur Berg Bochner

A mother and a son wrote this book together. It covers the basic money management topics, but what makes it special is that the son is 11, so this book is kid-friendly.

Capitate Your Kids : Teaching Your Teens Financial Independence
by Dr. John E. Whitcomb

Dr. Whitcomb's idea for teaching financial responsibilities to kids is to make them almost completely independent, money-wise. His idea is that after giving kids money, parents have no say as to what they do with it. This is not just an allowance, but all money needs for school, clothes, etc. This forces kids to learn what it will be like when they grow up and have to live on only what they make for an income. Find out more at www.capitateyourkids.com. The author provides rules and contracts for negotiations between you and your kids over purchases such as clothing or cars. This is a good way to give your kids an example of how the real world of money works.

How To Go To College Almost For Free
by Benjamin R. Kaplan
A Harvard graduate who won over $90,000 in scholarships to attend college explains how he did it and how your kids can too.

Kids' Allowances - How Much, How Often & How Come, Guide for Parents
by David McCurrach
This two book set will teach all about allowance in one and in the other lets you create your own with your child.

Kids, Parents & Money: Teaching Personal Finance from Piggy Bank to Prom
by Willard S. Stawski
Willard S. Stawski not only tells what should be done, but how to do it in a program that will teach kids the basics of money management.

How to Raise a Family on Less Than Two Incomes: The Complete Guide to Managing Your Money Better So You Can Spend More Time with Your Kids
by Denise M. Topolnicki
If you want to have more time with your kids, but think it's impossible to live without two incomes, this book is full of ideas, worksheets, and real-life stories that will help you find ways to save and live on only one income.

Smart-Money Moves for Kids
by Judith Briles
Easy to understand even for kids, this book covers the basics of money management and keeps kids interested with games and puzzles throughout.

If You Made a Million
by David M. Schwartz
The character Marvelosissimo the Mathematical Magician and friends go through a variety of chores in order to make money and figure out what can be done with a million dollars.

Neale S. Godfrey's Ultimate Kids' Money Book
by Neale S. Godfrey and Randy Verougstraete (Illustrator)
Meant for ages 8-12, this book covers many topics including the basics of money management plus taxes, inflation, and more. To keep it interesting and fun for kids, it's colorful and includes games and quizzes.

Dollars and Sense for College Students: Or How Not to Run Out of Money by Midterms
by Ellen Braitman
With so many students leaving college with huge debts, new college students should be required to read this book to learn about dealing with credit, effective budgeting, how to be a smart shopper, and more.

In the Black: The African-American Parent's Guide to Raising Financially Responsible Children
by Fran Harris
While this book would be good for any parent to learn to teach kids good money skills, this book also deals with problems specific to African-Americans.

Appendix B

Allowances: Dollars and Sense
by Paul Lermitte

Learn about the financial dangers that kids can face and the opportunities they will come across in dealing with money, saving, spending, loans, and college expenses. Lermitte introduces his "The Making Allowances System" and the "Universal Principals" in terms of money, provides tips and budgeting forms, and explains how you can be creative with your kids, try different things and use what works — just like he did when he developed his ideas. One of the author's ideas is the "Pizza method of getting rich," which relates buying a pizza to buying mutual funds. This is an easy and interesting way for kids to learn about investing. Find out more at www.makingallowances.com/index-fs – which includes information and advice for teens and parents.

Confessions of a Shopaholic and Shopaholic Takes Manhattan
Both by Sophie Kinsella

Great just for pleasure reading for a teenager or above, these two books follow Becky Bloomwood, a financial writer who is, herself, a shopaholic in debt. Most girls will understand Becky's infatuation with shopping and this book will teach them the serious consequences of being a shopaholic in a humorous and enjoyable manner.

General Commercial Resources

Ric Edelman
www.ricedelman.com/planning/kidsncash

Ric Edelman is a practicing financial planner who has authored several books and has also had a prominent media presence. This section of his web site has several articles specifically dealing with kids and money.

Baby Center
www.babycenter.com/refcap/baby/babyfinance

Beyond all the baby stuff for sale, parents can find informative articles focusing mostly on insurance, taxes, and wills that all have to do with having children. There's also a place where you can ask questions if you can't find your answer on the site.

Ms. Money
www.msmoney.com/mm/women/kidsmoney

Ms. Money is designed especially for women, with a section on kids and money. With links to other sources, articles about ways to raise financially able children, and lists of games and other ways to make learning about money more fun for your kids, it's a very good site to go for information even if you're not a Ms. – so don't Ms. it!

Money Experience for Kids
www.edu4kids.com/money

Are you game for these three games: Making Change, Spending Money, and Piggy Bank Breakin? They'll help your kids learn about adding up money and not overspending.

Headbone
www.headbone.com/wtvrags

This site features a game in which the object is to raise $5,000 by managing a rock and roll band. There are different options of how to do it, and if you get a high enough score, you're eligible for a prize.

InvestorGuide
www.investorguide.com/kidsmore

The list of links for teaching kids about money includes one site with a competition involving stocks, some with games and activities, and others that are more information-based on saving and other money-practices. There's a link for young kids in particular, which features cartoons to help kids learn.

Girl Zone

www.girlzone.com/html/funds

Because girls love to shop, this site is for girls and has tips on spending wisely, buying gifts, tipping, saving, and more.

TeenVestor

www.teenvestor.com

Teens can learn about investing and becoming young entrepreneurs. If they like what they see, they can buy the Teenvestor books on these subjects.

Bernie Bucks

www.berniebucks.com

Bernie gives you a free lesson plan that teaches kids about earning, saving, and investing. It also allows families to maintain and monitor accounts on a computer. You can also order books, software, and games related to financial matters.

Student Credit

www.studentcredit.com

It's geared to high school and college students, but this web site is for anyone who needs to learn more about credit. It teaches all about credit and how to choose the right card for what you need. You can apply for a credit card on the site and there are cards specifically for high school and college students and cards for all other consumers. Sorry, even though you'll be a credit whiz by the time you're done, you can't earn any academic credit here for it.

Young Monthly

www.YoungMonthly.com

Young people in their beginning days of investing will find many articles about all types of investing along with cartoons and a question board. They can also invest online with as little as $50 and enter an investing contest with a $1000 scholarship reward.

Young Investor

www.younginvestor.com

The cool graphics and sound effects will draw kids right in. They'll find 10 money games, questions of the month for kids, parents, and experts, a survey for kids to take and compare their money smarts to other kids, information on money and investing, a dictionary of terms, and calculators for chore wages, saving, and more.

Young Biz

www.youngbiz.com/money_smartz/ yb_money_smartz

In addition to substantial information about credit and investing, visitors can read personal stories about young kids who have become successful by starting their own businesses, and stories about how people have solved money dilemmas, and more. It's a great site for inspiring your kids, getting them thinking creatively, setting goals, and showing them that there are ways to make money at a young age.

Bonehead Finance

http://ourworld.compuserve.com/homepages/ Bonehead_Finance/bone4c1c

Don't let the name insult you. Use the calculator that estimates your net income by subtracting expenses and taxes.

Money Factory

www.moneyfactory.com

Do you want to enlist your kids' help in cutting your budget? Here they can learn about counterfeit money – and if they use it well it might allow you to move to a smaller house while the government pays for their room and board. There are two different sections for different age groups and both are animated and made fun for kids. They both have facts, quizzes, and games to make the learning experience fun.

Appendix B

Big Change

www.bigchange.com

This site touts itself as an "online allowance center" where you can convert your kids' allowance into "didtz" that allow them to make online purchases. Despite its heavy commercialism, it does have some interesting features that make it worth a look.

Escape From Knab

www.escapefromknab.com

This great game helps kids learn about managing money. The scenario is that you're on a trip to another planet that smells bad so to get back you have to earn $10,000 for a ticket. While you're there you have to get a job and pay expenses. Different situations involving money come up along the way. This is a really fun way for kids to learn.

Fun Brain

www.funbrain.com/cashreg

This game is great for your kids who are starting to learn about making change. Beginners practice making change from a dollar, and as they learn, they work with larger amounts.

C

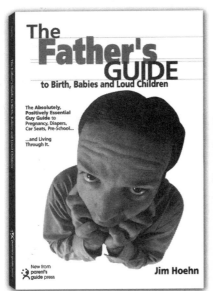